The World Bank Group

WORKING FOR A WORLD FREE OF POVERTY

The World Bank Group consists of five institutions – the International Bank for Reconstruction and Development (IBRD), the International Finance Corporation (IFC), the International Development Association (IDA), the Multilateral Investment Guarantee Agency (MIGA), and the International Centre for the Settlement of Investment Disputes (ICSID). Its mission is to fight poverty for lasting results and to help people help themselves and their environment by providing resources, sharing knowledge, building capacity, and forging partnerships in the public and private sectors.

The Independent Evaluation Group

IMPROVING THE WORLD BANK GROUP'S DEVELOPMENT RESULTS THROUGH EXCELLENCE IN EVALUATION

The Independent Evaluation Group (IEG) is an independent unit within the World Bank Group. It reports directly to the Board of Executive Directors, which oversees IEG's work through its Committee on Development Effectiveness. IEG is charged with evaluating the activities of the World Bank (the International Bank for Reconstruction and Development and the International Development Association), the work of the International Finance Corporation in private sector development, and the guarantee projects and services of the Multilateral Investment Guarantee Agency.

The goals of evaluation are to learn from experience, to provide an objective basis for assessing the results of the Bank Group's work, and to provide accountability in the achievement of its objectives. It also improves Bank Group work by identifying and disseminating the lessons learned from experience and by framing recommendations drawn from evaluation findings.

Liberia Country Program Evaluation: 2004–2011

Liberia Country Program Evaluation: 2004–2011

Evaluation of The World Bank Group Program

Contents

Abbreviations

AAA	Analytical and Advisory Assistance
ACE	Africa Coast to Europe (telecommunications cable)
AfDB	African Development Bank
AFREA	Africa Renewable Energy Access
AIDP	Agriculture and Infrastructure Project
ASYCUDA	Automated System for Customs Data
BRF	Buchanan Renewables Fuel Inc.
CAS	Country Assistance Strategy
CASPR	Country Assistance Strategy Progress Report
CCT	Cross-Cutting Themes
CEA	Country Environmental Analysis
CIVPOL	United Nations Civilian Police
CO2	Carbon dioxide
CPA	Comprehensive Peace Agreement
CRN	Country Reengagement Note
CSO	Civil society organization
DBOM	Design-build-operate and maintain
DfID	British Department for International Development
EC	European Commission (of the European Union)
ECOWAS	Economic Community of West African States
EFA/FTI	Education for All/Fast Track Initiative
EGIRP	Economic Governance and Institutional Reform Project
EIP	Emergency Infrastructure Project
EITI	Extractive Industries Transparency Initiative
EPA	Environment Protection Agency
EPAG	Economic Empowerment of Adolescent Girls Project
ESP	Education Sector Plan
ESW	Economic and sector work
FAO	Food and Agriculture Organization
FBO	Faith-based organization
FDA	Forest Development Authority
FIAS	Foreign Investment Advisory Service
FMC	Forest Management Contract
GAC	General Audit Commission
GBV	Gender-based violence
GDP	Gross domestic product
GEF	Global Environment Facility
GEMAP	Governance and Economic Management Assistance Program
GIZ	German Company for International Development

GNI	Gross national income
GPOBA	Global Partnership of Output-Based Aid
HIPC	Heavily Indebted Poor Country
IBRD	International Bank for Reconstruction and Development
IDA	International Development Agency
IDP	Internally-displaced persons
IEG	Independent Evaluation Group
IFAD	International Fund for Agricultural Development
IFC	International Financial Corporation
IFI	International financial institution
IFMIS	Integrated Financial Management Information System
IIU	Infrastructure Implementation Unit
ILO	International Labor Organization
IMF	International Monetary Fund
ISN	Joint Interim Strategy Note
LACE	Senior Executive Service
LEC	Liberia Electricity Corporation
LIBRAMP	Liberia Road Asset Management Project
LICUS	Low-Income Countries Under Stress
LIFM	Liberian Institute of Financial Management
LIPA	Liberia Institute for Public Administration
LRTF	Liberia Reconstruction Trust Fund
LTA	Liberia Telecommunications Authority
LTC	Liberia Telecommunications Corporation
LWSC	Liberia Water and Sewer Corporation
MCC	Monrovia City Corporation
MDRI	Multilateral Debt Relief Initiative
MIGA	Multilateral Investment Guarantee Agency
MTEF	Medium-Term Expenditure Framework
NEP	National Energy Policy
NGO	Nongovernmental organization
NTGL	National Transitional Government of Liberia
ODA	Official development assistance
OECD	Organisation for Economic Co-operation and Development
OPRC	Output and Performance –Based Road Contract
PEFA	Public Expenditure and Financial Accountability Assessment
PER	Public Expenditure Review
PEMFAR	Public Expenditure Management and Fiduciary Accountability Review
PFM	Public Financial Management
PMU	Project Management Unit

PPA	Project Preparation Advance
PPP	Purchasing power parity
PROFOR	Programme for Forests
PRS	Poverty Reduction Strategy
PRSP	Poverty Reduction Strategy Policy
PSD	Private sector development
RFTF	Results Focused Transitional Framework
RIA	Roberts International Airport
ROSC	Report on Observation of Standards and Codes
RREA	Rural and Renewable Energy Agency
SEA	Strategic Environmental Assessment
SES	Senior Executive Service
SESA	Strategic Environmental and Social Assessment
SIU	Special Implementation Unit
SOE	State-owned enterprise
TFLIB	Liberia Trust Fund
TMC	Timber Management Contract
TSC	Timber Sale Contract
TVET	Technical and Vocational Education and Training
UN	United Nations
UNDP	United Nations Development Programme
UNEP	United Nations Environment Programme
UNESCO	United Nations Educational, Scientific and Cultural Organization
UNICEF	United Nations Children's Fund
UNIFEM	United Nations Development Fund for Women
UNOPS	United Nations Office for Project Services
UNMIL	United Nations Mission in Liberia
URIRP	Urban and Rural Infrastructure Rehabilitation Project
USAID	United States Agency for International Development
VSAT	Very small aperture terminal
WAPP	West African Power Pool
WARCIP	West African Regional Communications Infrastructure Project
WBI	World Bank Institute
WFP	World Food Program
WHO	World Health Organization
YES	Youth Employment and Skills

Acknowledgments

The report was prepared by Chad Leechor (Task Team Leader, IEGCC), with background papers and substantive inputs from Basil Kavalsky, Peter Freeman, Lauren Kelly, Albert Martinez, Ursula Martinez, Mary Breeding, Carla Pazce, John Redwood, Elaine Ooi and Jorge Claro.

The task team wishes to acknowledge the excellent cooperation and support of the government of Liberia, generously provided during the visits of IEG missions to collect information (November-December 2011) and to discuss the draft report (June 2012). The task team also wishes to thank members of the Liberia Country Team of the World Bank Group for their valuable assistance, through the time and efforts unsparingly given during the fact-finding phase and through detailed comments on the draft report. We note in particular the kind support of Coleen Littlejohn, Lemu Makain and Sergiy Kulyk.

The evaluation was prepared under the supervision of Ali Khadr (Senior Manager, IEGCC) and the overall direction of Caroline Heider, (Director-General, Evaluation). It has benefited from the comments of peer reviewers: Stephen O'Brien (Consultant, IEGCC), Soniya Carvalho and Navin Girishankar (Lead Evaluation Officers, IEGPS), as well as from comments of IEG colleagues received during the review process, especially those from Daniela Gressani, Christine Wallich, Anis Dani, and Pia Schneider. Vikki Taaka and Corky de Asis provided administrative support; William Hurlbut provided editorial input.

Overview
Liberia Country Program Evaluation

Highlights

This report evaluates the outcomes of World Bank Group support to Liberia from its post-war reengagement in 2003 through 2011.

The country has moved in just a few years from a state of total disarray to one with a solid foundation for inclusive development. Although development has not moved forward as quickly as hoped, substantial progress has been made. Public finance and key institutions have been rebuilt; crucial transport facilities have been restored; and hospitals, schools, and universities are operating. The debilitating burden of massive external debt has been eliminated. Although the government deserves most of the credit, this success would not have been possible without external development and security partners, including the World Bank Group.

Following re-engagement in 2003, the World Bank Group strategy in Liberia initially focused on two areas: (i) restoring the functionality of the state; and (ii) rebuilding infrastructure. Both were seen as reflecting Liberia's comparative advantage. Infrastructure, in particular, was considered by partners and the government as an area where the World Bank Group could play a special role. The Bank made a decision to put less emphasis, in this initial phase, on social sectors and the growth agenda where substantial assistance was available from other partners— although in later years the Bank's emphasis on these areas increased. It was deemed necessary first to put in place the basic institutional and physical infrastructure needed for service delivery and private sector development. In addition, the World Bank Group designated three priorities as cross-cutting themes: capacity-building, gender equality, and environmental sustainability, with the aim of reflecting these in all interventions.

Regarding the outcomes, the rebuilding of public institutions has seen substantial progress, with important achievements in restoring public finances and reforming the civil service. With respect to the rehabilitation of infrastructure, the World Bank Group has helped improve the conditions of roads, ports, power supply, and water and sanitation. As for facilitating growth, however, World Bank Group financial support has been relatively modest, but it has helped with policy advice and in filling gaps left by other partners.

With regard to the three cross-cutting themes, some effective programs were carried out, including capacity development at several core public finance-related agencies. However, the integration of these themes across World Bank Group interventions, which was the underlying intent, still needs a vision and better articulated strategy.

Finally, the Bank (together with the International Monetary Fund) led efforts to reduce Liberia's inherited external debt burden under the enhanced Highly-Indebted Poor Country (HIPC) Initiative and the Multi-lateral Debt Relief Initiative (MDRI) mechanisms. Cancelation of Liberia's debt burden, which was attained in 2010, was a crucial step in boosting the country's development efforts and normalizing aid flows.

In the past year or two, most development partners have faced the task of transitioning from support for emergency reconstruction to support for sustained development. This is a significant challenge for the World Bank Group, coming at a time when the dynamism which characterized its emergency support is widely perceived to be abating. Major staffing changes at the regional and country levels, along with the 2011 political campaigns in Liberia, have contributed to a slowdown in the program. Of particular concern are a hiatus in the largest transport project (the road from Monrovia to the Guinean border) and the absence of prompt corrective action.

Although the evaluation is in broad agreement with the approach of the Liberia program, two issues merit greater attention. One is the stewardship of natural resources, including the need to systematically enhance the quality of governance across the value chain of resources— with the overarching goal of sharing the benefits among all Liberians. The second issue is the need to create job opportunities, especially among youth who also need skills development, to address the pervasive unemployment or underemployment problem.

The new program cycle of the World Bank Group to be set out in the next country strategy for Liberia presents an opportunity to strengthen the relevance and effectiveness of its assistance. First, the World Bank Group could help deepen Liberia's achievements under the Extractive Industries Transparency Initiative (EITI) by supporting the establishment of institutional arrangements to ensure that resource revenues are used for the benefit of all. Second, it could help develop a new growth strategy that is truly pro-poor; that is, one that focuses on job creation among the targeted beneficiaries in its interventions and that upgrades the investment climate for businesses. Finally, the World Bank Group could speed up implementation of its program by finding pragmatic ways around the many obstacles, such as procurement practices and competition for management attention.

Introduction and Context

Liberia was founded in 1821 by former American slaves. Until recently, their descendants, a small minority of the population, controlled most of the political and economic power. This social imbalance was a source of friction, particularly given the country's rich natural resources, with an abundance of iron ore, timber, diamonds, gold and rubber.

The legacy of discontent. The economy grew rapidly after World War II, as subsistence agriculture gave way to rubber plantations, large-scale forestry and industrial mining. Propelled by a commodity boom, Liberia became a lower middle-income country in the early 1970s. The performance, however, masked a darker side. Weak governance kept the vast majority of Liberians poor and uneducated. Liberia's growth was not accompanied by meaningful development.

In April 1980, a coup d'état, caused partly by long-standing resentment against the ruling regime, set off a protracted calamity. Years of violence followed. The destruction of war was on a scale seldom seen in the modern world. Eight percent of the population lost their lives and twice as many were displaced. More than half of the women were sexually assaulted. Most schools and health facilities were destroyed. Power, water and sanitation ceased to function while roads crumbled from lack of maintenance. A generation of young Liberians never attended school, or saw their education irreparably disrupted.

After the war, the world community responded with uncommon solidarity. Led by the United Nations Mission in Liberia (UNMIL) and the Economic Community of West African States (ECOWAS), many development partners soon arrived. The overriding goals were to disarm combatants, maintain peace, and provide emergency humanitarian relief. From 2003 until the end of 2005, the National Transitional Government of Liberia (NTGL), consisting of the former belligerent groups and civil society was in charge, but under the supervision of international peacekeeping forces. Presidential and legislative elections were held in November 2005 and certified by independent observers as fair and free. Former World Bank economist Ellen Johnson Sirleaf won and became the first female head of state in Africa.

A new hope. Guided by the vision of a more open and inclusive society, the elected government set out a framework to secure political stability, economic recovery, and basic services. The framework has four pillars:

- Expanding peace and security;
- Revitalizing the economy;
- Strengthening governance; and
- Rehabilitating infrastructure and delivering basic services.

It was derived from a broadly-based consultative process which led to the Interim Poverty Reduction Strategy in 2007 and the full Poverty Reduction Strategy in 2008.

The period from 2006 to 2011 saw steady progress in restoring government provision of services, strengthening the capacity of the civil service, and starting to deal with poverty reduction. This progress was rewarded in 2010 when Liberia's development partners and foreign creditors canceled almost all of Liberia's external debt, which stood at $4.8 billion in 2003 (see figure A).

Figure A — Liberia's External and Domestic Debt (US$ billion)

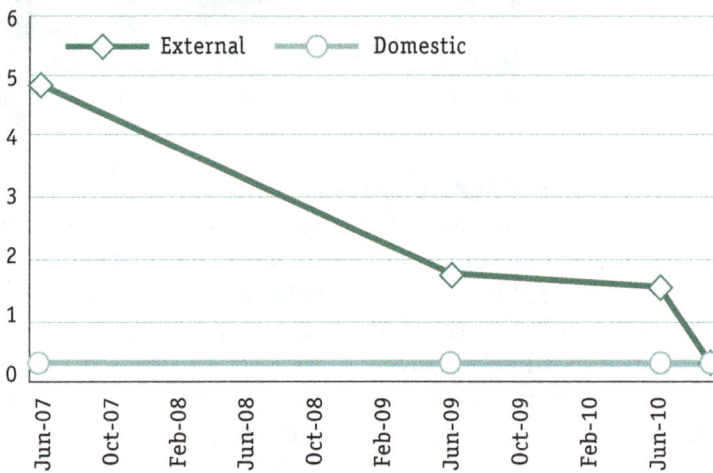

The World Bank Group's Liberia Program

The World Bank Group strategy for Liberia that was common to successive strategy documents can be summarized under three pillars of activities:

- Rebuilding core state functions;
- Rehabilitating infrastructure; and
- Facilitating pro-poor growth.

Three cross-cutting themes were also identified: capacity development, gender equality, and the environment— all to be increasingly mainstreamed into World Bank Group interventions in Liberia. Initially, the World Bank Group support was envisioned from the Bank only; later, the International Finance Corporation (IFC) and the Multilateral Investment Guarantee Agency (MIGA) began participating. Among the most important modalities of Bank support—while clearly not directed at specific pillars/themes—was the debt relief provided to Liberia under the enhanced Highly-Indebted Poor countries (HIPC) and Multilateral Debt Reduction (MDRI) initiatives.

PILLAR ONE: REBUILDING CORE STATE FUNCTIONS

World Bank Group Objectives. The 2004 Country Re-engagement Note (CRN) set out to restore the bare minimum of governance, including the monitoring of aid-financed spending. The 2007 Interim Strategy Note (ISN) formulated more ambitious objectives to support public sector restructuring. The main objectives were:

- Fiscal policy and financial management—putting in place fundamental public financial management (PFM) systems;

- Comprehensive civil service reform—putting in place a reformed civil service with appropriate staffing and compensation policies and upgraded capacity; and

- Rule of law and respect for human rights—putting in place a functioning and reformed judicial system, including courts, corrections, administration, and so on.

The 2009 Country Assistance Strategy (CAS) pursued the same set of objectives, but with new and more precisely specified targets.

Outcomes. The achievements in terms of addressing the objectives are significant— exceeding what might reasonably have been expected in the chaos in 2003. Major progress has been made in the Ministries of Finance, Planning and Health; the Civil Service Agency; the General Audit Commission (GAC); and the Liberian Agency for Community Empowerment. Among other things, by 2009 Liberia was able to win the designation of an EITI compliant country – the second country ever to achieve this distinction.

The results in civil service reform (CSR) are also strong. Among the difficult tasks completed are: the completion of a CSR strategy; the restructuring of 9 key ministries, which led to a reduction by 2010 of 11,000 employees including ghost workers; a biometric identification framework and management information systems. However, some tasks are still ongoing including the review of mandates and functions in the remaining ministries and the code of conduct for employees.

There has also been progress in setting up anti-corruption safeguards. Beyond those reviewed under PFM and CSR, achievements include the establishment of a functioning GAC, adoption of public sector accounting standards, and modernization of customs. Although corruption cannot be measured directly, Transparency International's 2010 Corruption Perceptions Index ranked Liberia 11th out of 47 sub-Saharan African countries. Globally, Liberia improved from 138th to 87th place in four years.

World Bank Group Contribution. Under the Transitional Government (2003–05), the World Bank helped restore fiscal discipline through a joint supervision of spending by the government and development partners, under the Governance and Economic Management Assistance Program (GEMAP). Since 2006, the elected government has shown a strong commitment and ownership that enhances the contribution of the World Bank.

In support of setting up PFM systems, the World Bank used a judicious mix of budget support operations and technical assistance projects, underpinned by analytical work such as the 2008 Public Expenditure Management and Financial Accountability Review (PEMFAR). Building a strong PFM Unit in the Ministry of Finance to provide centralized disbursement and expenditure controls for development projects proved highly effective. Furthermore, the World Bank supported the civil service reform through the recruitment of qualified individuals from abroad and modernization of the management information system for human resources.

This pillar showed shortcomings in three areas. First, it did not prioritize public procurement issues to the extent needed to meet the milestones. In addition, vesting control over procurement in multiple project management units was not effective. Although desirable in the long run, decentralizing the procurement function carries considerable risk. Second, the Bank did not provide support for in-service training at the Liberian Institute for Public Administration until 2010. Third, after some initial support, the Bank withdrew its support for judicial reform. In some of these cases, there were differences in views between Bank staff and key members of these agencies.

PILLAR TWO: REHABILITATING INFRASTRUCTURE

World Bank Group Objectives. During the immediate post-conflict period, this pillar focused on the restoration of critical infrastructure. In December 2003, following the peace agreement, the United Nations Development Programme (UNDP) and the Bank undertook a joint needs assessment, which led to the development of a Results-Focused Transitional Framework.

Following this framework, specific objectives under this pillar focused on emergency repairs to restore critical transport routes, assist returning refugees and create temporary jobs. The World Bank Group also sought to enable functionality of key public services through improvements to water supply and electricity distribution as well as to sewerage systems, solid waste disposal, and city street rehabilitation. In addition, the international airport and the seaport were to be made secure and functional. In rural areas, priorities were on restoring access to hubs and corridors serving larger towns.

Outcomes. The achievements have been considerable. There have been significant improvements in transport, including the rehabilitation of major roads, privatization of port operations, upgrading of the airport and improvement of access roads. Waste management in Monrovia is working well. The power supply is restored and reaching more people. Despite considerable progress, there is scope for efficiency improvements, even within this difficult environment. A clear symptom can be seen in the widespread delays in infrastructure implementation.

World Bank Group Contribution. Initially, a grant of $30 million was approved in June 2004 for emergency repairs. The International Development Association (IDA) later approved six grant-financed infrastructure projects under special rapid response procedures to restore functionality to a broader range of infrastructure services. Since the debt relief, IDA has approved two more credits covering road asset management and telecommunications.

These interventions addressed the country's needs as articulated in the CAS and the government's Poverty Reduction Strategy (PRS). They helped restore critical transport functionality and essential urban services. In the power sector, the IFC made a major contribution through its support for the Liberian Electricity Corporation, which led to a management contract with Manitoba Hydro International.

Before 2010, time pressure and budget constraints precluded the development of an adequate results framework or a system for tracking progress. Task teams followed a flexible and pragmatic approach, adapting to changing priorities and circumstances. Project implementation tended to encounter delays, and none of the infrastructure projects closed as scheduled. Many projects needed additional finance or were restructured to change the scope of works due to exogenous factors or policy changes.

The World Bank has committed to an Output and Performance-Based Road Contract (OPRC) combining construction and maintenance. The expanded role of the private sector has proved beneficial in some countries and the OPRC approach seems appropriate for Liberia— as it requires much less capacity of the government and, by agreement, places the implementation risk on the contractor.

PILLAR THREE: FACILITATING PRO-POOR GROWTH

World Bank Group Objectives. The World Bank Group sought to help revitalize the economy in an inclusive manner. Initially, the assistance was to be provided mainly through IFC knowledge products, collaboration with other donors, and small grants and technical assistance in agriculture and mining. Following arrears clearance and the PRS, the World Bank Group began pursuing the following:

- Improving the management of agriculture and natural resources;
- Upgrading the investment climate, including finance; and
- Increasing access to social protection and social services.

The planned support remained small compared to the other two pillars, with expected lending of less than 10 percent of the total indicative program.

Under this pillar, a significant role was envisioned for IFC and MIGA. Through the post-conflict initiative for Africa, IFC assistance sought to:

- Support improvements in the investment climate;
- Strengthen the financial sector;
- Promote private participation in the real sector and infrastructure; and
- Support selected agribusinesses or mining ventures.

MIGA sought to catalyze foreign investment to develop Liberia's natural resources by offering guarantees against political risk, as well as technical assistance in investment promotion.

Outcomes. For the most part, the program under this pillar reflects an initial exploratory engagement rather than the full-scale support. In the agriculture sector, the desired gains on output and productivity of domestic food crops have not materialized. The mining sector has seen progress on transparency and the legal framework, but artisanal mining has not had any gains. In the forest management sector, the United Nations lifted the sanctions on timber exports in June 2006. A legal framework has been established, as has a chain of custody system to curb illegal timber harvesting. Nevertheless, forestry practice has not been pro-poor, nor has it adequately taken into account community and conservation needs.

Under the investment climate agenda, the Better Business Forum and a business registry were established. IFC also made direct investments in private businesses, and MIGA provided a guarantee. However, thornier issues, such as land tenure or enforcement of contracts, have yet to show tangible progress.

In the health sector, core functions of the ministry were strengthened along with improvements in basic health care. Access to primary education and certain technical and vocational programs improved, but sector-wide issues such as shortages of teachers have not been tackled. Regarding social protection, war-torn communities received assistance and the adverse effects of the 2007-08 food crises were mitigated. The capacity of the Liberia Agency for Community Empowerment (LACE) was also enhanced.

World Bank Group Contribution. In the *agriculture* sector, the World Bank Group's program was small and came on stream too late to achieve the milestones. In the *mining* sector, World Bank Group support helped improve the regulatory framework, but did not cover artisanal mining, which involves 40 percent of the rural population. Regarding *forest management,* initial World Bank Group support to the multi-donor Liberia Forest Initiative helped lift the UN sanctions, but subsequent support was not sufficiently pro-poor.

World Bank Group support for the *investment climate* effectively addressed important business issues by helping to establish the Better Business Forum and company registry. IFC also invested in private firms, and in 2011 MIGA provided a guarantee of $142 million to a foreign direct investment project.

The World Bank Group also helped the Ministry of Health and Social Welfare with planning, development, and administration through the Health System Reconstruction Project. This assistance complemented other partners' programs, which focused on basic health services. In the education sector, the World Bank Group supported basic education under the Education for All Initiative and assisted vocational and technical education through the Youth Employment and Skills project. Regarding social protection, the World Bank Group was instrumental in developing the capacity of LACE and in financing relief programs for food crises.

With respect to facilitating pro-poor growth, the modest results were commensurate with the limited financial assistance. However, more analytic work would have been useful in the development of strategies and key institutions. For example, the World Bank Group could have raised the question of whether the reliance on large-scale concessions in mining, forestry, and agriculture can adequately serve the majority of Liberia's rural population. Analytic work on such questions should be of high priority for the World Bank Group.

Cross-Cutting Themes

The 2009 CAS identified three cross-cutting themes: capacity-building, gender, and environmental sustainability. Each of the themes was to be: (i) supported by a set of core programs, usually carried out by specialized units; and (ii) reflected in all sector-level interventions. The CAS provided little guidance, however, as to the objectives and modalities of support for these cross-cutting themes.

Outcomes. *Capacity-building* is defined as a locally-driven process of learning by relevant actors that leads to actions and change to advance development goals. At the institutional level, it requires well-defined objectives, as well as the operational structures and staffing to attain them. In addition, it requires adequate provision of information systems, equipment, and facilities. Perhaps the most important quality needed is effective leadership to provide motivation and trust. The development of capacity for core public sector management functions has made significant progress, with strengthening of institutions such as the Ministries of Finance and Planning, the Civil Service Agency, the General Audit Commission, and the EITI. For instance, the Ministry of Finance has made good progress on the functions of budgeting, financial controls and tax administration.

The evaluation found that each of these agencies had a clear sense of their objectives and well-developed operational programs and staffing designed to achieve them. In large part, this reflects broad and sustained efforts on the part of the Bank combined with a holistic vision. At the sector level, however, the achievements so far have been modest. No sector has an integrated approach that one finds in the core programs.

Regarding *gender,* the design of World Bank assistance focused narrowly on women's economic empowerment, as with the Adolescent Girls Initiative (EPAG) and the Results-Based Initiative. CAS objectives, in contrast, were to promote gender equality in a broader sense. Thus far, the Bank has not adequately addressed large gender disparities in health and education. The Bank has also recognized the gravity of gender-based violence as an impediment to progress, but no assistance aimed specifically at this has been provided. In addition, gender-sensitive design has appeared in more Bank projects, but has still not been addressed in the majority of cases.

Progress in addressing gender disparities in Liberia has been substantial, although very little of it is attributable to the World Bank Group. The one contribution of the Bank is through the EPAG, which is showing positive results in terms of employment for project participants. More generally, a large number of women are in high-level positions in the country, including the head of state and chief executives of agencies. A gender-sensitive management approach is emerging in the public sector, including the Gender Ministry and the Executive Office, although there is scope for further mainstreaming.

Although *environmental sustainability* was explicitly identified as a cross-cutting theme in the CAS, World Bank Group interventions have been modest, not well articulated, and essentially confined to biodiversity and safeguards policies. Furthermore, the reliance on the Global Environment Facility for support provided by the Bank has put global priorities ahead of national priorities, which remain to be defined.

Overall, the approach for advancing the objectives of cross-cutting themes shows the need for revision in the upcoming CAS. Thematic visions at the sector level (gender issues in health, for instance) need to be defined and implemented, with monitoring to track progress.

Strengthening World Bank Group Program Implementation

Today, there is a perception among many stakeholders that the responsiveness of the World Bank is abating, especially on implementation support. A particular issue that has contributed to this perception is the hiatus in the implementation of infrastructure projects, as well as the absence of prompt corrective actions. A failure to address this concern will pose a reputational risk for the World Bank.

In order to be responsive, the country team requires many types of organizational support, including adequate budgets, incentives, staffing, managerial attention and appropriate guidance for meeting the special demands of fragile and conflict-affected states (FCSs). The experience of the Liberia program in recent years shows that often the organizational support falls short.

For example, the country team has operated under a tight administrative budget that limits the engagement and staffing needed for operations. In addition, the incentives for attracting experienced staff to work on Liberia are relatively modest, and not commensurate with the challenging local conditions. Moreover, there is inadequate guidance for staff on managing the procurement process, which is particularly problematic in Liberia due to the scarcity of professional skills. Finally, the Liberia program faces stiff competition for managerial attention. Sector management has to contend with a very large span of control, while the Country Director needs to divide his attention among three important countries (Ghana and Sierra Leone, in addition to Liberia).

Despite these constraints, the Bank has been, for many years, able to deliver timely and relevant support. This achievement reflects, among other things, the resourcefulness and extra-ordinary efforts of the country team members. However, in the past year or two, a variety of factors have converged to challenge the responsiveness. First, as the World Bank Group moves from emergency to standard procedures, the sense of urgency is also abating. Second, the 2011 national elections brought a lull to development programs. Third, there have been many staffing changes in the Bank, both at the regional and country levels. The country director position, for example, was vacant for nine months until March 2012. Although the country team alone may not be able to deal with these constraints systematically, it is nonetheless essential to find pragmatic, if ad-hoc, ways around them.

Relevance of the World Bank Group Program

Because the evaluation is structured around the Country Assistance Strategy, it inevitably focuses on those aspects of the World Bank Group program that are included in the strategy. It is also important, however, to consider whether the strategy itself represented the right choices in terms of where to concentrate the World Bank Group's efforts. The strategy represented a deliberate choice to focus on restoring the functionality of the state, and rebuilding infrastructure. Both were seen as reflecting the comparative advantage of the World Bank Group (and specifically the World Bank).

Thus, a deliberate choice was made to put less emphasis in the initial phase of Bank involvement on the social sectors and growth agenda. There was already substantial involvement of other partners in the social sectors. As far as the growth agenda was concerned, the essential precondition for this was judged to be the governance framework and the basic institutional infrastructure needed for private sector development. At the same time, three cross-cutting priorities— capacity building, gender, and environmental sustainability—were defined, both to ensure that these were reflected in sector programs and to provide an overall strategic framework into which individual programs could be prioritized.

Although the evaluation is in broad agreement with the World Bank Group strategy, two significant areas could usefully be brought into a sharper strategic focus in the next program cycle. One concerns institutional arrangements spanning the entire value chain of Liberia's main natural resources to ensure that the wealth translates into service delivery for the benefit of all. The second concerns efforts to tackle the pervasive unemployment or under-employment, especially among youth.

An analysis of Liberia's history gives ample evidence of the role that rents derived from its natural resources has played in propagating conflict and political instability. In the long run, it is essential that Liberia develop systems of natural resource management that channel the wealth to good use and equitable distribution of the benefits. An example of such systems is the integrated "value chain" framework in natural resource management, which the World Bank has supported in many natural resource-based economies.

A second area that merits a sharper strategic focus is job opportunities. The World Bank analyzed employment during the period and found that it was much lower than had been previously thought. Under-employment and unpaid or low-paid informal employment are estimated at between 20 and 30 percent of total employment. The problem is particularly serious for youth. In Monrovia, for example, much of the employment consists of pushing small wheelbarrows in the market or selling a few items on the roadside. The capacity to steadily expand employment to absorb these youth, who include a large number of ex-combatants, would help Liberia manage social tensions, conflict, and political instability.

Overall Assessment

Liberia has now reached a point where it is well positioned to reduce poverty and build a more inclusive society. The World Bank Group has contributed through analytic work that supports the overall efforts – through assistance for public finance and institution building, and through major support for infrastructure. Although the World Bank Group has not been a key player in the agenda for growth and human development, it has made a good start and supported other partners.

A key part of the World Bank Group's contribution has been its role in coordinating the assistance of many partners. In some areas, the World Bank Group has taken the lead, but even in areas led by other partners, it has been willing to fill gaps. If the Liberia program succeeds, it will be judged as one of the better examples of a concerted program where partners work together to limit transaction costs to the government – as well as an instance where the common good took precedence over institutional prerogatives.

Lessons

The Liberia program has been distinctive in many ways, including the initial conditions of total collapse, which are seldom seen among member countries. Since 2006, the government has shown exceptional ownership of the assistance program. These factors have enabled the World Bank Group to tackle many difficult issues – often with good results. Some of the lessons gleaned from this experience are:

In developing the capacity of public-sector agencies in FCSs, an integrated package of policy advice, financial and technical assistance as well as logistic support, can help deliver results. This is illustrated by the assistance of the World Bank on public financial management, where the package included economic and sector work, technical assistance projects, budget support, as well as the contractual provision of consultants and professional staff, and training and facilities.

In FCSs, unemployment is likely to be pervasive and often constitutes a major risk factor for peace and stability. It may be helpful to integrate explicit job creation objectives in the assistance program. In Liberia, job creation took on an increasingly larger role over time in World Bank Group assistance. Early projects sometimes needed funding supplements or were restructured for this purpose, which delayed project completion.

In supporting infrastructure, a programmatic approach may provide more scope for efficiency gains compared to a series of investment projects. With a flexible program in place, the World Bank Group is better equipped to respond to unexpected changes, such as the collapse of a bridge or a shift in government priorities, which have occurred from time to time in Liberia.

Partnerships with the private sector (foreign or domestic) can help address major issues, such as shortages of capital, management and skills. In Liberia, the experiences with the landlord port, where a private operator handles commercial services, and the power sector, where a private firm operates under a management contract, have been very positive. The government is now expanding the scope of public-private partnerships (PPPs).

In supporting private sector development, rapid response and quick results can enhance the credibility of the World Bank Group. This is illustrated in the case of Liberia by the IFC assistance in improving, among other things, public-private sector dialogue and the business registry. This has generated goodwill and publicity for the World Bank Group. In pursuing quick results, however, the World Bank Group should not overlook analytical work and fundamental issues.

When the needs of the World Bank Group's intended beneficiaries in FCSs (such as the rural poor) are not explicitly assessed and documented, perhaps through economic and sector work, the resulting interventions may not be compatible with the desired outcomes. This is illustrated by the experience of the forest sector in Liberia. The intended beneficiaries were the residents of the regions where timber concessions were being granted. However, the residents' needs and capacity, including their ability to make a deal and monitor the actions of logging companies, were not adequately taken into account. As a result, little gains accrued to the intended beneficiaries.

In the development of procurement capacity for public sector agencies, which often requires total rebuilding from the ground up, it can help to start with a system-wide vision, rather than ad-hoc, project-by-project assistance. Procurement capacity should be considered as an integral part of public financial management needed across a range of public services. In Liberia, procurement capacity development did not benefit from such a holistic perspective, and the results have been uneven across agencies and functions.

Recommendations

During the next CAS period (2012–15), Liberia will face new and different challenges. First, the shift from emergency assistance to long-term development will continue, as the government takes on bolder reform programs during its second term. Second, to the extent that the global economy recovers and commodity prices rise, foreign direct investment in Liberia may grow while bottlenecks in finance, infrastructure and human resources are progressively removed. Thus, the Liberian economy may continue to gain strength. However, the expected withdrawal of the UNMIL could act as strong head winds to slow growth unless the pull-out process is carefully phased or is offset by private-sector initiatives. The new CAS should anticipate these emerging challenges while positioning the institution to take advantage of new possibilities. Among the key considerations are:

The growth agenda: The World Bank Group can help the government and other partners develop a new strategic framework for growth with the following characteristics:

- It is explicitly pro-poor and inclusive, taking into account the needs and circumstances of intended beneficiaries based on careful socio-political assessments. The pro-poor focus would be enhanced by integrating the role of indigenous communities and civil society in the design of interventions.

- It reexamines the "concession model" that has been traditionally applied in mining, forestry and plantations. A key question is to what extent such concessions are pro-poor when they often involve pitting local communities with limited capacity against far more sophisticated operators.

- It focuses on job creation and employment, especially for youth. Although job schemes under social protection will remain, ultimately most of the jobs will need to be created in the private sector. Measures to enhance the investment climate may be an essential element of the strategy.

- It addresses systemic issues such as land tenure, access to credit, and skill development to meet the demands of private businesses. This effort would be facilitated by supporting post-primary education, which would alleviate the shortages of teachers while expanding the scale and quality of education.

Sharing the wealth of natural resources: The government will increasingly face the challenge of matching the quality of governance with the expanding impact of natural resources. The World Bank Group can assist the government in the development of an integrated regime for natural resource management based on the "value chain" approach. It can serve as an organizing framework for improving transparency at each of the key decision points. The general process involves the following steps:

- Setting objectives, policy, and an institutional framework;

- Deciding to extract natural resources based on policy and consultations with stakeholders;

- Obtaining a good deal from investors through a competitive bidding process and favorable agreements. In addition, it is essential to ensure the transparency of revenue flow, which Liberia is well placed to do—thanks to the progress made under the Extractive Industries Transparency Initiative.

- Managing volatile revenues to smooth out spending and minimize disruptions in the funding of essential programs — often by saving for the rainy day; and

- Ensuring that the benefits are distributed equitably while social and environmental safeguards are observed.

Strengthening implementation support: The World Bank's program implementation in Liberia has been constrained by some of the organizational arrangements, including administrative budgets, staffing, and management attention. It has also been constrained by inadequate guidance on managing procurement, including how to develop the necessary capacity. The World Bank can provide more effective implementation support by:

- Formally empowering the Bank's Liberia Country Manager to make critical decisions on the country program, coupled with holding the Manager accountable for tracking results and country portfolio performance— in light of the Country Director's responsibility for multiple country programs.

- Designating a person (or persons) to serve as a focal point on each of the cross-cutting themes (capacity building, gender, and the environment), with the responsibility for providing guidelines to sector staff and monitoring progress.

- Developing a strategic vision for procurement capacity enhancement as an integral part of public financial management. In the short-term, this effort would need the support of a team of specialists to provide day-to-day procurement services and develop local capacity, possibly through private-public partnerships or management contracts akin to that of Manitoba Hydro. Special attention is needed in the road sector to determine whether to manage the sector from the Bank's Washington headquarters or from the field.

- There is an urgent need to reinvigorate the capacity of the Infrastructure Implementation Unit (IIU) at the Ministry of Public Works. In particular, the technical assistance on procurement of an international firm (under the Roads Asset Management Project) should be quickly restored, along with the resumption of recruitment of qualified staff as mandated by the IIU's implementation framework.

Management Action Record

IEG Findings	IEG Recommendations
Developing a new growth agenda: Although the focus on public financial management and infrastructure was understandable in the initial period, the Bank now needs to pay greater attention to the overall growth strategy and reconsider the traditional approach the government has relied on to develop natural resources.	The World Bank Group can help the government and other partners develop a new strategic framework for growth with the following characteristics: • It is explicitly pro-poor and inclusive, taking into account the needs and circumstances of intended beneficiaries based on careful socio-political assessments. The pro-poor focus would be enhanced by integrating the role of indigenous communities and civil society in the design of interventions. • It reexamines the "concession model" that has been traditionally applied in mining, forestry and plantations. A key question is to what extent such concessions are pro-poor when they often involve pitting local communities with limited capacity against far more sophisticated operators. • It focuses on job creation and employment, especially for youth. Although job schemes under social protection will remain, ultimately most of the jobs will need to be created in the private sector. Measures to enhance the investment climate may be an essential element of the strategy. • It addresses systemic issues such as land tenure, access to credit and skill development to meet the demands of private businesses. This effort would be facilitated by supporting post primary education, which would alleviate the shortages of teachers while expanding the scale and quality of education.

Acceptance by Management	Management Response
Agree/ongoing This recommendation goes along with the current work of the World Bank Group and will find an adequate reflection in the planned policy dialogue, analytical work and the partnerships with other donors for the next Country Partnership Strategy (to be completed in November 2012). Moreover, the World Bank Group intends to pass all operations through a "fragility filter" in which issues of geographical, ethnic, gender and age exclusion as well as capacity building will be analyzed per operation and throughout the portfolio.	The World Bank Group is providing considerable support to the government in designing strategies and implementation frameworks. These include: growth diagnostic, social protection diagnostic, options for financing infrastructure, energy sector development plan, private sector strategy, post-basic education and training strategy, as well as technical assistance to articulate the government's new Poverty Reduction Strategy (PRS) which is explicitly pro-poor and embraces all the characteristics suggested by IEG. One of the economic governance goals of the new PRS is to improve the negotiation management and monitoring of concessions to ensure that they effectively contribute to broad-based economic and social development. Through the analytical work of the Bank, the government has recognized the limitation of the concessions sector in creating jobs and is consequently emphasizing measures to enhance the environment for both domestic and foreign investors. With an active participation of the IFC, we will assess possibilities for structuring more holistic public-private partnership (PPP) options cutting across individual transactions (multi-user ports; rail, roads, power, technical training), which would strengthen the Liberian government's capacity to deliver better public infrastructure outcomes. Job creation has been accorded a high priority in the new PRS, acknowledging its cross-cutting nature. The government also recognizes that job creation has to be addressed from both the demand and supply side including addressing the issue of employability through emphasis on skills training. The Human Development, Sustainable Development Network and Private Sector Development teams are collaborating on several studies to inform the government's youth empowerment and employment strategy. This will be followed up with the Technical Assistance Project in FY 2013 to assist the government in designing concrete interventions in these areas. The interventions will be based on the lessons learned from the successful Bank-supported Economic Empowerment of Adolescent Girls pilot project which was a cornerstone of the Bank's efforts to focus on the issue of women's economic empowerment. It should be mentioned that even more effort will be made in the upcoming CAS to mainstream gender in all operations and not just those specific interventions designed for women and girls. The World Bank Group is also working with the government to address the complex issue of land tenure. Notable progress has been made with the establishment of the Land Commission and the initiation of the digitization of the land deeds supported by the World Bank Group and other donors. Further analytical work will be continued in FY 2013, which could provide the basis for an IDA or State and Peace Building Fund supported initiative; other development partners are interested in a greater Bank involvement in this priority area of the second PRS. Special consideration will continue to be given to the issue of land and women/youth.

IEG Findings	IEG Recommendations
Sharing the wealth of natural resources: The government will increasingly face the challenge of matching the quality of governance with the expanding impact of natural resources.	The World Bank Group can assist the government in the development of an integrated regime for natural resource management based on the "value chain" approach. It can serve as an organizing framework for improving transparency at each of the key decisions points. The general process includes the following steps: • Setting objectives, policy and institutional framework; • Deciding to extract natural resources based on policy and consultations with stakeholders; • Getting a good deal from investors through a competitive bidding process and favorable agreements; • Managing volatile revenue to smooth out spending and minimize disruptions in the funding of essential programs -- often by saving for the rainy day; • Ensuring that the benefits are distributed equitably while social and environmental safeguards are observed.

Acceptance by Management	Management Response
Agree/ongoing A case will be made in the dialogue with the government for a small IDA allocation combined with economic and sector work (ESW), and trust funds, including Multi-Donor Trust Funds. To date the government's preference is to use the limited IDA allocation almost exclusively for energy and other infrastructure in the upcoming Country Partnership Strategy (CPS).	A transparent, better managed, and inclusive extractive industries sector could play a leading role in promoting broad-based growth and in preserving peace and stability. The Bank is involved in a number of activities to improve the management of natural resources : • Supporting revision of the Minerals and Mining Act to ensure that mining deals follow competitive bidding as well as licensing where appropriate, and ensuring that environmental and social safeguards are observed; • Advising on the establishment of a mining inspectorate to better track mining operations and monitor compliance with contractual provisions; • Supporting improvement to the mining cadastre to monitor payments of surface rental rights and relinquishment provisions to enable the government to auction off properties which are not longer in compliance; • Supporting Liberia's Extractive Industries Transparency Initiative effort to build capacity to track revenue use from extractive industries. The Bank is in the process of preparing a policy note to identify reforms through the EITI++ value chain approach and an analysis of the gaps of implementation. The note will identify linkage opportunities through local procurement by private companies and the National Investment Commission effort to establish local procurement capacity. As part of the new CPS, the World Bank Group is planning two policy notes for FY 13 and 14, including one on extractive industries and another on petroleum sector management. These notes should inform the preparation of the new Technical Assistance Project focused on supporting pro-poor focus, strengthening governance and fostering private sector linkages and competitiveness in Liberia. Given the growing importance of the mining and petroleum sectors in Africa, the Region is exploring the possibility of establishing an informal "extractive industries practice" —drawing expertise from across the Bank to undertake work on thematic issues across the region, pool and share knowledge on emerging systemic issues, and respond more nimbly to client demand for knowledge and advice.

IEG Findings	IEG Recommendations
Strengthening program implementation: The World Bank's program implementation in Liberia has been constrained by some of the organizational arrangements, including administrative budgets, staffing, management attention, as well as inadequate guidance on managing procurement, including how to develop the necessary capacity.	The World Bank can provide more effective implementation support by: • Formally empowering the Liberia Country Manager to make critical decisions on the country program, coupled with holding the Manager accountable for tracking results and country portfolio performance, in light the Country Director's responsibility for multiple country programs. • Designating a person (or persons) to serve as a focal point on each of the cross-cutting themes (capacity building, gender and environment), with the responsibility for providing guidelines to sector staff and monitoring progress. • Developing a strategic vision for procurement capacity enhancement as an integral part of public financial management. In the short-term, this effort would need the support of a team of specialists to provide day-to-day procurement services and develop local capacity, possibly through private-public partnerships or management contracts akin to that of Manitoba Hydro. Special attention is needed in the road sector to determine whether to manage the sector from Washington or from the field. • There is an urgent need to reinvigorate the capacity of the Infrastructure Implementation Unit (IIU) at the Ministry of Public Works. In particular, the technical assistance on procurement of an international firm (under the Roads Asset Management Project) should be quickly restored, along with the resumption of recruitment of qualified staff as mandated by the IIU's implementation framework.

Acceptance by Management	Management Response
Agree	The Country Director assumed his post in early 2012. A clear division of responsibilities has been put in place ensuring delegation of authority and accountability for designing and implementing country program in Liberia. These internal procedures reinforce the formal Business Management Accountabilities of the Country Manager to, among other things: • Develop and implement the Country Assistance Strategy; • Lead the Bank's dialogue; • Take accountability for the results outlined in the CAS for the client country in coordination with operational staff, sectoral technical staff, and the country management team; • Support the development of high quality work programs and sector strategies based on the CAS and attuned to client demand and country contexts; • Provide oversight on portfolio management and quality issues, working with clients and the country teams to address implementation issues, and working to ensure high quality and results on the ground. The field-based Senior Operations Officer, coordinating with sector colleagues, will serve as the focal point for the cross-cutting themes, including capacity building, gender and the environment and any others that are identified in the new Country Partnership Strategy. For the upcoming fiscal year the Bank's budgetary allocation for Liberia has been increased by 28 percent, which reflects management's priority and realization of challenges of program development in a fragile environment. A strategic vision for enhancing procurement capacity will be presented as part of the governance strategy in the upcoming CPS. Procurement, together with contract management, is a key component in the overall objective of capacity building of the IIU. That capacity building will involve the engagement of the specialists through a professional firm (Transport Support Group-TSG) who will also provide for the necessary support, quality control and liability. The procurement process has started but has produced a very weak shortlist; the IIU has contacted additional consulting firms and the expanded shortlist will be submitted to the Bank shortly. During the last mission (April 2012), it was agreed that recruitment of a contracts manager and procurement specialist with international experience be carried out as an immediate interim measure until the intended consultancy firm (TSG) has been hired. The Ministry of Public Works is also increasing their efforts to retain qualified and experienced nationals, especially engineers, recruited both locally and from the Diaspora.

Report to the Board from the Committee on Development Effectiveness (CODE)— Sub-Committee Report

On September 7, 2012, the Sub-Committee (SC) of the Committee on Development Effectiveness (CODE) considered an Independent Evaluation Group (IEG) report entitled the *Liberia Country Program Evaluation, 2004–2011* (CODE2012-0033).

Summary[1]

Members welcomed the timeliness of the report and commended IEG and management for exemplary collaboration efforts , while maintaining IEG's due independence. They noted that the report will help sharpen the World Bank Group's focus and relevance in Liberia; and that its findings and recommendations will be reflected by Management in the upcoming Country Partnership Strategy (CPS) for 2013–15.

Concurring with IEG's overall evaluation, the Committee recalled the severely distressed state Liberia was in ten years ago and noted the remarkable progress that has been achieved. Members supported IEG's findings and recommendations, namely, fighting corruption by strengthening governance practices across the value chain of extractive industries; refocusing the growth agenda to make it more broad-based and inclusive; and strengthening implementation support through capacity development, especially in procurement. Despite progress in the country, members agreed that many challenges remain. Nevertheless, they were encouraged by the Bank's recent support and actions in several areas: (i) shifting from emergency assistance to a long-term development mode; (ii) addressing security risks and fiscal challenges resulting from the planned UN mission draw-down; (iii) enhancing project implementation and procurement capacity without undermining efforts to strengthen institutional capacity; and, (iv) addressing staffing constraints.

Members noted that the IEG report was not adequately linked to the 2011 World Development Report (WDR) on Conflict, Security and Development. Members proposed that in their recommendations IEG provide specific suggestions to help country teams set priorities when preparing Country Assistance Strategies, while taking into consideration limited International Development Association (IDA) resources. They also encouraged IEG not only to present lessons learned, but also to identify successes that could possibly be replicated. Some members noted that gender issues did not receive adequate attention. Recognizing the need for further analysis on an appropriate methodology to assess the World Bank's work in Fragile and Conflict States (FCS), IEG informed Committee members that this topic would be covered in its Thematic Evaluation of World Bank support to FCS, on which an approach paper will be presented to members in October.

Recommendations and Next Steps

The Committee asked that flagged issues, such as regional integration, staffing, reconciliation filter, gender and other cross-cutting issues should be added to the IEG approach paper on FCS. Management indicated that it will take into account the IEG's findings and recommendations in preparing the new CPS, assuring members that it will include a clear analysis of the gender dimension.

Main Issues Discussed

Staffing issues. Members noted that having sufficient staffing in FCS is essential to preserve the quality of the WBG's interventions and urged management to address this issue systematically. They favored, when possible, deployment of staff to the field, and a proposal was made to create an incentive system to attract experienced staff to work in Liberia. Some inquired how the Nairobi Hub could be used to help address staffing challenges. Management agreed that it was better to have experienced in-country staff but, as seen in the Afghanistan evaluation, it was not realistic or financially feasible to deploy global expertise for every Bank program in the country. Management indicated that they were working on building a flexible staffing model within existing budgetary and other constraints to address this in Liberia, including by frequently drawing on senior expertise from near-by countries. Furthermore, management informed members that the Nairobi Hub was being staffed-up, and that it would be used selectively where its fields of expertise coincided with Liberia's needs. Acknowledging that staffing issues were critical and not unique to Liberia, members asked IEG to include the topic in its FCS evaluation.

Natural resources. Members agreed on the need to systematically enhance the quality of governance across the value chain of resource extraction with the overarching goal of sharing the benefits among all Liberians. A suggestion was made to facilitate practical exchanges across the regions, such as learning from the Latin America and Caribbean (LAC) experience in this matter. Management confirmed that they intended to carry forward the recommendations on thematic emphasis, reflecting a more robust poverty reduction agenda. To this end, they were undertaking analytical work on natural resources and the forestry sector, which they considered the most appropriate areas to direct future assistance.

Donor coordination. Members noted the efficient donor coordination under the government's leadership and the size and scale of assistance, but expressed concern about the impacts of United Nations Mission in Liberia (UNMIL) withdrawal. In response, management explained that the government would need to scale up own security efforts, noting that this would have a budgetary impact. Recognizing that withdrawal of UN troops was common among post-conflict or in-conflict states, it was suggested that a framework be developed to analyze the impact of such withdrawals.

Procurement. Members concurred with IEG that procurement capacity be considered integral to public financial management across all public services.

Management provided assurances that procurement management would take a more holistic approach moving forward.

Private sector. Members recognized the importance of the private sector and encouraged management to support public-private partnership (PPP) development in the new programming cycle. IEG noted that the private sector had a crucial role to play but that needed to be balanced by realistic expectations of the existence of an enabling business environment.

Other issues. Members noted that attempts should be made to mainstream gender into future operations and stressed that much needed to be done in relation to prevention of gender-based violence and to close the gender gap in education and health. In response to comments that a reconciliation filter would be useful for Liberia and other FCS, management explained they were working on developing one with the Nairobi Hub to screen programs and activities and to address drivers of conflict. On the question of the Bank's interventions in agriculture, Management replied that agriculture was critical for job creation in Liberia and that there would be three agricultural operations active during the CPS period, and those would be complemented by investments in health and education.

Anna Brandt, Chairperson

Note

1. In accordance with the World Bank Access to Information Policy, the summary portion of this Report to the Board will be disclosed when it is finalized.

Chapter 1

Introduction

The objective of this country program evaluation (CPE) is to learn from previous experience of providing assistance in Liberia and to draw lessons for improving the effectiveness of future World Bank Group operations – both in Liberia and in other fragile and conflict-affected states (FCSs). The CPE reviews the outcomes of World Bank Group interventions, including lending, non-lending services, debt relief and the harmonization and alignment of development assistance. The evaluation takes into account Liberia's unique circumstances, including the initial conditions of a fractured society, the near total destruction caused by the war, and the overriding need to prevent renewed hostilities.

This evaluation also provides a platform to review how some of the key issues faced by FCSs, including those highlighted in the 2011 World Development Report, have played out in relation to World Bank Group support to Liberia. The primary challenge for most of these countries is to break the cycle of violence by strengthening legitimate institutions and enabling them to provide security, justice, and support job creation. The report examines how the World Bank Group has helped Liberia meet this challenge by examining how the issues have been tackled and what progress has been made. The report also reviews the extent to which Liberia has experienced some of the common limitations in World Bank Group support, including slow internal processes and segregation of its operations from those specialized in security or humanitarian relief.

Approach. This report uses the Independent Evaluation Group (IEG) standard methodology and rating criteria for Country Program Evaluations – as presented in Appendix B: Guide to Country Program Evaluation Methodology. In addition, the report also incorporates the following considerations.

First, the test of relevance is made more fragility-sensitive, recognizing special factors such as the need to support social inclusiveness, in addition to the alignment with government plans and World Bank Group strategies.

Second, the evaluation looks beyond the achievement of objectives to consider, among other things, unintended effects of pursuing targets and reasons why progress varies. It also reviews the responsiveness of World Bank Group interventions.

Third, the report places a special emphasis on learning, with a focus on the challenges of a post-conflict situation and finding workable modalities of assistance.

Scope. The report takes FY04–FY11 as the period of review, corresponding approximately to the interval between the release of the Country Reengagement Note (March 2004) and that of the Country Assistance Strategy (CAS) Progress Report (June 2011).[1] The coverage includes the full range of World Bank Group activities, irrespective of whether they are funded by the International Development Association (IDA) or trust fund resources. The role of the World Bank Group in harmonizing development partner assistance and aligning it with country priorities is also taken into account. In addition, this evaluation covers the World Bank (IDA), the International Finance Corporation (IFC), the

Multilateral Investment Guarantee Agency (MIGA) and trust-fund programs in an integrated manner, reflecting the contribution of the World Bank Group as a whole in achieving its objectives. It is understood, however, that IFC was not active in Liberia until FY2006 and MIGA until FY2010.

Structure of the Report

This report consists of three parts: (i) an introduction (chapters 1 and 2); (ii) the main body of the report (chapters 3, 4, 5 and 6); and (iii) a perspective on the overall country program (chapters 7 and 8). This chapter sets out the objectives of the evaluation, followed by background information on the country context. Chapter 2 then introduces the World Bank Group country program in relation to Liberia's objectives and the programs of other partners.

The main body of the report is organized by pillar and cross-cutting theme as set forth in the strategy documents. Thus, chapter 3 reviews the outcome of World Bank Group support for rebuilding core state functions. Chapter 4 reviews the outcome on rehabilitating infrastructure, and chapter 5 on facilitating pro-poor growth. Chapter 6 reviews cross-cutting themes, including capacity building, gender equality and environmental sustainability. The rest of the report reviews the program as a whole. Chapter 7 discusses the organizational support for the Liberia program, which have major implications on the implementation support and portfolio management of the World Bank Group. Chapter 8 gives an overall assessment and conclusions of this evaluation. Finally, appendix A presents the standard Independent Evaluation Group (IEG) ratings, and overall assessment of the Liberia program.

The Country Context

Founded in 1821 by former American slaves, Liberia is rich in natural resources, with an abundance of iron ore, timber, diamonds, gold, vast hydro-power potential, offshore oil fields, and a climate favorable for agriculture. This wealth has played a key role in setting the course of Liberia's history, including inflicting the symptoms of a resource curse (See box 1.1). Until 1980, the descendants of settlers (Americo-Liberians), which represent a small minority (5 percent) of the population, had controlled political power. Indeed, they remain a dominant force today. A representative democracy, Liberia has a multi-party system, with 15 counties under a unitary central government and an elected president. The legislature consists of a Senate with 30 elected members and a House of Representatives with 64 members.

Growth without development. From its founding until the 1980s, Liberia enjoyed an extended economic expansion. After World War II, the economy grew rapidly, as subsistence agriculture gave way to large-scale rubber plantations, commercial forestry and mining. Propelled by strong commodity prices, Liberia reached the status of a lower middle-income country by the early 1970s. The performance, however, masked a darker side. Poor governance and social

Box 1.1	Were Natural Resources a Curse to Liberia?

Liberia is very well endowed with natural resources. Natural resources have led the economy since World War II, dominating the formal sector and accounting for more than 90 percent of exports in peacetime.[a] (See table A below.) But has this wealth been a curse to Liberia?

It seems so, although the storyline is somewhat unusual. The resources did not bring about poor governance. Indeed, the exercise of authority has been problematic long before natural resources were developed and harvested. As Liberia's 2008 Poverty Reduction Strategy (PRS) states (World Bank 2008): "The founding constitution was designed for the needs of the settler population and subjugated the indigenous people for over a century." In addition, the resource revenue collected was not entirely wasted, except perhaps during the war. Although little of the money went into service delivery, much of it was used to buy peace in the country through patronage payments that kept regional warlords from engaging in violence (Reno 1997).

Table A	Share of Natural Resources in GDP (percent)		
	1965	1987/89	2004/05
Natural Resources	37	21	32
Of which, Rubber	10	6	20
Forestry	2	5	12
Mining*	25	10	0

Source: World Bank 2008c.
Note:* Mining production was depressed by the war in the 1980s and terminated in the 1990s.
GDP= gross domestic product.

Nonetheless, natural resources were still a curse in that they undermined stability and prolonged the civil war. The corrosive feature was the large swings in price. The commodity boom of the 1960s brought peace and prosperity to Liberia. But when commodity prices were depressed in the 1970s, government revenue plummeted, as did the largesse available to regional warlords. Unrest began to spread, leading to a military coup in 1980. During the war, various warlords took up arms to gain control over timber and diamonds. Proceeds from the sale of these items financed the war and kept it going for two decades. Not until the United Nations applied sanctions on diamonds (2001) and timber (2003) did the cash dry up, bringing an end to the war in August 2003.

The war's destruction was so profound that it has taken the resource sector almost a decade to recover. Less than 10 percent of forest concessions are in operation today, while iron ore exports did not begin until November 2011. Nonetheless, there is no doubt that natural resources will rebound and once again dominate the economy.

Managing the resource sector effectively is of central importance to Liberia's future. Although good progress has been made, especially with the Liberia Extractive Industries Transparency Initiative (EITI) and robust public financial management, much remains to be done to ensure that the revenues from Liberia's natural resources can reliably translate into better public services for the benefit of all. (See box 8.1 in chapter 8.)

Source: IEG.

a. Ministry of Planning and Economic Affairs. "External Trade of Liberia." Various issues: 1971–81.

exclusion kept the vast majority of Liberians in poverty and inhibited social cohesion. Contemporary scholars noted that it was a case of growth without development (Clower and others 1966).

The coup d'état of April 1980 marked the beginning of a protracted calamity, as the country unraveled and plunged into a deep decline. A multitude of factors precipitated the war.

Social injustice and oppression of human rights. Through the years, political institutions deprived most Liberians, especially women and rural residents, of basic human rights. According to the Liberia Poverty Reduction Strategy (PRS):

> The founding constitution was designed for the needs of the settlers, with less involvement of the indigenous people. In the early days, land and property rights of the majority of Liberians were severely limited. Later, marginalization was perpetuated by the urban-based policies of successive administrations. Political power was concentrated at the Presidency. Most infrastructure and basic services were concentrated in Monrovia. Marginalization of youths and women was widespread (Government of Liberia 2008).

Outside the capital, some tribal customs suppressed the rights of ordinary people. Village heads and tribal chiefs controlled the resources and often used their power to the detriment of local people (see box 1.2).

Loss of external funding. Historically, political leaders protected domestic stability by distributing the largesse from abroad to tribal strongmen, who were often well armed, in exchange for peace. But in the late 1980s, the collapse of the Soviet Union ended the Cold War. The willingness of the West and Eastern Bloc to buy favor from strategic allies diminished, which together with depressed commodity prices, cut deeply into the economic assistance for countries like Liberia. The loss of foreign funding also interrupted the flow of

---

Box 1.2	Agrarian Roots of Conflict

Here is one illustration of how traditional customs deprive people of basic human rights:

The resentments of impoverished villagers in the Mano River region are deeply rooted. Non-elite families do not enjoy secure land, labor or marital rights. Many young people view local systems of land tenure and marriage payments as instruments of exploitation by chiefs. There is enough evidence to suggest that land grabbing and the exploitation of labor through marriage have been powerful sources of conflict in rural Liberia. Further evidence that peace in this region is undermined by agrarian discontent is provided by the armed conflict in Cote d'Ivoire, a country lacking diamonds and timber but riddled with agrarian tensions. In all cases, reform of rural rights is as urgent as tracking diamond and timber smugglers. Under systems prevailing for several centuries, rights belonged only to the children of chiefs.

Source: Richards 2005.

money going to tribal warlords around the country, leading to more unrest and a breakout of violence (see box 1.3).

As turbulence spread and intensified, Liberia splintered into numerous **factions**. Some attempted to take over state power, as with the National Patriotic Front of Liberia (NPFL) led by Charles Taylor, while others aimed to capture smaller territories. The breakdown of law and order put an end to large-scale operations in mining, forestry and rubber. The formal economy collapsed, driving households into subsistence farming. Economic hardship, in turn, drove more factions into desperate tactics of plunder and random violence. For a time, the war became self-perpetuating.

The Devastation. All told, the 14 years of conflict (1989–03) resulted in a scale of destruction seldom seen in the modern world. About 220,000 people (or 8 percent of the population) lost their lives; and twice as many were displaced. More than half of the women were sexually assaulted. Most schools and health facilities were destroyed. Infant and maternal mortality rose to shockingly high levels (196 per 1000 and 578 per 100,000 live births, respectively). In cities, water, electricity and other public services ceased. Roads crumbled under the erosion of perennial rains and lack of maintenance. The economy was in ruins, with the formal sector, particularly large-scale mining and rubber plantations, crippled. By 2003 when the violence stopped, four out of five workers were without jobs. A generation of young Liberians never attended school—or saw their education disrupted.

Peacekeeping. After the war, the world community responded with uncommon solidarity. Led by the United Nations Mission in Liberia (UNMIL) and the Economic Community of West African States (ECOWAS), a large number of

---

| **Box 1.3** | How Geopolitics Undermined Liberia's Stability |

Geopolitics undermined Liberia's stability in many ways.

In Liberia, warfare followed the breakdown of strategies that Cold War-era rulers used to control resources and enhance their own power. Previously, they converted formal aspects of the state—its institutions, laws, creditworthiness and capacity to attract aid from outsiders—into patronage that they could distribute to followers. Rulers consciously undermined their own bureaucracies. Effective bureaucrats might acquire interests at odds with those of the ruler. In this context, state spending on health services, education, or agriculture diverted scarce political resources that could be used to bolster the ruler's personal power.

The end of the Cold War brought declining aid from abroad and the imposition of an external mandate for reform. Rulers of African states suddenly lost the economic tools that they had previously used to exercise power. Having abjured building long-term legitimacy through meeting the needs of their people, rulers could not draw upon popular support when enterprising strongmen began to build their own power bases. Pressure from outsiders to promote economic and political liberalization further undermined the stability of these states.

Source: Reno 1997.

development partners soon arrived. Initially, the overriding goal was to disarm combatants and maintain peace. To be effective, a broad agenda was needed, encompassing security, humanitarian relief, human rights and reconstruction. An international force of 15,000 troops was mobilized from 40 countries, including military personnel, civilian police and an all-female squadron with a mandate to protect women and girls.

Transition to Democracy. Over time, more than 100,000 former combatants were disarmed and returned to normal life, although many remained unemployed. Nascent hostilities were effectively dealt with. More than 300,000 internally displaced people benefited from the support and facilities provided. Training was given to a large number of police and military personnel. The international community also created the Governance and Economic Management Assistance Program (GEMAP) which, in essence, was a system of fiduciary controls designed to curb corruption, as will be discussed later in chapter 3. In addition to official assistance, civil society organizations (CSOs) have played a crucial role. They have been active in health, education and civil rights. In the health sector, CSOs managed some 60 percent of development partners' funds in 2008, a role larger than that of the Ministry of Health. Three-quarters of Liberia's health facilities are now operated by nongovernmental organizations (NGOs) or faith-based organizations (FBOs).

The 2005 Elections. From October 2003 until January 2006, the National Transitional Government of Liberia (NTGL), which comprised the former belligerent groups, was in charge— but under extensive protection of international peacekeeping forces. Presidential and legislative elections were held in November 2005, and certified by independent observers as fair and free. Former World Bank Group economist Ellen Johnson-Sirleaf won the election, and became the first female head of state in Africa. In 2011, she was awarded the Nobel Peace Prize and won a second six-year term of office.

The Economy

Poverty. The civil war turned Liberia from a relatively well-off country — albeit one marked by extreme income inequality —to one of the poorest countries in the world. The per capita income, which reached a peak of $833 in 1972, collapsed during the war to US$135 per capita in 2003. The incidence of poverty was unusually high and close to universal in rural areas. According to a 2007 survey,[2] poverty was far more widespread in Liberia than in Sierra Leone where the conflict ended a year earlier, with 84 percent of Liberians earning less than US$1.25 per day, compared to 53 percent in Sierra Leone.

Since the war ended, growth has been positive but not impressive. The "peace dividend" has been modest, with gross domestic product (GDP) growth lower than that of Sierra Leone in the years following the Peace Accord (see table 1.1). The strong growth experienced in Sierra Leone right after the war did not materialize in Liberia.

Table 1.1	Comparative Growth – Liberia and Sierra Leone							
	Years after Peace Accord (Real GDP Growth (%))							
	0	1	2	3	4	5	6	7
Liberia (2003)	–31.3	2.6	5.3	7.8	9.4	7.1	NA	NA
Sierra Leone (2001)	18.2	27.4	9.5	7.4	7.2	7.3	6.4	5.5

Source: World Development Indicators.
Note: GDP= gross domestic product; NA= not available.

To a large extent, the subdued performance reflects the sanctions on timber and diamond exports which were imposed in July 2001. These sanctions were not lifted until 2006 (timber) and 2007 (diamonds). There were also delays in the production of iron ore due to a renegotiation of the contract with ArcelorMittal, and the need to rehabilitate the railway. Exports of iron ore did not resume until November 2011. Timber production was held back by regulatory and logistical issues including inadequate roads, land disputes, and a revocation of forest concessions in 2006.

Gender. Women have been the backbone of the economy. They account for 60 percent of agricultural production (food and cash crops) and 80 percent of trading activities in rural areas, which serve as a link between rural and urban markets. Nonetheless, with the exception of microcredit in the Monrovia area, women have less access than men to land, credit, training and technology (World Bank 2007). They have also been under-represented in politics, except during the war when they briefly established political authority within the camps for Internally Displaced Persons (IDP). Another exception is under the incumbent administration, where women are well represented as senior executives in key public agencies. Recent studies conducted in ten of the fifteen counties show a prevalence of gender-based violence (GBV), which appears to be rooted in cultural beliefs and exacerbated by a continuation of behavior prevalent during the war.

Debt Relief. External debt accumulated since the 1980s stood at $4.8 billion in 2003 (800 percent of GDP), making Liberia one of the most heavily-indebted countries (see table 1.2 below). However, by June 2010 when Liberia reached the completion point under the Heavily-Indebted Poor Countries' Initiative (HIPC), a variety of mechanisms for debt relief took effect. Thereafter, Liberia benefited from debt reduction provided by the World Bank Group, the International Monetary Fund (IMF), and the African Development Bank under the Multilateral Debt Relief Initiative (MDRI). The European Union (EU) also provided additional debt relief under its Special Debt Relief Initiative. In September 2010, Liberia reached agreement with the Paris Club (sovereign) creditors for a 100 percent cancellation of the remaining debt. Many bilateral agreements reduced the remaining debt. In all, 95 percent of the initial debt has been canceled.

Table 1.2	Liberia's Overall Debt Position (US$ millions)				
	JUN-07	JUN-09	JUN-10	SEP-10	MAR-11
Total External	4,892.3	1,782.0	1,553.0	282.5	224.3
Multilateral	1,619.2	1,070.7	1,006.7	138.8	102.3
Bilateral	1,587.3	690.8	525.8	123.2	121.5
Commercial	1,685.8	20.5	20.5	20.5	0.5
Domestic	307.9	298.1	292.2	282.2	281.0
Total Debt	5,200.2	2,080.1	1,845.2	564.7	505.3

Source: Government of Liberia 2011.

Notes

1. The AfDB is not planning to conduct a review of its assistance to Liberia in the near future.

2. Core Welfare Indicators Questionnaire. 2007.

References

Government of Liberia. 2011. "Third Quarter 2010–11 Public Debt Management Report." Ministry of Finance Debt Management Unit. Liberia: Ministry of Finance.

Liberia Institute of Statistics and Geo-Information. 2007. Core Welfare Indicators Questionnaire.

Reno, W. 1997. "Humanitarian Emergencies and Warlord Economic in Liberia and Sierra Leone." Working Paper No. 140. Helsinki, Finland: The United Nations University, World Institute for Development Economics Research.

Richards, Paul. 2005. "To Fight or to Farm? Agrarian Dimensions of the Mano River Conflicts." *Oxford Journals* 104(417): 571–590.

World Bank. 2011. "Liberia – Country Assistance Strategy Progress Report for the Period FY09–FY12." Report No. 59772. Washington, D.C.: World Bank.

———. 2008. *Lift Liberia: A Poverty Reduction Strategy.* Washington, D.C.: World Bank.

———. 2007. *Liberia: Toward Women's Economic Empowerment: A Gender Needs Assessment.* Report prepared by the World Bank's Gender and Development Group in collaboration with the Liberian Ministry of Gender and Development. Washington, D.C.: World Bank.

———. 2004. "Liberia – Country Reengagement Note." Report No. 28387. Washington, D.C.: World Bank.

Chapter 2
The Liberia Program

"Across the country, Liberians speak of building a country where a child can live in safety, go to a school with good teachers, get clean water and medicine, and study by electric light."
—Ellen Johnson Sirleaf, in Liberia Poverty Reduction Strategy (2008)

Liberia's Objectives: Breaking with the Past

The vision of a more inclusive and open society emerged from the elected government. In its plan for the first 150 days (from January 16, 2006), the government set out a framework with four pillars designed to secure political stability, socially-inclusive recovery, and restoration of basic services. The pillars were: (i) expanding peace and security; (ii) revitalizing the economy; (iii) strengthening governance and the rule of law; and (iv) rehabilitating infrastructure and delivering basic services. This framework was subsequently reaffirmed in the interim poverty reduction strategy (World Bank 2007b) and the full poverty reduction strategy (World Bank 2008b).

The government wished to break away from the exploitative rule of the past and move toward a more humane future. (See box 2.1.) It embarked on a broadly-based consultative process in the development of a poverty reduction strategy. Consultations took place with all segments of society, including civil society organizations and the private sector. The Liberia Reconstruction and Development Committee (LRDC), a high-level steering group chaired by the President and including partners like the World Bank Group, coordinated the process. This approach was a repudiation of the country's legacy of exclusion, which led to discontent and conflicts. The new poverty reduction strategy was seen as an instrument for healing and rebuilding national cohesion.

Reflecting the long-suppressed needs of Liberians and overwhelming material scarcity, the PRS was infused with a keen sense of urgency. The targets were ambitious, far exceeding available resources and implementation capacity. The government envisioned an active campaign to attract additional assistance from foreign partners and greater involvement of the private sector, both domestic and international. The government also established a mechanism for monitoring and evaluation to ensure prompt corrective actions where needed.

Before the arrival of the elected government, policymaking under the National Transitional Government of Liberia (NTGL) was guided in part by the exigencies of a humanitarian crisis and in part by the preparation for the 2005 elections. The Results Focused Transitional Framework (RFTF), endorsed by the international community at the landmark Liberia Reconstruction Conference in New York in February 2004, set the overall direction. The priorities of the RFTF reflected the findings of an emergency needs assessment conducted immediately after the peace agreement. With a horizon of two years, the RFTF mainly targeted post-war demobilization, reintegration of former combatants, and paving the way for the elections in 2005. The contents of RFTF, grouped in ten clusters, also served as a terms of reference for the NTGL.

| Box 2.1 | Healing the Deep Wounds of Civil War |

The 2008 Poverty Reduction Strategy sets out the following vision for Liberia:

The new Liberia aims to acknowledge and begin to move beyond the divisions, marginalization, and exclusion of the past and to create circumstances where differences are discussed, not fought over. Liberia cannot simply recreate the economic and political structures of the past. It must respond to the deep wounds of the civil war while taking strong steps to establish the foundation for sustained stability and peace in the future.

It must therefore create much greater economic and political opportunities for all Liberians, and not simply for a small elite class. Liberia must ensure that the benefits from growth, and the provision of basic health and education services, are spread much more equitably throughout the population, including women, children, youths and persons with disabilities.

It must address the social consequences of the war, including gender based violence (GBV) and the transmission of HIV and AIDS, which continue to permeate society today. It must grant more political power to the counties and districts, build transparency and accountability into government decision-making, and create stronger checks and balances across all three branches of government.

Source: World Bank 2008b.

Objectives of the World Bank Group

The World Bank Group program in Liberia is more challenging than most country programs. The war's destruction on human and physical capital was so profound that it was difficult to formulate a strategy. In addition, the World Bank Group had gone through a long period of disengagement, with an erosion of institutional knowledge about the country (see box 2.2). In addition, it was not just a question of how best to help, but how to pay for it. The funding issue arose from Liberia's non-accrual status[1] at the time of World Bank Group reengagement, which disqualified the country from IDA assistance. It was not until the arrears were cleared (2007) and the HIPC process was completed (2010) that Liberia again became eligible for assistance.

In mobilizing resources, the World Bank Group made use of unconventional funding sources, including sector-specific trust funds and trust funds designed for low-income countries under stress, which Liberia could access in spite of its arrears. The World Bank Group also established an additional trust fund specifically tailored to Liberia's needs (the Liberia Reconstruction Trust Fund - LRTF), drawing on special allocations from IBRD surpluses. Overall, trust funds supported $342 million of the $1.282 billion (27 percent) of assistance from FY04–FY11.[2] In terms of administrative costs, trust fund sources have played a larger role than the World Bank Group's own administrative budget. Over the review period, trust funds accounted for 54 percent of total administrative costs.

For nearly two decades, from December 1986 to April 2004, Liberia received no assistance from the World Bank. During most of this period, the country was engulfed in one of the longest, deadliest and most devastating civil wars. When the World Bank reengaged after the peace agreement, Liberia laid covered under the ashes of war.

After joining the World Bank in 1962, Liberia had been an active client, with a cumulative total of 37 projects. When the assistance was suspended in 1986, Liberia had an outstanding balance of $141 million from 22 International Bank for Reconstruction and Development (IBRD) loans and $44 million from 17 IDA credits. The large share of IBRD loans was unusual for a country in the region, and was indicative of Liberia's position at the time as a relatively well-off country. The portfolio at the time was well diversified, with projects ranging from infrastructure to forestry to education and urban services.

In the 1980s, under the double burden of depressed rubber prices, on the one hand, and protracted social turmoil, on the other, Liberia's economy faltered. By the end of 1986, the government failed to meet its scheduled debt service obligations, prompting the World Bank to suspend all disbursements. In June 1987, Liberia's loans were placed in non-accrual status.

Thereafter, the conflict in Liberia intensified and prevented further efforts by the World Bank to provide humanitarian assistance or stay engaged. The absence of financial support continued until 2004, when two emergency projects were approved under special funding arrangements for member countries under non-accrual status. One was a community empowerment project (of $4 million) financed by the Low-Income Countries Under Stress (LICUS) Trust Fund, and the other an infrastructure project (of $25 million) financed by a special grant from IBRD surplus. IBRD surplus funds may be used to finance projects in countries that are not sovereign (such as the West Bank and Gaza), are not World Bank members (such as Kosovo and Bosnia after the Balkan wars), or are in payment arrears.

Source: IEG.

Drivers of World Bank Group assistance. Although resources were very constrained, the needs for assistance were also very substantial in every area. In allocating its limited resources, the World Bank Group has generally been guided by three factors. First and foremost, it has been guided by the government's strategic direction, as well as by its own comparative advantage in particular areas, and available support from other partners or funding options.

In Liberia, the task of aligning the assistance with government priorities and coordinating with other partners has been facilitated by structured consultations among stakeholders. The principal areas of World Bank Group engagement were seldom in doubt during the review period. From the beginning, the international community looked to the World Bank Group for assistance in rebuilding core institutions and revitalizing the economy. However, it was also deemed necessary to create transitional delivery mechanisms to handle the flow of aid while the non-existent country systems were being rebuilt.

During the transitional period (2004–05), governance and expenditure control were the key areas of World Bank Group engagement. Thereafter, the Bank supported three out of the four pillars of the government's priorities, including economic recovery, governance, and infrastructure. The remaining pillar on peace and security was handled by the UNMIL and other partners. The budget constraints on the World Bank Group narrowed the range and limited the number of areas it could support, but did not prevent it from engaging in what it considered to be crucial interventions.

World Bank Group strategy documents. During the review period, the key strategies were contained in: The Country Reengagement Note (CRN) for the period March 2004–June 2007; The Interim Strategy Note (ISN) covering the period July 2007–June 2009; and The Joint Country Assistance Strategy (CAS) for June 2009–June 2011. Since June 2011, the CAS Progress Report (CASPR) has been in effect. Table 2.1 below provides a schematic presentation of World Bank Group objectives in the various strategy documents, from which the objectives assessed in this evaluation are derived.

Presented to the Board in March 2004 —half a year after the cessation of hostilities, the CRN envisioned a mission of "delivering fast and visible results on the ground." The main goal for this period was to assist in Liberia's transition to peace by supporting implementation of the RFTF. The areas of support were to include: rapid economic revival through labor-intensive public and community projects; the establishment of the state and basic economic governance; and the establishment of a multi-donor monitoring mechanism for the RFTF.

In addition, a major initiative was to enable Liberia to pay off the $1.7 billion of arrears owed to multilateral creditors, which precluded Liberia's access to major sources of assistance including that of IDA. Another priority was to help set the stage for the United Nations to lift sanctions on timber and diamonds. In June 2007, five months after the launch of the government's Interim Poverty Reduction Strategy (iPRS), the World Bank Group issued its ISN to guide the Liberia program over two years. Like the CRN, the overarching objective was to support Liberia's transition from post-conflict relief to long-term development. A strategic agenda was to fully restore normal relations with the international financial institutions, which required the clearance of existing arrears as well as obtaining debt relief under the enhanced HIPC and MDRI Initiatives. As the ISN was presented to the Bank's Board, the sanctions on timber and diamonds had been lifted and multilateral creditors, including IDA, were ready to remove the non-accrual status. A program was put in place to facilitate compliance with the requirements for debt relief. (See box 2.3 below).

The interim strategy was based on the government's iPRS, both in terms of substance and speed of delivery. The assistance was to support three of the four clusters of the iPRS: (i) revitalizing the economy; (ii) strengthening governance and the rule of law; and (iii) rehabilitating infrastructure and delivering basic services. The ISN also pledged to deliver "discernable impact in terms of dialogue, reforms and infrastructure rehabilitation" within one year. Specific targets were spelled out in a results matrix.

Early in 2008, having paid off the arrears to multilateral creditors (including the IMF and the World Bank), Liberia was accepted into the enhanced Heavily-Indebted Poor Countries (HIPC) Initiative. About two years later, it fulfilled the "completion point" requirements of the program and received full debt relief.

The World Bank Group, in partnership with the IMF, played a key role in supporting Liberia's efforts. Apart from administering the HIPC process, and conducting the analysis with the IMF to establish Liberia's eligibility (IMF 2008), the World Bank Group also:

- Mobilized resources to cover debt service payments before the debt relief;

- Helped clear arrears on commercial debt through the IDA Debt Reduction Facility; and

- Provided technical assistance for the preparation of the PRS and reforms in public financial management (as discussed in chapter 3).

When the debt relief took effect, president Sirleaf said: "Today is a day for Liberians to celebrate." Among the benefits that debt relief under the HIPC process brought to Liberia were:

- Cancelation of nearly $5 billion in external debt in 2010 (Lipsky 2010);

- Normalization of relations with foreign officials and private creditors;

- External support in revitalizing the economy (as discussed in chapters 3-6);

- Policy and institutional reforms as mandated under the program; and

- Resumption of foreign direct investments, especially in natural resources.

Without these benefits, the country would have been trapped, stagnating under the weight of a debilitating debt, with no access to external assistance beyond humanitarian relief. Any significant economic recovery and growth would have been difficult to achieve.

Source: IEG.

As with the CRN and ISN, the objective of the first full CAS was to support Liberia's transition from post-conflict recovery to long-term development. It was prepared jointly with the African Development Bank (AfDB) and presented to the Board in April 2009, to cover the period from July 2009 to June 2011. Overall lending was conservatively estimated at $139 million. As the CAS took effect, Liberia was current on its debt repayments, but the service obligations were still unmanageable. As indicated earlier, debt relief was a major goal supported by the Bank under the enhanced HIPC and MDRI initiatives.

The CAS was organized around three pillars of activities: rebuilding core state functions and institutions; rehabilitating infrastructure to jump-start economic growth; and facilitating pro-poor growth. The CAS also identified the crosscutting themes of capacity development, gender and the environment to be increasingly mainstreamed into World Bank Group programs. Since the CAS program is the most comprehensive and encompassing of all of the objectives stated in the preceding documents, as well as new elements not previously envisaged, it will also serve as the basis for the assessment to be made in the remainder of this report (table 2.1).

Table 2.1	Objectives of the World Bank Group to be Evaluated in This Report
Objectives of the World Bank Group	
Country Reengagement Note (CRN)	1. Support for social and economic revival.
	2. Support for the establishment of institutions and governance reforms.
	3. Capacity building to establish systems for donor coordination and the effective use of aid.
	Results Framework: None. RFTF served as a guiding tool.
Joint Interim Strategy Note (ISN)	1. Revitalizing the economy.
	2. Strengthening governance and the rule of law.
	3. Rehabilitating infrastructure and delivering basic services.
	Cross –cutting themes: gender, capacity building.
	Results Framework: includes milestones but not outcome measures.
Country Assistance Strategy (CAS)	1. Rebuilding core state functions and institutions.
	2. Rehabilitating infrastructure to jump-start economic growth.
	3. Facilitating pro-poor growth.
	Cross–cutting objective: capacity development.
	Strategic mainstreaming: gender, environmental sustainability.
	Results Framework: contains outcomes as well as milestones.
↓ ↓ ↓	
World Bank Group Objectives used in this Evaluation	
Pillars	1. Rebuilding core state functions and institutions
	• Fiscal policy and financial management
	• Comprehensive civil service reform
	• Improving governance and the rule of law
	2. Rehabilitating infrastructure to jump-start economic growth
	• Transport: Rehabilitating the transport network and institutions
	• Energy: Restoring critical infrastructure on an emergency basis
	• Water and Sanitation: Restoring critical services
	• Telecommunications: Reducing the cost of telecom services
	3. Facilitating pro-poor growth
	• Agriculture and fishery
	• Mining
	• Forest management
	• Investment climate
	• Human development
Cross–Cutting Themes:	Capacity development; Gender; Environmental sustainability

Source: World Bank Group strategy documents.

Note: RFTF= Results-Focused Transition Framework.

The CAS was guided by the PRS, both in substance and in the sense of urgency. As the World Bank Group stated: "The CAS has been designed with a strong focus on achieving and demonstrating results on the ground. The CAS Results Framework uses Liberia's PRS as its starting point, and narrows down the range of PRS objectives to those that the World Bank Group (and AfDB) can demonstrably contribute to during the CAS period."(World Bank 2009a) In effect, the assistance intended to help the government not just to achieve its goals, but also to achieve them according to the government's own timeframe.

To pursue these objectives, each of the strategy's pillars proposed a program of interventions, including lending and non-lending services. Table 2.2 gives an overview of the planned support.

The country team presented the CAS Progress Report to the Board in June 2011. It provided an update on CAS implementation, upheld the strategic approach, and extended the period of CAS coverage by one year to July 2012. In addition, drawing on larger than expected resources that became available, the CASPR proposed a substantially larger program of assistance than envisaged in the CAS, increasing the size of credit in the pipeline, adding new projects and expanding non-lending activities.

Results Frameworks Underlying the World Bank Group Program

The World Bank Group strategies have made use of progressively more elaborate results frameworks. The 2004 CRN did not clearly indicate how results were to be achieved or monitored. Instead, it referred to the government's Results-Focused Transitional Framework, which was developed with the help of Bank staff. The 2007 ISN was to cover a short period of twelve months; it made use of a rudimentary framework with no specific "outcomes" or indicators. A

Table 2.2	Overview of Planned Interventions*			
Strategy	Period	Number of AAAs	Number of Projects	Indicative Commitments ($ millions)
Country Reengagement Note	FY05–07	17	9	29
Interim Strategy Note	FY08	5	6	521
Country Assistance Strategy	FY09–11	15	12	138
CAS Progress Report	FY12	6	5	65

Source: IEG.

* Refers to the Base Case Scenario indicative program.

Note: The Country Reengagement Note indicating $29 million in commitments includes $4 million from the Low-Income Countries Under Stress (LICUS) Trust Fund and $25 million from surplus allocation. Country strategies do not specify planned operations for IFC or MIGA.

AAA= analytic and advisory activity; CAS= Country Assistance Strategy; FY= fiscal year.

series of "milestones"—intermediate steps or outputs, but generally not the ultimate outcomes—were identified, including four for core state functions; 17 for infrastructure; and eight for economic revitalization.

The CAS includes a more detailed results framework that identifies the outcomes (mostly of intermediate nature) to be achieved, as well as the activities of the World Bank Group (and the African Development Bank) that are expected to help bring them to fruition. In addition, a series of milestones are given for different years. In practice, however, monitoring activities of the country team have been conducted on the basis of milestones, such as completion of certain audits or resurfacing of particular roads. The 2011 CAS Progress Report revised the CAS results framework to create a leaner version, and extended the program by one year. Primary education was added as a component and some indicator targets were revised.

Analytical and Advisory Activities

In terms of financial support, the World Bank Group is merely one of many large actors and also a late entrant due to Liberia's non-accrual status. In conveying developmental knowledge, however, it has a distinctive niche—with its role being much valued and sought after.

Technical assistance started immediately after the peace agreement in 2003. Bank staff, along with representatives of the United Nations, were among the first development partners to arrive in Liberia. Much of the knowledge work was conducted under two small operations supported by the LICUS trust funds. Initially, the Bank collaborated with the United Nations Development Programme (UNDP) in the Joint Needs Assessment for the transitional government. Bank staff helped address a broad range of critical issues, including policy actions needed to: (i) lift the sanctions on timber and diamonds; (ii) develop a regulatory framework to re-launch power transmission; and (iii) reactivate public financial management; and (iv) restore port operations in Monrovia.

Several Analytic and Advisory Activities (AAAs) were of particular importance including a Rapid Social Assessment (Richards and others 2005), which built the crucial knowledge base for World Bank Group interventions in community empowerment and social protection. The creation of GEMAP – the Governance and Economic Management Assistance Program, helped provide much needed integrity to public finance. It mitigated donor concerns about the diversion of their assistance, and included a large-scale, multi-sector technical assistance project, supported by the Liberia Reconstruction Trust Fund. It covered roads, ports, airports, energy, water and sanitation. The resulting assessments identified the most critical areas for urgent World Bank Group assistance, which led to the first wave of projects, and produced pre-feasibility studies of follow-on interventions.

A series of analytical studies (or activities or products) began to emerge around FY2007, including advisory services of the IFC and larger economic and sector work. A broad range of issues was examined, both to address urgent needs and to prepare for future operations. Most of the knowledge work, however, related to the first (core state functions) and third (pro-poor growth) pillars. Among the products noted by the government and other partners are: the 2007 Public Expenditure and Financial Accountability (PEFA) Assessment; the 2008 Insecurity of Land Tenure and Land Law, and; the 2009 Public Expenditure Management and Financial Accountability Review (PEMFAR). Overall, 35 knowledge activities were completed during the review period, including seven advisory service activities of the IFC.

Overview of Lending

The World Bank Group has been one of Liberia's principal development partners, providing both technical and financial assistance. In financial terms, it is one of the largest, along with the United States, the African Development Bank, and the IMF. Between FY04 and FY11, the World Bank Group committed a total of $1.284 billion, including $1.121 billion from IDA and trust funds, $21 million from the IFC, and $142 million from MIGA (see table 2.3).

Early Bank projects were based on emergency procedures and addressed the needs of war-affected areas, including road work and community empowerment. Implementation arrangements were improvised based on practicality, with reliance on the newly-created autonomous agency, the Liberation Agency for Community Empowerment (LACE), with the UNDP as executor. Over time, and in addition to transport and community empowerment, the engagement broadened to encompass public sector reforms. In FY10 and FY11, as the debt relief allowed greater access to IDA assistance, World Bank Group activities proliferated, with new projects in urban development, information technology, agriculture, energy and education.

World Bank Group support has been heavily concentrated in the rehabilitation of infrastructure, that is, pillar 2 of the assistance strategy. In terms of new assistance (and excluding arrears clearance), $468 million out of a total of $854 million (55 percent) was allocated to infrastructure projects. Within this pillar, the majority (90 percent) was devoted to transport, primarily to road rehabilitation and maintenance. Apart from the arrears clearance, the first pillar (core state functions) generated new commitments of $84 million. The third pillar (pro-poor growth) generated $302 million, although more than $200 million of those commitments were made in FY2011, including MIGA's $142 million guarantee.

The size of assistance during this period, however, was significantly influenced by two large operations. One was the $430 million grant for the Reengagement and Reform Support Program (RRSP) in FY2008 which was designed to pay off the IDA arrears and end Liberia's non-accrual status. However, it was not intended to inject funds into new development programs. The other was an FY11 MIGA guarantee of $142 million provided in support of a foreign direct investment in a natural resource project. This project does not involve any disbursements from the World Bank Group to Liberia.

Table 2.3	World Bank Group Financial Operations, 2004–11 (US$ million)							
Commitments	World Bank Group Total		IDA + Trust Fund		IFC		MIGA	
Sector	US$m	%	US$m	%	US$m	%	US$m	%
Pillar1. Rebuilding State Functions	514	40	514	46				
Pillar 2: Rehabilitating Infrastructure	468	36	468	42				
Pillar 3: Facilitating Pro-Poor Growth	302	24	139	12	21	100	142	100
Agriculture and Fishing	28	2	28	2	10			
Finance	11	1			11	52		
Natural Resource	162	13	10	1		48	142	100
Social Sectors	101	8	101	9				
Total	1,284	100	1,121	100	21	100	142	100

Source: World Bank Group Project databases.

Note: MIGA volumes represent guarantee values. IDA= International Development Association; IFC= International Finance Corporation; MIGA= Multilateral Investment Guarantee Agency.

A vastly different picture emerges when the RRSP and MIGA guarantee are excluded. Net of these two operations, World Bank Group assistance was considerably smaller, with total commitments of about $726 million – most of which were made in FY10 and FY11. Furthermore, total disbursements from World Bank Group operations between 2004 and 2010 amounted to $90 million (about 2 percent of total disbursements from official sources), nearly all of which ($82 million) came in FY09-10. Over this period (2004–10), average annual disbursement from the World Bank Group was small, about $11 million per year. Thus, the financial impact of the World Bank Group has been modest, although it has grown rapidly.

The actual operations during the period differed substantially from the plans presented. Of the 48 operations approved by the Board, about one half (24 operations) were not included in the proposed strategies. (See table 2.4) However, of the 27 projects explicitly mentioned in the strategies, 24 were delivered promptly as scheduled. These were the principal interventions of strategic importance to the program. Unplanned operations, considered for the most part less urgent or strategic, were added when unanticipated funding became available. Although large, the variance between planned and actual activities should not be surprising. First, the plans were made on the basis of severe data limitations. Second, the situation on the ground was fluid and changeable. Third, resource availability could not have been forecast accurately. Finally, the government frequently needed to amend its priorities.

Partnerships

When hostilities ended in 2003, the international community responded with generous support. Initially, the focus was on peacekeeping and humanitarian

Table 2.4	Planned and Actual Operations					
			Of which			Total
	Planned	Delivered	Delayed	Dropped	Unplanned	Approved
FY 2005–07	9	9	0	0		
FY08	6	4	0	2	2	11
FY09	2	2	0	0	8	12
FY10	3	2	0	1	5	7
FY11	7	7	0	0	5	7
TOTAL	27	24	0	3	4	11

Source: Internal World Bank database.

relief. The peaceful elections of November 2005 and the democratic transition opened the gateway for more assistance. Over the years, the track record of the government encouraged more aid flows. Official development assistance, which was about $213 million in 2004, expanded to $1.422 billion in 2010 (see Table 2.5). More than 50 official entities, both national and multilateral, contributed.

The World Bank Group has been one of Liberia's largest and most active development partners. In financial terms, it has been one of the principal contributors, with a share of about 11 percent of total disbursements (see figure 2.1). Other major providers of financial assistance are the United States, the IMF, Germany and the European Union.[3] In addition, the World Bank Group is one of the most active, as indicated by the number of sectors in which it has provided support. As shown in table 2.6, it has a total of 15 sector-level engagements (including the World Bank and IFC) and plays a leadership role in five sectors.[4] Other active partners are the United States and the United Nations, with 10

Table 2.5	Official Development Assistance to Liberia (Net disbursement in US$ million)								
Donor	2003	2004	2005	2006	2007	2008	2009	2010	Total 04–10
Bilateral donors									
DAC Total	70	163	144	187	229	819	340	702	2,586
Non-DAC Total	0	0	0	0	1	27	1	2	32
Multilaterals									
Multilateral Total	37	50	78	72	471	405	171	718	1,966
All Donors, Total	107	213	222	260	701	1,250.99	513	1,423	4,584

Source: Organisation for Economic Co-operation and Development (OECD), Development Assistance Committee (DAC).

Figure 2.1 — Share of Official Development Assistance by Partner

Based on cumulative disbursement during the period 2004-10

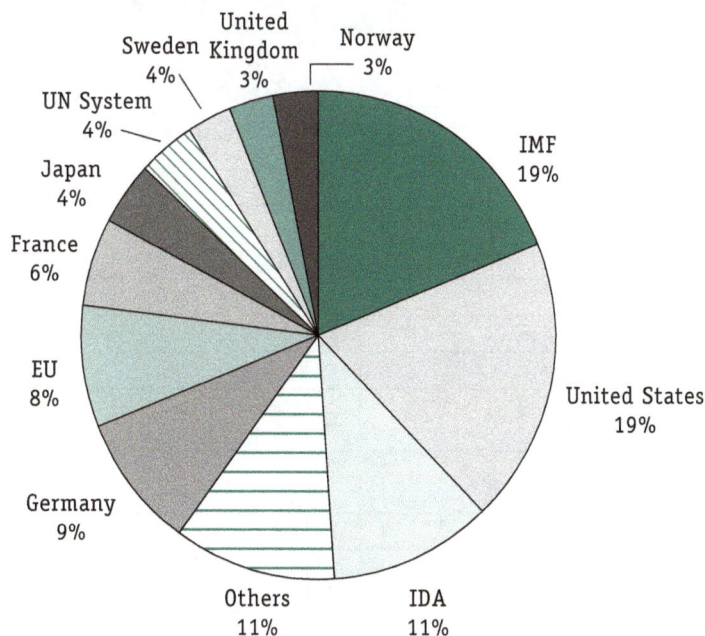

Sweden 4%
United Kingdom 3%
Norway 3%
UN System 4%
Japan 4%
France 6%
EU 8%
Germany 9%
Others 11%
IDA 11%
IMF 19%
United States 19%

Source: OECD-DAC database.

Note: EU= European Union; IDA= International Development Association; IMF= International Monetary Fund; UN= United Nations.

sector level engagements each, and Germany and the European Commission with 7 each.

Despite the multiplicity of donors and large sums involved, aid has been well harmonized. One facilitating factor is the close collaboration of key actors in the immediate aftermath of the conflict, under the leadership of the UNMIL and the United States Department of State. At that time, the World Bank Group played an active supporting role, contributing its expertise in the areas of economic governance and recovery. Since early 2006, President Sirleaf has played the key role in aid harmonization. The mechanism used is the Liberia Reconstruction and Development Committee (LRDC), which is chaired by the President. In addition, the Poverty Reduction Strategy serves as a guide for the activities of the LRDC.

Through regular consultations with partners, technical issues faced by the government are quickly recognized and addressed. Working groups have been set up to address the requirements of different areas of assistance. In addition, a wide range of stakeholders, including non-governmental organizations and private firms have contributed. In 2009, the government decided to deepen

Table 2.6   Development Partner Involvement by Sector

Sector/ Thematic Areas	EC	AfDB	France	Japan	UK	UN	US	IFC	WB	Denmark	Germany	China	Sweden	# Partners in Sector
Private Sector	X		X			X	X	X					X	6
Financial Sector								X						1
Transport	X	X				X	X		X		X	X		7
Trade							X		X				X	3
Agriculture	X			X		X	X	X	X	X	X	X	X	10
Health	X				X	X	X		X			X		6
Education	X					X	X				X	X	X	6
Environment						X	X		X					3
Water-Sanitation		X				X					X			3
Social Protection						X					X			2
Public Sector					X	X	X		X					4
Judicial Reform		X				X	X		X		X		X	4
Capacity Building	X	X			X	X	X		X		X		X	8
Security	X						X		X		X	X		5
Gender						X			X	X				3
# sectors engaged	7	4	1	1	3	10	10	5	10	2	7	5	6	

Source: World Bank 2009a.

Note: Shaded areas indicate the lead partners in each sector.

AfDB= African Development Bank; EC= European Community; IFC= International Finance Corporation; UK= United Kingdom; UN= United Nations; US= United States; WB= World Bank.

aid coordination by setting up additional working groups at sector levels. The expanded network has begun to function, although the 2011 elections slowed the pace somewhat.

The World Bank Group is generally looked upon as a leader and coordinator in the areas of its engagement.[5] Its intellectual role is particularly valued by other partners. The analytical work and policy advice provided by the World Bank Group has considerable impact on the programs of many partners.[6] The influence enjoyed by the World Bank Group, however, has also come at a price. Both the government and other partners generally expect a broader engagement by the Bank than is possible financially. Furthermore, the administrative budget limits the Bank's ability to deploy staff with the necessary skills and experience in the field. As a result, some of the partners have voiced frustrations about the Bank's level of responsiveness.

Notes

1. Liberia's external debt was in arrears or default, making the country ineligible to receive additional assistance from most of the international organizations.

2. See Appendix table 9B.

3. It should be noted, however, that the data on aid disbursement follows different definitions across countries and entities. For example, IDA disbursements do not include trust-fund resources. In addition, some entities include new loans made for the repayments of arrears.

4. The information on sectoral engagement in table 2.6 is based on 2009 data, while the activities of partners vary over time.

5. The findings in this paragraph are based on feedback provided by government officials and other development partners during a field visit by the Independent Evaluation Group (IEG) from November 28 through December 9, 2011. There was a broad consensus on the role and contributions of the World Bank Group.

6. The finding is based on interviews with government officials and development partners. In addition, an IEG review of studies conducted by development partners provided corroboration. For example, an independent report to the United States Congress on American assistance to Liberia (the largest official development assistance program) mentioned the World Bank 17 times and highlighted multiple collaborations between US agencies and the World Bank. See Cook 2010.

References

Cook, N. 2010. "Liberia's Post-War Development: key issues and U.S. Assistance." CRS Report for Congress Prepared for Members of Committees of Congress. Report No. 7-5700. Washington, D.C.: Congressional Research Center.

International Monetary Fund. 2008. "Liberia: Enhanced Initiative for Heavily-Indebted Poor Countries." Washington, D.C.: International Monetary Fund.

Lipsky, J. 2010. "Liberia: Life after Debt." Washington, D.C.: International Monetary Fund.

Richards, Paul. 2005. "To Fight or to Farm? Agrarian Dimensions of the Mano River Conflicts." *Oxford Journals* 104 (417): 571–590.

Richards, P.S. Archibald, B. Bruce, W. Modad, E. Mulbah, T. Varpilah, and J. Vincent. 2005. "Community Cohesion in Liberia. A Post-War Rapid Social Assessment." Social Development Papers: Conflict Prevention and Reconstruction. Paper No. 21. Washington, D.C.: World Bank.

World Bank. 2011. "Liberia- Country Assistance Strategy Progress Report for the Period FY09–12." Report No. 59772. Washington, D.C.: World Bank.

————. 2009a. International Development Association, International Finance Corporation and African Development Fund Joint Country Assistance Strategy for the Republic of Liberia for the Period FY09–11." Report No. 47928-LR. Washington, D.C.: World Bank and the African Development Bank.

————. 2009b. "International Development Association Program Document for the Second Re-engagement and Reform Support Program in the Amount of SDR 2.7 Million (US$4 million equivalent) to the Republic of Liberia." Report No. P46508-LR. Washington, D.C.: World Bank.

————. 2008a. "Liberia Public Expenditure Management and Financial Accountability Review." Report No. 43282-LR. Co-produced with the Government of Liberia, the African Development Bank, International Monetary fund, UNDP, DfID, and Swedish National Auditing Office. Washington, D.C.: World Bank.

————. 2008b. *Lift Liberia: A Poverty Reduction Strategy.* Washington, D.C.: World Bank.

————. 2007a. "Doing Business: Comparing Regulations in 178 Economies." Washington, D.C.: World Bank.

————. 2007b. "International Development Association and African Development Fund Joint Interim Strategy Note for the Republic of Liberia." Report No. 39821. Washington, D.C.: World Bank and African Development Bank.

————. 2007c. "Public Expenditure and Financial Accountability (PEFA) Assessment." Report No. 48282-LR. Co-produced with the Government of Liberia, African Development Bank, International Monetary Fund, UNDP, DfID, and the Swedish National Auditing Office. Washington, D.C.: World Bank.

————. 2004. "Liberia- Country Re-engagement Note." Report No. 28387. Washington, D.C.: World Bank.

Chapter 3
Rebuilding Core State Functions

The civil war left the Liberian government in dire straits. The provisional government set up in 2004 represented the three former warring factions. The implicit understanding was that each would appropriate the resulting rents from the portfolio it controlled back to the central government. The loss of former staff during the war, supplemented by thousands of "ghost" workers, along with seriously degraded facilities, left the civil service ineffective. Credible country systems for budgeting, procurement, financial management and supervision did not exist, forcing government and development partners to establish parallel mechanisms staffed at senior levels by expatriates. The government and development partners agreed that, in the immediate future, fiduciary management of external aid flows had to be expedited through *"project management units"* while core country systems were rebuilt from the foundation.

When the elected government took office in 2006, the stage was set for progress on the national agenda. A key step was the adoption of the Public Procurement and Concessions Act in January 2006, followed by the cancellation of all forest and other concession contracts awarded by the interim government, including major concessions such as the Container Park at the free port of Monrovia and the contract for the Liberian Petroleum Refining Company. A new forestry law was enacted with World Bank Group assistance.

The new government assigned high priority to the task of redesigning the architecture of governance. The Governance Commission, established in 2007, helped define policies and create special-purpose agencies, including those for Anti-Corruption, Public Procurement and Concessions and Land. In 2005, Liberia's executive law was amended to make the General Audit Commission (GAC) an independent supreme audit institution, with an expatriate in charge from mid-2007. GAC has since played a key role in exposing fraud and non-compliance.

Since 2006, Liberia has made a great deal of progress toward putting its fiscal system in order. Under the interim government in 2004 and 2005, there was no budgetary process in place to manage revenues of $70 million. Since 2006, the elected government has pursued a balanced cash budget and has made notable progress. Revenue collections rose from about $84.6 million in FY05/06 to $275 million in FY09/10. This increase was due to a combination of strong economic activity and improved tax administration. Among the key steps taken were: reinstituting pre-shipment inspection of imports to reduce the discretion of customs; strengthening of the large taxpayer unit; withholding of personal income tax and stationing controllers in the main state-owned enterprises (SOEs). Public expenditure has also expanded rapidly, from 11 percent of GDP in FY06/07 to an estimated 30 percent of GDP in FY09/10.

The budget is now prepared in a timely fashion and published. Budget controls are stringent, with allocations made against actual cash availabilities. The variance between the budget and the actual outcomes has been progressively reduced and is now under 10 percent. In FY10/11, the budget, following the new Public Financial Management Law, was cast in a medium-term framework articulated in the first Budget Policy Framework Paper. However, weak capacities in spending ministries — for expenditure planning, procurement and project management — continue to challenge effective budget execution. Large capital spending has been subject to delays. The government is taking corrective measures, including preparing a Public Sector Investment Program, to improve efficiency and transparency.

The restructuring of 15 state-owned enterprises has been underway. The history of SOEs is riddled with corruption, cronyism and mismanagement. The GEMAP and other initiatives began to change financial and operational performance at several state-owned companies, notably the Port Authority, the International Airport, the Forestry Development Authority, and the Petroleum Refinery Corporation. More recently, the government embarked on a two-pronged restructuring strategy. Initially it intends to dissolve or privatize SOEs that have become unnecessary or more appropriate for private ownership. There are also ongoing efforts to improve efficiency and corporate governance at the remaining SOEs.

In June 2008, Liberia started moving toward a more professional and efficient public sector by implementing a civil service reform (CSR) strategy. The CSR has six elements: (i) restructuring and right-sizing; (ii) pay and pension reform; (iii) improving public service delivery; (iv) managing human resources; (v) developing leadership; and (vi) gender equality.

The efforts to combat corruption present a mixed picture thus far, with some success in combating 'state capture.' Corruption is of two broad categories: (i) *state capture*, in which the various arms of government manipulate state functions for their own private gains; and (ii) *administrative (or petty) corruption* in which civil servants require a bribe in order to carry out their duties. Much progress has been made toward the goal of moving away from almost total state capture. Initially this was due to the GEMAP which established a system of shared sovereignty between the government and development partners. The GEMAP, which ended its operations in 2009, has been replaced by financial controls and the auditing of public accounts. Administrative corruption, however, continues to be a fact of life. In the 2009 Enterprise Survey (World Bank 2009e), over one-third of managers considered corruption a serious problem. Fifty-three percent paid a bribe.

The Liberia Anti-Corruption Commission was established in 2008 and today faces severe constraints due to the lack of subpoena and prosecutorial powers. Cases are referred to the Ministry of Justice, which is chronically overworked. Constraints within the judicial system are widely seen as serious impediments to improved governance and anti-corruption efforts. The UNMIL and UNDP have supported the Chief Justice of the Supreme Court in drafting a judicial reform plan and establishing a trust fund for the process. A Judicial Conference was held in March 2010 and a Law Reform Commission has been established to draft a reform program.

World Bank Group Objectives

The World Bank Group's Country Reengagement Note of 2004 noted the need to rebuild public services entirely. The CRN addressed the need during the two-year transitional period for national elections and the delivery of fast results on the ground. The CRN focused on three key objectives for the transition period, of which the second and third relate to the subsequent CAS first pillar: establishment and strengthening of state institutions and fundamental governance reforms; and establishment of an effective national coordinating and monitoring mechanism.

The Joint Interim Strategy Note of June 2007 defined specific sub-pillars for rebuilding state functions. The first was that of economic revitalization which includes a sub-category to *strengthen fiscal policy and financial management*. The second pillar is governance that is facilitating effective institutions to support democratic governance, justice, and security. Under this topic, there are two sub-categories: *implementing comprehensive civil service reform* and *strengthening the rule of law and respecting human rights*. These objectives are taken together as components of the first pillar:

- Fiscal policy and financial management: The objective was to put in place fundamental public financial management and procurement systems.

- Comprehensive civil service reform: The objective was to put in place a re-formed civil service with appropriate staffing, compensation and capacity.

- Rule of law and respect for human rights: The objective was to establish a reformed judicial system, including courts, corrections and administration.

The CAS of 2009 brought together public financial management (PFM) and governance issues within the first of its three strategic themes, namely that of Rebuilding Core State Functions and Institutions. (This in turn was aligned with the third pillar of the PRS). The first sub-category under this pillar was to improve PFM, and the second was to strengthen the effectiveness and efficiency of public institutions. It is notable that judicial reform, one of the areas of focus of the Interim Strategy was absent from the 2009 CAS. The two relevant objectives were to:

- Create a new framework for PFM: The focus was on the improved efficiency of budget preparation and execution, and enhanced revenue administration.

- Strengthen and enhance the effectiveness and efficiency of public institutions: The objective was to increase the professionalism and improve human resource management.

To pursue these objectives, the World Bank Group worked closely with a large number of partners, initially with the IMF, UNMIL, ECOWAS, the U.S. State Department, the United States Agency for International Development (USAID), and the UNDP. Since 2006, it has worked with a wider group of partners under the aegis of the Liberia Reconstruction and Development Committee.

Outcomes

With respect to achievements, there are two quite different outcomes. First, there are significant results on the build-up of institutional capacity (see box 3.1). Second, there are mixed achievements against the CAS milestones. As far as the broader achievements are concerned, these go substantially beyond what might reasonably have been expected when the new government took office in 2006.

A large number of institutions, which have been the focus of institution building efforts during the review period, were evaluated on criteria such as whether they have clearly-defined objectives and strategies, whether their operational programs support the achievement of these objectives, and whether they have the staff and organizational capacity to achieve these objectives. In the light of these criteria, the evaluation notes substantial achievement in the core area of public management including in the Ministries of Finance, Planning and Health, the Civil Service Agency and the General Audit Commission. Box 3.2 highlights some of the achievements in this regard.

Regarding civil service reform, important initial steps have been taken, but there is still a need for progress in developing an appropriate incentives framework as a basis for an efficient and effective civil service. The government is well aware of the need to increase the pay of civil servants (outside of the

---

Box 3.1   Capacity Development and How the World Bank Group Supported It

The World Bank Group defines capacity development as a locally-driven process of transformational learning — by leaders, coalitions, and other agents — that leads to actions that support changes in ownership, policy, and organizational behavior to advance development goals.[1]

In Liberia, the support in *capacity development* follows a pragmatic approach. It focuses on what is required in the areas of World Bank Group engagement, particularly core state functions and infrastructure. As discussed in greater detail later, the assistance entails providing key stakeholders with an integrated package of training, logistics, facilities and incentives through a series of analytical work and lending services.

In practice, a key part of capacity building is to find a way of closing the gap between the need to carry out the core functions of government and the weak civil service capacity that was then in place. The actual support has included the following components:

- Provide more competitive salaries at the Senior Executive Service, which enables the recruitment of qualified individuals from outside Liberia;

- Upgrade facilities, including computers and systems for use in government;

- Reform the civil service which provides the structures and incentives for efficiency;

- Create extensive training programs, including the Liberia Institute of Public Administration, which is providing a range of short courses for government officials; a special degree program to recruit staff for the Ministry of Finance; and a wide range of other capacity building activities, such as study tours to see 'good practice.'

Source: IEG.

Senior Executive Service program), and has already undertaken a number of modest increases, although there is still room for considerable improvement. The U.K.'s Department for International Development (DfID) has been the key partner in support of the civil service reform program, with active support from the World Bank Group and the UNDP. Among the difficult tasks completed are the development and launching of the CSR strategy, and the restructuring of 10 key ministries, which led to a reduction of 11,000 employees including ghost workers by 2010. In addition, a framework for the biometric registry and management information systems was established. Some tasks, however, are still ongoing including the review of mandates in the remaining ministries, redefining the roles and responsibilities of the principal secretary within the ministries, as well as the code of conduct for public employees. This includes dealing with the pervasive issue of patronage in civil service appointments. In general, outcomes of public financial management and civil service reforms have been effective and World Bank Group programs have provided the critical support.

At the same time, the achievements against specific milestones have been mixed.[2] Of the target values for 15 indicators, only 8 were achieved or showed good progress during the CAS period. Table 3.1 presents a summary of the outcomes and progress made under this pillar against the specific milestones stipulated in the CAS. Some of the CAS milestones seem unrealistic, given realities on the ground. The expectations for making the Integrated Financial Management Information System (IFMIS) and Medium-Term Expenditure Framework (MTEF) operational within three years go against experience in other African countries. Similarly, it is unrealistic to expect that performance-based management for civil servants could be fully implemented within the CAS period. In these cases, more modest steps toward the objectives would have been more appropriate. In addition, the design of the World Bank Group program on public financial management should have prioritized public procurement issues to a greater extent.

The various indices on perceptions suggest that there has been progress on the governance and anti-corruption agenda.[3] Although the CAS did not specify any milestones in this area, the World Bank Group's strong interest is implicit in the program design and in particular in the substantial oversight of public financial management. One indication, given by the Mo Ibrahim Index on the perception of governance in Africa released in October 2011, finds that Liberia's score has improved from 32 (out of 100) in 2005 to 45 in 2010. In another indication of the progress made, the Transparency International's 2010 Corruption Perceptions Index ranked Liberia 11th of 47 Sub-Saharan African countries included in the survey. Globally, Liberia's position improved dramatically, moving from 138th to 87th place in a few short years.

The improved perceptions rest on a long list of concrete achievements: the creation of the General Audit Commission; the EITI; the introduction of public sector accounting standards; the potential role of the IFMIS; the adoption of the Automated System for Custom's Data (ASYCUDA) by the Customs

Since the elections in 2005, development partners, spearheaded by the World Bank Group, have worked effectively to help the government rebuild the core institutions. Although some agencies continue to need more support, there has been considerable success in the core agencies. Almost all of these have benefited from the support of the World Bank Group.

- **The General Audit Commission (GAC).** The strengthening of GAC was essential for HIPC completion because one of the core conditions was audits of five ministries (such as education, health, and public works). In 2006 when work started, it was necessary to do a clean sweep of the agency, and begin anew. The World Bank Group supported GAC in capacity building and brought in seasoned auditors to mentor staff and consultants. GAC has also audited the Petroleum Refinery, Monrovia Transport, Social Security, and National Housing. All audits are publicly disclosed. GAC is now supporting internal audits in ministries.

- **The Liberian Extractive Industries Transparency Initiative (LEITI).** In May 2008, the government established the Liberia EITI with membership from the government, civil society, the private sector and development partners to help ensure transparency in the mineral and forestry sectors. The LEITI Secretariat's first full audited report of receipts and payments from the extractive industries was published in February 2009. Liberia was designated an EITI-compliant country in October 2009 — the first country in Africa and the second in the world to receive such status.

- **The Ministry of Finance.** The achievements are illustrated by two units:

  - The Public Financial Management Unit (PFMU). The PFMU was set up six years ago in the Ministry of Finance to undertake the financial management of projects supported by development partners. The initial focus was on World Bank Group projects, but subsequently the unit also serviced those of other development partners. The unit now handles a $600 million portfolio and has two international staff and 24 Liberians. There is general agreement that the unit has operated effectively. Indeed, the GAC audit has uncovered no irregularities. Soon they will be mainstreaming the financial management of projects to the line ministries.

  - The Fiscal Unit is a think-tank of the Ministry of Finance, which was dysfunctional in 2006. The Senior Executive Service and the Economic Governance and Institution Reform projects helped build its capacity and attract qualified people. It now has 18 staff members including four senior economists in charge of forecasting, strategy and monitoring, as well as a monthly bulletin. The unit has worked with the World Bank Group on the Poverty Reduction and Strategy Papers (PRSPs).

Source: IEG.

Bureau; and the Freedom of Information Act. Although the government's program has been weak on the prosecution of cases of corruption brought by the anti-corruption commission, the publicity associated with bringing forward a case is proving a credible deterrent to corrupt practices. Progress on decentralization has been constrained by limited devolution of decision-making authority, although to some extent administrative functions are being transferred from central to local agencies (with officials appointed from the center).

Table 3.1	Progress Made under Specific CAS Milestones	
Objective/ Result Indicator	Actual Results (as of 12/2011)	Progress Made
A. Improved efficiency in budgeting and enhanced tax administration		
Budgeting. Eighty percent of vouchers approved and paid by the Ministry of Finance by 2009.	One hundred percent in 2010	Achieved
Quarterly expenditure reports posted within 6 weeks by 2009.	The Quarterly report is published in 45 days	Achieved
The IFMIS system operational by 2011.	One of 3 near completion	Some progress
Less than 20 percent of procurement on less competitive methods by 2010.	68.3 percent in 2010	Some progress
GAC audits five ministries by 2009.	Twenty-two audits in 2009	Achieved
Internal audits of three key ministries by 2009.	Decision made	Some progress
Budget linked to Medium-Term Expenditure Framework (MTEF) by 2010.	Not linked to MTEF.	Some progress
Tax Administration. New Integrated Tax Administration System (ITAS) by 2010.	ITAS started in Oct 2010	Achieved
Tax administration. Risk management implemented by 2010.	Not implemented	No progress
B. Increased professionalization and human resource management of the civil service		
Professionalization. Senior Executive Service (SES) has 70 percent staff by 2009.	Ninety-seven percent at post	Achieved
Three Ministries restructured based on new mandates, structures and staffing plans.	One implemented	Some progress
Civil Service Reform Strategy by 2009.	Strategy approved	Achieved
A plan for the Liberian Institute of Public Administration's training delivery by early 2009 and 25 staff trained by 2010.	No training plan	No progress
Performance based on merit designed and linked to compensation by 2011.	System is being designed	Some progress
Human Resource Management. Personnel records maintained with matching payroll records.	Records created with matching on-going	Good progress
Personnel file includes biometric information for 100 percent of employees.	Biometric ID for 45 percent of employees	Good progress
Rationalization of civil service grades and a well-defined salary structure.	Re-grading done; new pay strategy approved	Achieved
Retirement rules are fully enforced.	Fully implemented	Achieved

Source: IEG.

Contribution of the World Bank Group

A key initial step, supported by the Bank, was the establishment of the *Governance and Economic Management Assistance Program (GEMAP)*. This was set up to ensure that development partner support was not siphoned off to corrupt politicians. The motivation was the dysfunctional interim government, the NTGL, which continued the mode of business as usual, with the SOEs being treated as sources of rents for the party in control of the agency. Under the GEMAP, the government agreed with development partners to deploy international experts with binding co-signatory authority to improve financial management in selected institutions and enterprises. In 2005, the GEMAP was set up with an Economic Governance Steering Committee which met monthly with civil society and representatives of development partners.

A series of four *Reengagement and Reform Support Programs (RRSP)* (World Bank 2007b, 2009a, 2010b and 2011) provided budget support as part of a framework for improvement in public management. The first RRSP, approved in November 2007, was by far the largest and most important since it provided the bridge loan to pay off Liberian arrears owed to the IBRD and IDA. The Implementation Completion Report review by IEG concurred with the ratings of high relevance and substantial efficacy for the operation, and the overall satisfactory rating.

The objectives of the second RRSP, approved in May 2009, were aligned with the CAS pillar of rebuilding core state functions and institutions. IEG also concurred with the ratings of high relevance, substantial efficacy and overall satisfactory rating for this second operation.

The third RRSP, approved in September 2010 for completion in June 2011 has a focus on only two areas: (i) improving budget preparation and publication and; (ii) improving land administration to reduce conflicts and enhance the investment climate.

The fourth RRSP was approved in September 2011. It emphasizes improved public procurement practices through recruitment of a qualified procurement specialist in at least one key operating ministry, and the preparation and publishing of procurement plans in seven operating ministries. The remaining criteria relate to financial management, tax administration and land policy.

The Economic Governance and Institutional Reform Project (EGIRP) (World Bank 2008) provides the technical assistance needed to implement the RRSPs. The EGIRP was approved in April 2008 for a sum of $11 million, with $7 million more added in March 2011. Essentially the EGIRP is designed to provide the technical assistance needed to support the government's efforts to meet the policy conditions of the RRSP series. The objective of the operation was defined as "helping strengthen the capacity of the public administration to deliver key public services and manage natural resources, in order to ensure that scarce public resources are used efficiently and to restore confidence that they are used for the benefit of all and not just for factional interests." (World Bank 2008). The analytic work carried out for the PEMFAR (World Bank 2009d) played a major role in establishing the agenda of actions included in the EGIRP.

The EGIRP has two components. The first is to strengthen PFM and institutions involved in PFM training, including the support for decentralization and for the Liberian Agency for Community Empowerment. The second is to support the CSR program through performance contracts in selected state enterprises and the design of a comprehensive CSR program.

The *Senior Executive Service (SES)* program filled critical gaps in key management positions in ministries and agencies. In October 2007, the World Bank Group provided a credit of $2.3 million to support a trust fund administered by UNDP. It had been established for a project to provide the government with the assistance needed to develop a cadre of technical and managerial public servants. The idea was to cover the costs of recruiting, at salaries well above the civil service levels, qualified people to fill key technical and managerial position in ministries and agencies. The program covered 100 recruits on three-year contracts with 30 being hired at a monthly salary of $3,000; 30 at $2,000; and 40 at $1,000. The World Bank Group part of the program funded those receiving $2,000 a month. Recruitment was handled by an independent professional recruitment firm and was open to Liberians and others, but with the requirement that they be recruited from abroad.

The SES closed in 2010 but the government was not able to absorb the cost of the staff into its payroll. Such costs have subsequently been funded out of the EGIRP, with the intention that the government will take these expenditures over at the end of 2012. This is unlikely to be feasible. Although it is important for donors to continue to fund this program, it needs to be associated with an explicit program for building capacity in the ministries and an orderly phasing down of donor support.

A large number of grants have provided ad hoc support for core public financial management and governance institutions. Some of these grants, such as the support for the IFMIS, have been quite large. The World Bank Group has also provided a large number of small grants (usually in the 0.5 to $1 million range) to address various gaps or priority needs that came up during the course of program implementation. Beneficiaries have included the Civil Service Agency, the Judiciary, the Liberian Institute of Statistics and Geo-Information Services (LISGIS), the Liberian Extractive Industries Transparency Initiative (LEITI), the Liberian Institute for Public Administration (LIPA), the Public Procurement Commission, the Anti-Corruption Commission, as well as support for the Ministry of Planning (in preparing the PRS) and different units within the Ministry of Finance. The grants generally helped with formulating strategies, training of agency officials, including study tours, and logistics support through enhanced information systems, computers, and, where appropriate, vehicles. The impact of the grants on outcomes has been mixed, however. In cases where there was no follow up, for example, the grant for the judiciary, there has been limited impact.

The World Bank Group has also undertaken a range of Economic and Sector Work (ESW) to provide the analytic underpinnings for its operations. The key output for the first pillar is the Liberia 2008 Public Expenditure Management and Financial Accountability Review (PEMFAR), published in June 2009. This is the first comprehensive assessment of public expenditures and financial management since the peace accords. At the macroeconomic level, the PEMFAR describes the external economic opportunities and constraints that will drive growth and revenue mobilization over the medium term. It reviews the institutional structure that guides resource allocations and assesses the strengths and weaknesses of the current system. It then assesses how public expenditure has been allocated between sectors and priorities. Other relevant ESW included a Report on the Observance of Standards and Codes (ROSC), and the Investment Climate and Doing Business Assessments. The World Bank Group, working with the UNMIL, is preparing a new Public Expenditure Review (PER) that highlights security. World Bank Group ESW has made a significant contribution to operations and supported a number of the key outcomes specified in the CAS.

Relevance

Although initially the program in this pillar reflected mainly the views of the World Bank Group and development partners on what was needed, over time it has evolved toward genuine *ownership* by the Liberian authorities. It is now a close reflection of government priorities as noted in key government strategy documents and statements by leading public officials. Increasingly this is seen as the government's program rather than being partner-driven. A key factor is the PRS which has been used effectively as an instrument for building consensus through a participatory process, and as a monitoring framework by the President to hold ministers accountable for performance.

The focus of the World Bank Group's first pillar is on budget management and civil service reform. In Liberia, these areas represent the Bank's comparative advantage in which other development partners are reluctant to participate. The World Bank Group has taken up other topics selectively as opportunities presented themselves, often in response to specific requests from other development partners (the UNDP and European Union) or from the government. The overall results of this pillar are summarized in table 3.2 below.

There are questions, however, as to the advisability of introducing complex systems such as the Integrated Financial Management Information System and the Medium Term Expenditure Framework at this stage. Both the IFMIS and the MTEF have proven complex to implement and slow to yield outcomes in other African countries with higher levels of capacity. A case could be made that since post-conflict countries need to rebuild systems from the ground up, they are better off moving directly to a more sophisticated system rather than first restoring a more traditional approach. The key question is whether there is ownership and support for these systems at the ministerial and senior administrative levels. Without such commitment, the systems will in all likelihood not succeed. The officials need to be able to generate the reports and data that management needs and be willing to utilize them. With these systems now in place, the issue is whether the World Bank Group is doing enough to support the training and implementation that are required. The focus thus far seems to be mainly on getting the systems operational and not on how to use them effectively.

Table 3.2	Summary Results of Pillar 1 – Rebuilding Core State Functions
Outcomes	Contribution of the World Bank Group
Objective: Rebuilding the public financial management system	
From a chaotic beginning in 2006, the budget is now prepared on time and published. Recent budgets were cast in a medium-term context. Revenue collections rose from $85 million to $275 million in four years. Public spending has grown from 11 percent of GDP to 30 percent in 3 years, with improved controls. But capacity in spending ministries remains weak. Large capital spending is often delayed.	Assistance is provided through a comprehensive package of policy advice, technical assistance and budget support. Key operations are: the series of four Re-engagement and Reform Support Programs; and the Economic Governance and Institutional Reform Project. The World Bank Group has also conducted a variety of knowledge work, including the 2009 Public Expenditure Management and Financial Accountability Review (World Bank 2009).
Objective: Rebuilding the civil service	
The Civil Service Reform (CSR) strategy has been completed and implementation is now underway. Restructuring has taken place in nine ministries and in the Civil Service Agency, with a reduction of employees and ghost workers from 45,000 to 34,000 in four years. The linking of biometric IDs to the human resource information system is underway.	World Bank Group support was provided through the Senior Executive Service (SES) which helped with the recruitment qualified individuals from abroad, as well as a variety of grants for capacity development programs for civil servants, and the Economic Governance and Institutional Reform Project (EGIRP) which supported the implementation of the biometric system. In the next phase, the program needs to combine provision gradual phase down of the SES with further capacity building efforts.
Objective: Improving governance and the rule of law	
The Governance Commission has provided a mechanism for ongoing reforms. The General Audit Commission has exposed fraud and enhanced financial discipline. The Anti-Corruption Commission has not yet succeeded in bringing any cases to closure. However, by bringing cases to public attention, it is providing a credible deterrent. The management and staffing of procurement functions remain inadequate.	The World Bank Group was a key party in introducing the Governance and Economic Management Assistance Program 2005, which limited the scope for state capture. Further assistance was provided through a series of grants to support the Governance Commission and the agencies it created to improve transparency. The initial grant for judicial reform had a limited impact however, and the World Bank Group did not follow up until recently.

Source: IEG.

The program on judicial reform and anti-corruption has not been commensurate with the challenges. Judicial reform was given some prominence in the Interim Strategy Note, but in practice this only resulted in a small grant intervention with no supporting analytical work. An implicit decision was made to move away from this area in the full CAS, but a clearer explanation would have been warranted. The Bank has recently returned to the judicial reform agenda, however, both because of the importance of judicial reform to the anti-corruption agenda, and because the leadership in the Ministry of Justice shows more interest (see box 3.3 below).

An important gap in the government program thus far is the failure to develop a meaningful strategy for decentralization. This reflects in part the fact that the percentage of the total population living in Monrovia is one of the highest for any city on the African continent. However, in the future it would be appropriate for the government to put into place some pilot programs for local empowerment, with elected local governments in one or two of the more accessible towns in the interior.

A grant of $650,000 for judicial reform in 2006 was essentially intended to support a pro-gram initiated by a Swedish NGO. Liberia's Chief Justice refused to implement it, arguing that the real need was for training. The Bank revamped the program by adding a training component and a special focus on gender-based violence. The program also supported the provision of books and documents for the courts to enable justices to cite precedent. In addition, the program provided for the digitizing of the supreme court's decisions, as well as the provision of vehicles for public prosecutors. Once the funds had been disbursed, however, the Bank decided not to proceed with judicial reform. There was a large program of support from USAID, but overall there seemed little progress in the sector.

In FY12, the Bank decided to reengage in judicial reform. The decision was motivated in part by the increasing urgency of building a sound legal structure outside of Monrovia. The legal capacity will be developed in one or two regional hubs and through the piloting of community dispute resolution mechanisms. The Bank is working with the Carter Center, but this is still an area where the World Bank Group seems to be tentative. Despite the decision to reengage, the Bank has not participated in meetings with sector and NGO groups, such as the Rural Access to Justice.

Source: IEG.

Risks to First Pillar Achievements

Because this pillar is so intrinsically bound up with the functioning of the state, it is highly vulnerable to the basic political environment. A major risk, symptomatic of the resource curse (as discussed in box 1.1), is that of increasing high-level corruption through the public procurement process, revenue collection, and concession agreements. This is an area where Liberia cannot afford to simply maintain status quo. It needs to ensure that it continues to make progress. The World Bank Group needs to strengthen its support both to help the government establish an independent procurement function and to support strong enforcement efforts on the anti-corruption side. The link between natural resource revenues and the prevalence of corruption is well established. Thus far, Liberia's leadership has managed to steer a reasonable course between the need for additional revenues and the pressures to sign additional concession agreements that are demanded by political supporters. This is a delicate balance that could very easily tilt in the wrong direction.

Notes

1. See, for example, Capacity Development Resource Center, the World Bank. URL: http://web.worldbank.org/WBSITE/EXTERNAL/TOPICS/EXTCDRC/0,,contentMDK:20295295~menuPK:645091~pagePK:64169212~piPK:64169110~theSitePK:489952,00.html

2. The CAS milestones represent intermediate outcomes that are viewed as being achievable within the current CAS period, relative to objectives whose achievement is likely to extend over a number of CAS programs.

3. For a more detailed discussion on governance issues in Liberia, see IEG, 2011. "Liberia: World Bank Country Level Engagement on Governance and Anti-Corruption," Working Paper 2011/8, The World Bank. This is a country case study prepared for the IEG evaluation of Governance and Anti-Corruption. URL: http://ieg.worldbankgroup.org/content/dam/ieg/gac/backgroundpapers/GACLiberiaWPFinal.pdf

References

International Monetary Fund. 2008. "Liberia: Enhanced Initiative for Heavily-Indebted Poor Countries." Washington, D.C.: International Monetary Fund.

World Bank. 2011. "International Development Association Program Document on a Proposed Credit in the Amount of SDR 3.2 Million (US$5 million equivalent) to the Republic of Liberia for the Fourth Reengagement and Reform Support Program." Report No. P123196. Washington, D.C.: World Bank.

———. 2010a. "Doing Business 2011, Making a Difference for Entrepreneurs." Washington, D.C.: World Bank.

———. 2010b. "International Development Association Program Document for the Third Re-engagement and Reform Support Program in the amount of SDR 7.5 million (US$11 million equivalent) including SDR 4.1 million in Pilot CRW Resources (US$6.0 million equivalent) to the Republic of Liberia." Report No. 54493-LR. Washington, D.C.: World Bank.

———. 2009a. "International Development Association Program Document for the Second Re-engagement and Reform Support Program in the Amount of SDR 2.7 million (US$4 million equivalent) to the Republic of Liberia." Report No. P46508-LR. Washington, D.C.: World Bank.

———. 2009b. "International Development Association, International Finance Corporation and African Development Fund Joint Country Assistance Strategy for the Republic of Liberia for the Period FY09–11." Report NO. 47928-LR. Washington, D.C.: World Bank.

———. 2009c. "Liberia Public Expenditure Management and Fiduciary Accountability Review (PEMFAR). Washington, D.C.: World Bank.

———. 2009d. "Liberia 2008 Public Expenditure Management and Financial Accountability Review." Report No. 43282-LR. Co-produced with the Government of Liberia, the African Development Bank, the International Monetary Fund, the United Nations Development Programme, the UK Department for International Development, and the Swedish National Auditing Office. Washington, D.C.: World Bank.

———. 2009e. *Enterprise Surveys: Liberia Country Profile.* Washington, D.C.: World Bank and International Finance Corporation.

———. 2008. "Emergency Project Paper for an IDA Grant in the amount of SDR 6.7 million (US$11.0 million equivalent) to the Republic of Liberia for an Economic Governance and Institutional Reform Project." Report No. 42836-LR. Washington, D.C.: World Bank.

———. 2007a. "Doing Business 2008, Comparing Regulations in 178 Economies." Washington, D.C.: World Bank.

———. 2007b. "International Development Association and African Development Fund Joint Interim Strategy Note for the Republic of Liberia." Report No. 39821. Washington, D.C.: World Bank and African Development Bank.

———. 2004. "Liberia- Country Re-engagement Note." Report No. 28387. Washington, D.C.: World Bank.

Chapter 4
Rehabilitating Infrastructure

During the war, extensive destruction of basic infrastructure contributed to the collapse of the formal sector and reversion to a subsistence economy. As the World Bank Group began its reengagement, most of Liberia's existing roads were in extreme disrepair. The Monrovia international airport and seaport were damaged and suffered from acute mismanagement. The power supply, telecommunications, water and sanitation had ceased to function due to physical degradation, looting, and lack of maintenance. There was no local private industry, and the size and value of contracts did not attract international contractors. Moreover, there was a lack of basic equipment, making infrastructure work and implementation enormously challenging and expensive.

Rehabilitation of infrastructure was among the top priorities of the government. Both the transitional and elected governments recognized the urgency of rehabilitating infrastructure and the massive scale of investments needed. In addition, there was a consensus among stakeholders that the World Bank Group was uniquely well-qualified to take the lead in this major responsibility. In response, the World Bank Group designated infrastructure as its principal area of support in the CRN (World Bank 2004), the ISN (World Bank 2007) and the CAS (World Bank 2009).

Shortly after the peace agreement was signed, the UNDP and the World Bank Group undertook a joint mission to conduct a needs assessment. Following the 2005 elections, a grant of US$30 million was approved in June 2006 to provide emergency infrastructure assistance for the critical period before arrears could be cleared and regular IDA financing could be made available. The needs assessment took place in strategic partnership with UNMIL which had the only heavy equipment and engineering capacity in the country.

Simultaneously, a series of infrastructure assessments was undertaken, in the context of a major multi-sector technical assistance project supported by the Liberia Reconstruction Trust Fund (LRTF). This included technical studies and master planning for roads, the Port of Monrovia, the Roberts International Airport, water, sanitation, telecommunications and energy. The consultants handling this task, however, had to work in an environment with very limited data because the records had largely been destroyed in the war. Nevertheless, the studies were able to identify immediate priorities to be included in the first round of projects (such as the dredging of the port), as well as pre-feasibility assessments for the follow-on projects.

Under the circumstances, task teams had to focus on moving forward creatively one step at a time, often unable to foresee changing needs (such as the collapse of the Vai Town Bridge in Monrovia) or shifting priorities of the government. The approach was acceptable and pragmatic under the prevailing conditions. The project teams, in fact, are to be commended for their flexibility. It was also appropriate to have a few infrastructure umbrella projects to begin with since the entire spectrum of physical structures and equipment needed rehabilitation. Although the government attempted to spread infrastructure work around the country, it was necessary to focus on Monrovia initially in order to ensure that the government could function. In addition, it was important to start in Monrovia because the capital city is now home to more than a third of the country's population.

The emergency phase began in 2006 and ended with the debt relief agreement in June 2010. During this phase, IDA approved six infrastructure projects under special rapid response procedures, some of which had extensions or additional financing, and most of which are still active. Since 2010, IDA has approved two credits for infrastructure covering road asset management and telecommunications. The appraisal of these projects was subject to more normal preparation procedures.

The World Bank Group has also led the difficult task of donor coordination, fostering collaboration across sectors and administering the Liberia Reconstruction Trust Fund. Combining funds from the World Bank Group (including IDA) and the LRTF, more than US$460 million has been committed to date for rehabilitating infrastructure.

Transport

ROADS

The road network in Liberia is about 10,000 km, comprising 734 km of primary roads, 2,350 km of secondary roads, and 5,700 km of feeder roads. This is excluding forestry and community roads, but including urban main roads. Less than 10 percent of the network is paved, and 86 percent of the paved roads are in poor condition. Key issues identified include: (i) severely deteriorated and long- neglected infrastructure; (ii) fewer days available to do the work because of the long rainy season; and (iii) difficulties in attracting reputable engineering companies and contractors.

Drawing on international good practices, the National Transport Policy and Strategy (NTPS) set out in 2009 the following goals for the road sector (Government of Liberia 2009):

i.   *Institutional development.* The Ministry of Public Works would move incrementally away from force account (contracted construction work paid-for on the basis of time taken and material consumed). Road sector management would gradually be placed in the hands of an autonomous road authority supported by a Road Fund;

ii. *Contracting arrangements.* Partnerships with the private sector would be deployed; payments to contractors would be based on performance;

iii. *Maintenance strategy.* Most of the road network would first need to be rehabilitated to bring it to maintainable status. Once in stable condition, the maintenance would be done through contractors, but with community participation for local roads.

A Special Implementation Unit (SIU) was established under the Ministry of Public Works for the implementation of aid-funded infrastructure projects across the sector in early 2006. In 2009, the SIU was converted into a self-standing Infrastructure Implementation Unit (IIU), with greater decision-making authority under the leadership of a regionally-hired program director.

WORLD BANK GROUP OBJECTIVES

Initially, the Bank was to target emergency repairs to restore transport functionality, create temporary employment opportunities, and assist returning refugees. The projects in this phase also envisaged putting in place at least the minimum institutional capacity for implementation. Subsequently, the objectives were to be broadened to include transport of agricultural products at critical locations and to replace bridge crossings that had been destroyed. Once out of the initial emergency phase, the attention was to focus on larger highways connecting the major towns. Consideration was also to be given to planning for future sustainability by increasing expenditures for road maintenance. Emergency assistance was to be provided by IDA and through the LRTF, including contributions from the European Union, Germany, Ireland, and Sweden.

OUTCOMES

The World Bank Group, in collaboration with UNMIL and UNDP, successfully completed the temporary repairs of the main routes (World Bank 2006b, 2007). More substantial finished tasks included the main road from Monrovia to the international airport, the bitumen surfacing of 24 km of main streets in Monrovia, the replacement of the Vai Town Bridge, and rehabilitation of sections of rural primary roads in the south-east of the country, where the communities were cut off in the rainy season. Several other projects have started or are expected to commence shortly, including the completion of the road from the airport to Buchanan, and the Caldwell Bridge in Monrovia. The achievements of the emergency road projects are fairly substantial, taking into account frequent delays, changes in priority, and limited capacity. The milestones as stipulated by the 2009 CAS for this pillar are presented in table 4.1, along with a summary of the progress made. As shown, progress has been made across the board, although only three milestones (out of a total of eight) have been fully met at this stage. It should be noted, however, that since most of the projects have not yet closed, further progress is still being made. In addition, some of the achievements made under projects that were approved prior to the CAS are not reflected in this particular set of milestones.

The early road improvements brought functionality to the main routes, created temporary employment, and helped returning refugees to reach home. This emergency phase was followed by the Infrastructure and Agriculture Development Project, which included several small sub-components such as key bridge crossings to facilitate the movement of farm products. Later on, larger highway projects were supported. The most important of these was the Liberia Road Asset Management Project (World Bank 2011a) for the rehabilitation and

Table 4.1	Summary Results of Pillar 2 – Roads
Outcome	Contribution of the World Bank Group
Objective: Rehabilitating the transport network and institutions	
Roads. Early road projects were to help restore functionality to the main routes and create temporary employment. Later, many small sub-projects were devised to assist the movement of farm products and replace key bridge crossings. Other goals included the development of a National Transport Policy and Strategy, and compilation of traffic data to enable more informed decisions. Institutional capacity of the implementing agency was to be strengthened and maintenance was to receive more attention.	Through emergency projects, the World Bank Group assisted the Ministry of Public Works to upgrade the road network to good or fair condition. It also recommended a study of the best means for securing a stream of funding for maintenance needs, and advocated for a transport policy study (including data collection) which was funded by the German Society for International Cooperation (GIZ). However, several projects (although not those under OPRC) experienced delays or cost overruns, and the IIU was not adequately strengthened.
Source: IEG.	

upgrading of the road corridor from Monrovia to the Guinea border (LIBRAMP) and Monrovia (Red Light-Bokey Town-Buchanan Town Roads). These roads are a vital backbone for the post-war reconstruction, connecting some of the country's largest towns. All milestones have been or are likely to be met, on time and budget, as evidenced with the already completed Red Light-Bokey Town Road. However, the Monrovia Gbranga-Ganta- Guinea Border roads (LIBRAMP) have been delayed as the result of slow procurement and attempts by the client to have the contract awarded to an un-qualified contractor (Lot 1). In the meantime, the contract has been awarded and the works commenced. The second Lot will be re-tendered because of non-responsive bidders, while the first responsive bidder's offer was very high. A dialogue has begun on sustaining the road investments and for the first time there has been a budgetary line item for maintenance of main roads. In addition, the recommendations of a Transport Policy and Strategy study have been adopted.

CONTRIBUTION OF THE WORLD BANK GROUP

Through a series of projects, including the Emergency Infrastructure Project and the Agriculture and Infrastructure Development Project, the World Bank Group played an indispensable role in tackling the immediate pressing road needs and in ensuring there was a minimum capacity to engage with project implementation during the emergency phase. The team gave useful advice on standards, priorities and implementation issues. The World Bank Group also recommended that a detailed feasibility study of road financing options, including a "Road Fund," be done to consider the costs and benefits of different options for securing a sustainable stream of funding for road maintenance. The Bank ensured that a Transport Policy and Strategy Study be initiated; this was later completed and funded by the German Society for International Cooperation (GIZ). Under the emergency phase, the World Bank Group's rapid response to crises and emergencies was applied and the increased flexibility helped accelerate the preparation of Bank projects. With the advent of larger projects, the milestone approach evolved into full preparation using a results-based framework.

In hindsight, however, the predominantly roads-focused Emergency Infrastructure Project should have contained a labor-intensive component from the outset. When the government requested such an element be included, additional financing had to be hastily put in place after the project became effective. This might be a lesson for other post-conflict states where local unemployment and shortages of essential commodities are exacerbated by the influx of displaced people from the war. (The outcomes and World Bank Group contribution to the transport sector are summarized in table 4.2 below.)

Although it is too early to evaluate the efficacy of LIBRAMP, IEG noted with concern the delays in preparation, bidding process and start-up. A decision was made to pursue an output-based road contract (OPRC) instead of the traditional input-based contract. Under this OPRC, the contractor has to maintain the road in good condition for a ten-year period and ensure through a technical advisor that training of local staff takes place on a continuous basis. Similar contracts have been used in Liberia (including those for the Cotton Tree -Bokay road and Monrovia streets) and also elsewhere in Africa. OPRCs significantly expand the

Table 4.2	Progress Made Under Specific Milestones	
Objectives/result Indicator	Actual Results (as of 12/2011)	Progress Made
Improved access to key transport services		
Cotton Tree – Buchanan road corridor by 2010; Monrovia - Ganta corridor under OPRC by end 2011.	Cotton Tree - Bokay section complete. Bokay to Buchanan procured. Monrovia – Ganta lot 1 under construction, lot 2 to be re-bid.	Some progress
Draft legislation on Road Authority and Road Maintenance Fund by 2011	In preparation	Some progress
Twenty-four kms of Monrovia roads resurfaced	Twenty-four km resurfaced under OPRC.	Achieved
New Vai Town, Caldwell and several minor bridges built or improved by June 2011	Vai Town Bridge completed. Caldwell consultancy in process.	Good progress
Six hundred kms of roads under maintenance	Initial maintenance carried out and routine maintenance ongoing.	Achieved
Four hundred kms (World Bank) of rural feeder roads rehabilitated by 2011	Rehabilitation of 200 km of feeder roads started in 2011.	Some progress
One hundred and twenty-five km of primary roads rehabilitated by 2010 using labor-based methods	Rehabilitation of Fish Town – Harper and 125 km of primary roads commenced.	Some progress
Two hundred and twenty-nine drainage points constructed by 2010	Two hundred twenty-nine drainage points constructed at Fishtown-Harper Road.	Achieved

Source: IEG.

Note: OPRC=Output and Performance-Based Contracts.

role of the private sector, from the simple execution of works to the management and preservation of road assets. Unlike the traditional contract where the requirements on the IIU professional staff would be onerous, all implementation risks under the OPRC fall on the contractor. Payments under this contract are due only if milestones have been met with regard to contractual quality and quantity parameters. Although some development partners in Monrovia expressed concerns about introducing this type of contract in Liberia on a large project, IEG believes that the OPRC approach is reasonable. The underlying issue, however, is the lack of capacity in the IIU to engage the private sector and development partners, irrespective of the type of contract selected.

RELEVANCE

Although the expanded role of the private sector as envisaged in LIBRAMP has proved beneficial in several other countries, the launching of any major construction project on a large scale in Liberia -- by whatever contracting method – was premature because of the IIU's lack of capacity. The regionally-hired incumbents were expensive, but did not providing the level of expertise expected and hardly any local staff had been engaged to prepare for future key positions. Although the project team had repeatedly brought this issue to the attention of the government, there was limited action due to the 2011 elections and other pressing matters. The urgency of the problem was not recognized and decisions regarding the bid evaluation process were very slow. In the first few months of 2012, there are indications that renewed efforts are being made to address the capacity constraints at the IIU.

PORTS

Liberia has five ports: Monrovia, Buchanan, Greenville, Harper and Robertsport. Before the war, these ports handled about 200,000 tons of general cargo and 400,000 tons of petroleum products each year. Monrovia and Buchanan handled all iron ore exports, while Buchanan and Greenville accounted for most of the timber exports (World Bank 2006b). Civil war and United Nations sanctions disrupted port operations while extensive looting rendered many of the facilities useless. The ports were further hampered by the lack of maintenance. The National Ports Authority (NPA), a state-owned enterprise, was overstaffed and inefficient. A baseline audit funded by the European Commission and a needs assessment by the International Maritime Organization (IMO) found evidence of poor operational systems, non-existent financial controls, and widespread corruption (World Bank 2006a; United Nations/World Bank 2004).

THE WORLD BANK GROUP OBJECTIVE

The Bank's objective was to restore the Port of Monrovia operationally and institutionally so that it would apply modern international best practice with the separation of public sector ownership and private sector port operations. Through the Infrastructure Rehabilitation Project, the World Bank Group was able to support the upgrading of the port and assist in developing a medium-term strategy for an efficient port sector. Among the key activities planned were: the dredging of the entrance channel, improving productivity, the upgrading of the oil jetty and, improvement of the firefighting capability.

OUTCOMES

The port of Monrovia has been transformed from a state-owned enterprise into a *"landlord port,"* with a private operator (APM Terminals) providing commercial services for general cargo and containers, and the government serving as landlord and regulator responsible for public policy. This is a major achievement that has eluded some of the more advanced and stable countries in the region. It also fulfills the specific targets in the CAS, as shown in table 4.3.

In addition, a significant dredging operation was completed, and improvements of the facilities and safety procedures made. APM Terminals brought management skills and resources to upgrade the efficiency of port services, improving ship turnaround time and cutting theft by 90 percent through surveillance cameras. According to the 2012 World Bank's Doing Business Report, there have been important impacts from the transformation. The average time in Monrovia Port for a container is 14 days, compared to averages of 37 for sub-Saharan African ports and 11 for OECD countries. Similarly, the cost per container averages US$1,200 compared with US$1,960 (sub-Saharan Africa) and US$1,032 (Organisation for Economic Co-operation and Development).

CONTRIBUTION OF THE WORLD BANK GROUP

The World Bank Group financed the dredging operations and improvements in the Port of Monrovia, attracting bids from suitable private sector operators to enable the transformation of the port through a management contract with an experienced and qualified international firm. This support entailed technical assistance to develop a strategy and build capacity and to provide considerable advice for the government, which was faced with challenges ranging from occupation of part of the port area by displaced communities to security issues. The concession of Monrovia Port's general cargo and container operations was therefore a very important achievement that showed the commitment of the government to institutional reforms, no matter how difficult. The World Bank Group provided excellent technical advice based on its experiences globally

Table 4.3	Progress Made under Specific Milestones	
Improved port services		
Ports. Seventy percent of the general cargo operations by professional terminal operator by 2010	Private concession effective in 2010 and handles near 100 percent of general cargo	Achieved
Landlord Port Authority established by 2010		Achieved
Source: IEG.		

with port operations. (Table 4.4 provides a summary of the outcomes and World Bank Group contribution.)

The lack of qualified contractors, however, frustrated efforts to rehabilitate the oil jetty at the Monrovia Port. The jetty has physically deteriorated to the extent that it poses a severe risk to the country's fuel supply. There is no firefighting installation on the jetty and it is structurally unsafe until the planned replacement is constructed and the pipes to landfall are replaced (a new concept is now being pursued). In the future, a heavy oil facility is anticipated to be a cheaper solution for electricity generation. In the medium term, the National Ports Authority would like to see a similar facility provided at Buchanan, which could serve as an alternative in the event of a breakdown in Monrovia.

Restoration of the Port of Monrovia was highly relevant since it was Liberia's lifeline for imports and exports to the rest of the world. As the landlord owner/ operator model had worked successfully in many World Bank Group-financed projects, it made sense to introduce it in Liberia.

Airports. The Roberts International Airport (RIA), about 45 km outside Monrovia, is Liberia's only international airport and is managed by the International Airport Agency. During the war, the airport suffered severe damage and operations were suspended for several years. Following the peace agreement in 2003, UNMIL secured RIA with a large military presence. Today, security at RIA continues to be the full responsibility of UNMIL. The restoration and securing of the airport to enable international flights to resume were clearly very relevant and of the highest priority. The World Bank Group's small but vital role was to finance navigational, aeronautical and meteorological

Table 4.4	Summary Results of Pillar 2 – Ports and Airports
Outcome	Contribution of the World Bank Group
Objective: Rehabilitating the transport network and institutions	
Ports/Airports. The Monrovia port was to be transformed into a "landlord port," with the government acting as regulato r and a private operator providing commercial services. Major dredging operations and improvements of facilities and safety procedures were to be completed to restore the functionality of the port, thereby greatly facilitating maritime trade with Liberia. The international airport was to be restored to minimum International Civil Aviation Organization (ICAO) standards through the purchase of essential equipment, and international and regional flights were to be resumed. Master plans for future development were also to be drawn up.	The World Bank Group supported the government's transformation of the port sector through technical assistance to develop a strategic framework and build capacity using the landlord port model. The excellent technical advice was based on its global experiences. Cargo movements/ clearances were improved from 20 days in 2007 to 15 days in 2012. Theft fell by 90 percent during the same period. The service was expedited by creating a one-stop shop bringing together various agencies, and streamlining the inspection regime. Fees for customs clearance and port and terminal handling were reduced. At Roberts International Airport, vital equipment was procured and master plans prepared.
Source: IEG.	

equipment and provide technical assistance for master planning, including essential institutional advice regarding safety, security and legal issues.

Railways. The railway network in Liberia was constructed by mining companies to transport iron ore from the mines in the Mano River basin to the ports of Monrovia and Buchanan. The length of the network was about 500 km. By 1986, the last mine had closed, with the tracks and wagons subsequently damaged or looted. In 2006, ArcelorMittal renegotiated and accepted a mineral contract with more favorable terms for Liberia. The company repaired 240 km of railroad and the road from the mines in Yekepa to Buchanan. The World Bank Group has only been peripherally involved in these activities through the ports and roads master plans, but IFC is considering possible investments in mining.

Telecommunications

Liberia is among a handful of countries in the region not connected to the global network of broad-band fiber optic infrastructure. Civil unrest prevented the country from participating in the 2001 West Africa submarine cable project, SAT-3. Connectivity between Liberia and the outside world has relied exclusively on expensive satellite (VSAT) technology with limited bandwidth, resulting in high costs. Only 1.5 percent of the population has access to the internet and only 24 percent have access to fixed-line or cellular telephones.

The Liberia Telecommunications Authority (LTA) was the first regulatory authority to be established in post-conflict Liberia, with the Ministry of Posts and Telecommunications having the responsibility for sector policy. The West Africa Regional Communications Infrastructure Project (WARCIP) is expected to address connectivity gaps through the creation of a fully integrated network with affordable broadband services. This was made possible by the Bank's insistence that Liberia, Sierra Leone and Guinea not be left out of another chance to obtain broadband communications (World Bank 2010).

World Bank Group Objectives

The objective of WARCIP was to connect to international broadband networks and reduce the cost of communications services. The access to high-speed connectivity was very low even by regional standards. The Africa Coast to Europe (ACE) fiber-optic submarine cable, which stretches from Europe to South Africa, represented a unique opportunity for 23 countries on the western side of the continent.

Outcomes

The new submarine cable has now been brought ashore and the landing station is expected to be completed by September 2012. However, additional finance is being sought from other donors and the private sector to connect it to the country's backbone system. WARCIP was approved in January 2011 (World Bank 2011b), and became effective nine months later. It is too early to assess the outcome at this stage. Nonetheless, the specific milestone stipulated in the CAS has been met, since the feasibility study for telecommunications interconnections to Côte d'Ivoire, Guinea and Sierra Leone has been completed as scheduled.

CONTRIBUTION OF THE WORLD BANK GROUP

Over the last few years, the government embarked on telecommunication sector reforms with the help of World Bank multi-year technical assistance delivered through the PPIAF. The major achievement to date is the conclusion of negotiations resulting in bringing the cable ashore. Technical assistance has also been provided for training. Through this project, the World Bank Group is likely to make a significant contribution to Liberia and the West Africa Region more broadly.

The telecommunications project was initially anticipated to be a grant. However, because its approval in January 2011 was after the debt relief milestone, the IDA funds were provided instead as a credit with required repayment. Although parliamentary approval was not required for this, under the post-HPIC program, a debt management review was mandatory to demonstrate the business case for contracting such debt. This and other factors led to a delay in making the project effective. However, despite delays in effectiveness, payments were still made on schedule. The government will also receive proceeds from the private sector during the divestment of government shares in the cable. A summary of the outcomes and the World Bank Group contribution is presented in table 4.5 below.

RELEVANCE

Clearly, the upgrading of telecommunications infrastructure and services was critical for revitalizing the economy by enabling connectivity to improve from a dire to a more adequate level. Taking advantage of the opportunity presented by the laying of the new undersea cable was an obvious course to pursue.

Energy

Energy policy falls under the Ministry of Land, Mines and Energy. Before the civil war, Liberia utilized a total installed electricity capacity of 177 MW for

Table 4.5	Summary Results of Pillar 2 – Telecommunications
Outcome	Contribution of the World Bank Group
Objective: Rebuilding telecommunications network	
The expected outcome was to reduce the costs through improved networks and access.	The World Bank Group assisted with negotiations and preparation to tap into the new undersea cable being laid from Europe to South Africa. It is to be connected to the country's network by September 2012. Appropriate technical assistance was also provided. The project was prepared as a grant, but after the debt relief, the terms were amended to a credit and delayed the process.
Source: IEG.	

approximately 35,000 customers. The electricity subsector is centered in the Liberia Electricity Corporation (LEC), which has the mandate for generation, transmission and distribution in the country. In 1987, about 13 percent of the population had access to electricity. The system was constrained by technical and commercial inefficiencies. Blackouts and load shedding were frequent. By the end of the civil war, the power sector had been largely destroyed, including the hydropower plant and all of the transmission lines. LEC ceased operations.

WORLD BANK GROUP OBJECTIVES

The main objective was to help restore critical infrastructure on an emergency basis, but this was only possible through restoring the functionality of LEC. An energy policy (as opposed to an electricity policy) was also to be established.

OUTCOMES

With the collapse of the LEC, the government sought the assistance of IFC to bring private management to resuscitate the corporation. However, support for a fully privatized option was limited. Thus, the government decided instead to implement a five-year management contract with the objective of improving the financial and operational performance of LEC, rebuilding the electricity system in Monrovia, and significantly expanding access to electricity. It also included piloting projects to provide modern renewable energy services to off-grid users.

CONTRIBUTION OF THE WORLD BANK GROUP

In this venture, the IFC fostered close coordination among the various partners to achieve a commitment from the government on an incentive-based structure for the management contract. Manitoba Hydro International (MHI) of Canada (IFC 2010) was awarded the contract under international competitive bidding and took over LEC operations on July 1, 2010. It commenced a comprehensive training scheme throughout the organization, but it is too soon to assess its effectiveness. The successful selection of MHI and implementation of the management contract also represented the specific milestones stipulated in the CAS. See appendix B for details.

Although the CASPR (World Bank 2011a) presented to the Board early in FY12 did not contemplate additional investments in energy, two additional operations were prepared as a result of an urgent government request during the Annual Meetings of 2011. The first will finance 10 MW of a heavy fuel oil-fired power plant to provide thermal back up to Mount Coffee Hydro. The second, the West Africa Power Pool project (US$ 150 million), will unite the region and provide a good part of the transmission and distribution network for the country. The World Bank Group has assisted Liberia in making plans for the sustainability of the energy sector. For electricity, the short-term solution has been to introduce private sector participation to ensure effective operations. In the power sector, however, there will likely be a short-term imbalance between demand and supply as the number of connections increases, until Liberia can be connected to the West African power grid.

The final project under the emergency phase was the World Bank supported Liberia Electricity Enhancement Project (World Bank 2010). Its objective is to improve and increase access to electricity in Liberia. This project comprises $10 million from IDA, with parallel financing of $29 million from the government of Norway, $10 million from the Global Partnership of Output-Based Aid (GPOBA), and $2 million from the Africa Renewable Energy Access (AFREA) trust fund for pilot projects. The World Bank Group and the government of Norway are collaborating to build capacity in LEC and MLME to support their Energy Access Plan to achieve accelerated connection rates to potential consumers (70 percent for Monrovia and 30 percent for the country by 2030). The government of Norway is providing assistance through Norconsult, and the Bank is providing assistance to the Ministry though two high-level consultants with over 35 years of experience in power engineering in West Africa. IFC's key role was to ensure that a competitively bid private sector company secured a management contract with incentives for performance. Manitoba Hydro will receive a bonus or a penalty according to how many household connections are made compared to an agreed target. It is too early to assess the outcome, but IFC is to be commended for helping Liberia put in place a strong private sector management contract. Table 4.6 gives a summary of the outcomes and World Bank Group contribution.

RELEVANCE

Providing electricity on an emergency basis to enable the government to function was highly relevant. The plan to bring in the private sector also made a great deal of sense given the weak state of the LEC. An overarching energy policy enabled the authorities to tackle longer term supply adequacy, including importing electricity from neighboring states, as well as the feasibility of supplying power to select remote communities. Recent moves to improve sustainability include strengthening local capacity and accelerating the rate of household connections.

Table 4.6	Summary of Results – Energy
Outcome	Contribution of the World Bank Group
Objective: Restoring energy services and institutions	
A management contract was awarded by mid-2011 to an international firm. An electricity connection program was rolled out to be completed over several years. An energy policy was formulated and adopted and new projects are in implementation.	IFC provided technical assistance to establish a management contract to run the Liberia Electricity Corporation for 5 years. To date, it has been successful and LEC personnel are being trained. The World Bank Group has assisted in ensuring sustainability. A national energy policy has been approved which has established a basis for participation by other partners. Two new projects have been launched to ensure a thermal back up and will link with the West Africa Power Pool.
Source: IEG.	

Water, Sanitation and Urban Infrastructure

Prior to the war, Monrovia and several nearby towns had a functioning water supply system providing service via communal and individual water points. In the sanitation sector, Monrovia also had a sewer network —an uncommon asset in West Africa. In 1980, a water treatment plant and primary water mains were completed with a capacity of 16 million gallons per day to serve Monrovia's 450,000 inhabitants. The war damaged the purification plant, cutting the capacity to less than 10 percent of the original amount. It now has to serve a Monrovian population of more than a million. The sewer network was also in a state of disrepair. The Liberian Water and Sewer Corporation (LWSC) is the entity responsible for drinking water supply and sewerage services in Monrovia, secondary cities and rural areas. Urban roads, solid waste disposal and related services were the responsibility of the Monrovia City Corporation.

WORLD BANK GROUP OBJECTIVES

The objective was to help the government restore critical services on an emergency basis. The urban projects, which focused on Monrovia, covered a broad range of basic urban services, including the bitumen resurfacing of main streets, and the restoration of water, drainage, sanitation and electricity services. Some projects such as those involving public works were specifically designed to create employment opportunities. In addition, the assistance for solid waste management was designed to increase the participation of small businesses.

OUTCOMES

Regarding urban road improvements and sanitation, progress has been substantial. The massive backlog of uncollected waste in Monrovia has been addressed and the Fiamah dump (an environmental and community disaster) has been closed. A state of the art landfill, probably one of the best in Africa, is now being developed. More solid waste collection businesses have been established than planned, and special arrangements have been made for small businesses to become involved in the disposal operations. A DfID officer advised IEG that it regards the results and methodology to date as best practice in the region. Capacity has also been strengthened considerably in Monrovia City Corporation (MCC). As for water, however, the outcomes are mixed at this stage. Treated water in Monrovia is currently delivered below target and household water connections can only be completed once the supply infrastructure is finished. Therefore, actual data were unavailable. Sewer repairs are ongoing. See table 4.7 below.

CONTRIBUTION OF THE WORLD BANK GROUP

Water connections have made slow progress. They were delayed mainly by procurement issues affecting delivery of the supply infrastructure. The IIU appears to be a bottleneck in this regard, but there are other issues because LWSC has not always provided information requested in a timely manner. Water policy reforms also made limited headway until recently. However, the agenda is now moving ahead after a new managing director was appointed.

Table 4.7	Progress Made under Specific Milestones: Water		
Milestone		Actual Results	Progress Made
Household water connections in Monrovia to 50,000 by 2010.		Delayed due to lack of supplies	Not achieved
Seventy-five km of Transmission Mains and 200 km of distribution lines rehabilitated by 2010.		Not available	Not available
Treated water in Monrovia increased from 2 million gallons per day (MGD) to 6 MGD by 2010.		4.2 MGD in Oct 2010	Some progress
One sewage stabilization pond, and 31 public toilets, rehabilitated/constructed by 2010.		Not available	Not available
Forty percent of solid waste disposed of in a sanitary manner annually (compared to original capacity of 25 percent).		Forty percent of solid waste collected and disposed	Achieved
Special Purpose Company for regional transmission operation formed by 2010.		Special Service Company not set up	No progress
Source: IEG.			

One of the problems has been that no ministry was charged with providing a vision for the sector. Through its ESW, the Bank has encouraged engagement by other donors. The African Development Bank has agreed to take responsibility for the White Plains Water Treatment Plant in Monrovia to bring it to full pre-war capacity and to provide 17 new boreholes covering several towns. The Bank financed an assessment of the rehabilitation of the water treatment plant, but instructed the consultants to use the AfDB bidding document format. The Water and Sanitation Program has provided analytical and diagnostic work and is set to put a full time professional in place to continue providing technical assistance to the sector. The World Bank Group provided crucial support in Monrovia through multiple interventions. Bitumen surfacing of 24 km of urban roads in Monrovia has been completed. The Emergency Infrastructure Project covered a one-time major clean-up in Monrovia and a rudimentary collection system for 30 percent of the city.

However, it soon became clear that a major solid waste disposal facility would be needed. The World Bank Group's new urban sanitation project has expanded the access to solid waste collection services. This was achieved with technical assistance to the Monrovia City Corporation (MCC) to enhance revenue collection, financial management and provision of services. In addition, the World Bank Group also supported a primary and secondary collection system to dispose of captured waste, as well as a public education campaign on the handling of solid waste. A summary of the outcomes and World Bank Group contribution is provided in table 4.8.

RELEVANCE

The restoration of basic services in the capital city and its environs was of the highest priority, but the water and sanitation program design is only now

Table 4.8	Summary of Results – Urban Services
Outcome	Contribution of the World Bank Group
Objective: Restoring and increasing access to urban services	
Access to the solid waste collection service has been expanded through technical assistance to the Monrovia City Corporation. Advice has been given to improve traffic management and the main roads have been resurfaced.	The World Bank Group has supported multiple interventions to restore basic urban services in Monrovia including, urban road and bridge improvements, a onetime major clean-up in the city and the introduction of a highly satisfactory solid waste disposal system. On the water side, slow progress has been made due to procurement delays and, until recently, a lack of policy direction. The Bank assisted AfDB to engage in the sector.
Source: IEG.	

taking on broad problems associated with weak institutional capacity. To some extent for LWSC, an arrangement with a private sector partner (similar to the LEC arrangement) might have been a better solution. Arrangements with MCC have worked extremely well.

OVERALL INFRASTRUCTURE OUTCOMES

Although progress has been made, there is room for improvement in the efficiency of assistance. In areas where the private sector has been involved, such as the port and the electricity utility, performance has been better than in the public sector-driven projects. The lack of capacity in the IIU is a major concern. A clear symptom is the widespread delays in project implementation. To date, none of the infrastructure projects have closed as planned. Some projects encountered unexpected bottlenecks in the procurement process, while others experienced cost overruns. An important cause of the delays was the need to change the scope or design of projects. Of course, such changes are not necessarily inefficient. Often, by restructuring existing projects, task teams are able to respond to evolving needs, thereby avoiding spending more time to appraise a new project.

It is important to highlight that many achievements were made in difficult circumstances, including: (i) repair of farm-to-market roads; (ii) rehabilitation of important urban streets and rural road sections; (iii) cleanup of solid waste in Monrovia; (iv) procurement of essential equipment at the international airport; (v) an agreement to connect to a new undersea cable to improve internet and telephone connectivity; (vi) the introduction of a private sector port operator; (vii) a private sector company to manage the electricity corporation; (viii) short-term improvements to the potable water supply; and (ix) more assurance of an adequate fuel supply for generators in Monrovia. These first steps were vital to restarting the economy and the outcomes are reported under the various respective sector tables in this chapter.

Procurement in infrastructure projects, however, poses a special challenge. Even today, markets for contractors, specialized equipment and finance, which atrophied during the civil war, have yet to fully recover. It is still difficult to attract firms to bid on large contracts. Given the extremely weak capacity in the first years of donor support, a program approach instead of a project approach for procurement could have been adopted from the beginning. To some extent this is what the IIU attempted to do, but in practice, it failed. A partnership with a private sector management company could have provided the necessary expertise and its performance would have been measured against the degree to which an effective capacity building program was implemented. In fairness, this is what the transport team is still trying to achieve. The capacity building is to involve the engagement of specialists through a professional firm to provide a "Transport Support Group." The initial list of interested parties was weak, but has now been expanded to provide a wider selection and better competition.

The frequency of project amendments also suggests that a more programmatic approach with greater flexibility might work better in an emergency situation. In the end, some of the projects became a repository for miscellaneous needs, making progress quite difficult to monitor. Some components migrated from one project to another as funding diminished. A more flexible approach would involve additional contingent funds that could be allocated once actual needs become clear. A programmatic approach would create an umbrella emergency program where detailed requirements would be worked out as the need arises.

Risk to Development Outcome

Sustainability of outcomes is a concern as infrastructure is highly vulnerable. It is critical that the infrastructure be adequately maintained. Effective maintenance in turn requires a strategy, adequate funds for implementation, sufficient human skills capacity, and appropriate supporting systems. At the World Bank Group's insistence, a line item for road maintenance has appeared on the national budget for the first time. However, it will be some years before a fully functional Road Agency and Road Fund (or other appropriate financial mechanism) can be properly established.

The port, airport, utilities and other services can, however, more easily charge enough to cover maintenance, but the risk is that these charges will not keep pace with rising costs over time or that they are collected inefficiently. To create a sustainable environment, adequate human resources need to be made available over a period that far exceeds the life of individual projects. The involvement of private firms will enhance sustainability, but there needs to be significant efforts to build capacity in the appropriate line departments and within the IIU. As with other sectors, there is a risk of increasing state capture through the public procurement process and revenue collections. Strong enforcement efforts are essential on anti-corruption and other governance aspects.

References

Government of Liberia. 2009. "National Transport Policy and Strategy." Liberia: Ministry of Transport and Public Works.

International Finance Corporation. 2010. "IFC Helps Liberia Select Partner to Improve and Expand Electricity Services: Partnership Expected to Connect Thousands of New Customers to the Grid." Press Release. April 19. http://www.ifc.org/IFCExt/pressroom/IFCPressRoom.nsf/0/6903F976A4BB77E88525770A004C11D9?OpenDocument

United Nations/World Bank. 2004. "Joint Needs Assessment for the National Transitional Government of Liberia.

World Bank. 2011a. "Project Appraisal Document on a Proposed Credit in the Amount of SDR 43.1 Million (US$67.7 Million Equivalent) and a Grant from the Liberia Reconstruction Trust Fund in the Amount of US$108.9 Million to the Republic of Liberia for a Road Asset Management Project." Report No. 58304-LR. Washington, D.C.: World Bank.

————. 2011b. "Project Appraisal Document for Proposed IDA Grants in the Amount Equal to US$8 Million the Republic of Liberia for the 3rd Series of Projects Under the Phase of the West Africa Agricultural Productivity Program (WAAPP-1C)." Report No. 58328-AFR. February 2011. Washington, D.C.: World Bank.

————. 2010. "West Africa Mineral Sector Strategic Assessment: An Environmental and Social Strategic Assessment for the Development of the Mineral Sector in the Mano River Union." Report No. 53738-AFR-West Africa. Washington, D.C.: World Bank.

————. 2009. "International Development Association, International Finance Corporation and African Development Fund Joint Country Assistance Strategy for the Republic of Liberia for the Period FY09–11." Report No. 47928-LR. Washington, D.C.: World Bank and African Development Bank.

————. 2007. "International Development Association and African Development Fund Joint Interim Strategy Note for the Republic of Liberia." Report No. 39821. Washington, D.C.: World Bank and African Development Bank.

————. 2006a. "Project Appraisal Document for the Trust Fund for Liberia in the Amount of $8.5 Million for a Liberia Infrastructure Rehabilitation Project." Report No. 36778-LR. Washington, D.C.: World Bank.

————. 2006b. "Project Paper on a Proposed Additional Financing (Grant) in the Amount of SDR 11.20 Million (US$16.5 Million Equivalent) to the Republic of Liberia for an Emergency Infrastructure Project Supplemental Component." Report No. 37408-LR. Washington, D.C.: World Bank.

————. 2004. "Liberia – Country Reengagement Note." Report No. 28387. Washington, D.C: World Bank.

Chapter 5

Facilitating Pro-Poor Growth

In addition to rebuilding core state functions and infrastructure, the World Bank Group's program in Liberia has also sought to revitalize the economy. This goal has always been central, but at the outset the World Bank Group recognized that many of the preconditions were not in place. In the early phase, the growth agenda was modest, supported by advisory services and technical assistance projects. In 2009, following the arrears clearance and introduction of the PRS (World Bank 2008c), the World Bank Group began to focus on revitalizing the economy. The CAS (World Bank 2009b) envisioned: (iv) improving the management of agriculture and natural resources; (ii) upgrading the investment climate, including finance; and (iii) increasing access to social protection and social services.

The support envisaged for the CAS period was small in comparison to the other two pillars, with planned IDA assistance of US$ 12 million over three years out of a total indicative program of US$ 138 million. This assistance was to be supplemented by resources from the IFC, MIGA and trust funds. In addition, the program was to leverage IDA funds through regional initiatives involving other donors. As it happened, the actual support for this pillar was much larger than planned, reaching $63 million. In addition, MIGA issued a guarantee of US$ 142 million.

The sequencing of the World Bank Group program reflects a pragmatic adaptation to necessity. Administrative budgets were tight in the early years, as Liberia's non-accrual status restricted IDA lending. An early or deep engagement on this agenda would have been difficult and possibly disruptive to programs elsewhere. After the debt relief took effect in 2010, the World Bank Group expanded the assistance rapidly. The phasing of this agenda, however, has meant that the Bank has been a latecomer in the support of critical areas, such as education, health, banking and land tenure.

This chapter reviews the interventions to facilitate pro-poor growth, including the following areas:

- Agriculture and fisheries;
- Mining;
- Sustainable forest management;
- Investment climate; and,
- Human development.

Agriculture and Fisheries

Agriculture has been the primary source of livelihood, providing both food and income for the majority of Liberians. The war severely damaged the road network and limited access to markets. After the peace agreement, favorable commodity prices assisted the recovery of cash crops (for example, coffee cocoa, rubber, and palm oil). But the rest of agriculture, especially rice and cassava production, which was dominated by smaller-holder subsistence farming, remained depressed.

The PRS identified the following major challenges for revitalizing agriculture including: (i) increasing yields and the production of cash crops in the smallholder sector; (ii) supporting efficient supply chains and value-added crops; (iii) enhancing food security by stimulating food crop production; and (iv) reforming and modernizing the system of land tenure (see box 5.1 below).

WORLD BANK GROUP OBJECTIVES

Recognizing the central role of agriculture in facilitating pro-poor growth, the World Bank Group sought to: (i) revitalize the agriculture sector to contribute to equitable and sustainable economic growth; (ii) ensure food security; (iii) increase employment and income; and (iv) reduce poverty. The CAS established a number of "milestones" for its initial operations in the sector to support the government's programs for increasing small-holder production and yield.

OUTCOMES

Due to a combination of procurement and institutional problems, most of the Bank-supported investments in the agricultural sector had not yet started implementation at the time of the IEG mission to Liberia in December 2011. As a consequence, the CAS objectives and "milestones" for the agricultural sector have not been met (see table 5.1). In the case of rice, the estimated 2010 output levels were still below those registered in 1988 during the conflict.

Recent activities, however, are more promising. The support for fisheries is off to a very promising start, but it is still too early to definitively evaluate results. In the meantime, financial assistance to curb illegal fishing and help coastal communities that rely on fisheries is now in effect. The Bank project has the potential to substantially strengthen governance and sustainability of this key natural resource, including through disclosure of fishing licenses

---

Box 5.1. A Primer on Land Tenure in Liberia

Most Liberians do not have adequate access to land. Those who do often find their title invalid or non-exclusive.

The issue of land tenure is deeply rooted in Liberia's history, stemming from tribal customs, discriminatory laws, wartime occupation, and the taking of land for mining or forestry concessions. Land titles are insecure because different authorities have issued conflicting claims on the same property. Moreover, land administration is in disarray, with incomplete surveys and missing or contradictory ownership records. Apart from depressing investment and economic growth, these unresolved issues are also capable of reigniting violence. Resentment and discontent among agrarian youths contributed significantly to the spread of conflict in the 1980s and 1990s. Today, land disputes remain prevalent, involving an estimated one-quarter of rural residents. They also account for a high percentage of verbal abuse, threats and assaults (Blair and others 2011). Furthermore, Liberians often think that the next war will be about land (Sawyer 2009).

Source: IEG.

Table 5.1	Progress Made against Specific Country Assistance Strategy Milestones— Agriculture		
Objective / Result Indicator	Actual Results (as of 12/2011)	Progress Made
Markets for seed rice increased from three to seven by 2009	-	No progress
Local facility with 1000 metric tons of certified seed	-	No progress
Two new sector policies completed by 2010	-	Achieved
At least three markets constructed by 2010	-	No progress
Reduced tariffs on rice and farm inputs	Not Available	Not Available
Source: IEG.		

and revenues (on the model of EITI), registration of artisanal fishing boats, establishment of a full-time fisheries monitoring center, undertaking regular patrols, and arrests of unauthorized vessels. Investment support to help raise rice and cassava output and productivity is expected to start. A new project to assist smallholders for the production of tree crops, particularly cocoa and coffee, will reintroduce agricultural credit for small farmers in Liberia. This project is expected to go to the Board in June 2012.

CONTRIBUTION OF THE WORLD BANK GROUP

The most relevant part of the World Bank Group contribution in the agriculture sector to date has been policy advice and technical assistance. A particularly important output is the study of land tenure insecurity, which has implications reaching far beyond agriculture— although it has not contributed to the outcome envisaged within the horizon of the CAS. The Bank has also helped the Ministry of Agriculture to develop several new policies for the sector and, together with USAID, establish and strengthen its implementing capacity by supporting an internal Project Management Unit (PMU).

In terms of lending, the World Bank Group approved one small grant operation for the sector in 2007: the $5 million agricultural component of the $37 million Agriculture and Infrastructure Development Project (AIDP) (World Bank 2007a). The main objective of this project was to rehabilitate road infrastructure. The agriculture component focused on production and marketing of smallholder tree and food crops. Another $3 million was added in May 2008 to support increased rice and cassava production as part of a $10 million Bank response to the global food price crisis. The focus of this earlier project has now shifted entirely to food crop production and marketing. A new Bank project will support smallholder tree crop production, and is likely to soon be underway. In addition, the World Bank Group is providing support to Liberia's agriculture and fisheries through two regional initiatives, which are still at relatively early stages of implementation:

- The West Africa Regional Fisheries Project, approved in October 2011 (World Bank 2011); and

Table 5.2	Summary Results of Pillar 3 – Agriculture
Outcome	Contributing Activities of the World Bank Group
Expected improvements in food and tree crop output and productivity have been delayed. World Bank Group investment support has been ineffective due to procurement and institutional problems.	The World Bank Group's main contribution has included analytical work carried out in cooperation with the Food and Agriculture Organization (FAO) and the International Fund for Agricultural Development (IFAD), and policy and technical support to the Ministry of Agriculture for smallholders, coastal fisheries and land tenure issues.
Source: IEG.	

- The West Africa Agricultural Productivity Project, approved in March 2011 (World Bank 2011b).

The World Bank Group has also played a key role in donor partner coordination, and chaired a technical working group on agriculture. Initially, the assistance took the form of analytical work carried out jointly with the Food and Agriculture Organization (FAO) and the International Fund for Agricultural Development (IFAD). Over time, the sector has attracted the support of additional development partners, including AfDB, USAID, and the Japan International Cooperation Agency (JICA), with the World Bank Group playing a key coordinating role.

Table 5.2 presents a summary of the outcomes and World Bank Group contribution to agriculture.

Mining

In the mining sector, iron ore played a major role in the economy before the conflict, accounting for a quarter of GDP. In addition, artisanal mining of gold and diamonds engaged the employment of as much as 40 percent of rural residents. However, much of the diamond and gold output was smuggled out of the country and not captured by official statistics. The civil war ended large-scale mining operations due to the destruction of associated rail and port infrastructure. United Nations sanctions further depressed small-scale diamond mining activities. Today, substantial foreign direct investment, which has started to return through new/or renegotiated concession agreements, is still needed to rehabilitate or build new large-scale iron ore mining facilities and associated transport infrastructure.

WORLD BANK GROUP OBJECTIVES

In the 2009 CAS, the goal of the World Bank Group was to: (i) rapidly expand mining as an engine of economic growth and social development; (ii) ensure that the benefits from mining activities are widely shared; (iii) diversify the mining sector into new and downstream activities; and (iv) improve support to local miners. The mining-related CAS indicator was to attain the Extractive Industry Transparency

Initiative (EITI) compliant status by 2011. The indicator for the sector was to increase the volume of iron ore exported from zero to 3 million tons by 2011.

OUTCOMES

The rehabilitation of needed rail and port infrastructure was delayed by the global economic and financial crisis. Iron ore exports only resumed in July 2011 and were estimated to be between 1.2 and 1.3 million tons by the end of the year, thus falling short of the 3 million ton target (see table 5.3). However, they are expected to rise to as much as 4 million tons a year in 2012 and thereafter.

CONTRIBUTION OF THE WORLD BANK GROUP

The World Bank Group has worked closely with USAID to help modernize and reform Liberia's legal framework in the mining sector. To help the country attain EITI compliance, the Bank provided assistance through the mining component of the EGIRP (World Bank 2008a), and subsequently through supplementary financing for this project in March 2011. The technical assistance provided by the Bank in 2007 and 2008 helped develop a new mining policy, law and regulations, mining cadastre, and model mining development agreements.

This technical assistance made it possible, among other things, for the government to renegotiate one major iron ore concession (with Arcelor Mittal) and to start new contract negotiations with other foreign companies. The World Bank Group has also launched an effort to harmonize mining regulations in the Mano River Union, which includes Liberia, Sierra Leone, and Guinea. More assistance is needed, however, to help Liberia regulate and disseminate to all affected parties the strengthened environmental and social measures that have been included in the new national mining legislation.

Table 5.4 below presents a summary of the outcomes and World Bank Group contribution to the mining sector.

RELEVANCE

Although substantially relevant, World Bank Group assistance has not thus far focused sufficiently on the crucial area of artisanal or small-scale mining,

Table 5.3	Progress Made against Specific CAS Milestones — Mining	
Objective / Result Indicator	Actual Results (as of 12/2011)	Progress Made
Large-scale exploration and mining licenses issued through mining cadastral system.	All new licenses are issued	Achieved
Transparent and competitive mineral asset tendering procedures are applied.	New mining contracts are completed	Achieved
Two reports of payments are published.	Reports are published	Achieved
New environmental and social frameworks.	Update is delayed	Partially Achieved
Source: IEG.		

Table 5.4	Summary Results of Pillar 3 — Mining
Outcome	Contributing Activities of the World Bank Group
Iron ore exports restarted late in 2011 at a level below the CAS target; new large-scale mining concessions show good prospects. Greater attention is still needed for small-scale gold and diamond mining which generates much greater employment.	World Bank Group support to the Extractive Industries Transparency Initiative (EITI) process, and reform legislation and regulatory regime in the mining sector, including concession arrangements, has been very positive. Efforts to improve harmonization in mining in the Manu River Union have yet to show results.

Source: IEG.

which is of greater importance from an employment (if not foreign exchange) standpoint. Geographically dispersed and difficult to reach, artisanal mining suffers from a lack of information and support services, poor access to markets, and inadequate standards and regulations. The sector also generates negative social and environmental effects, including attracting illegal operators who may be armed and dangerous. This is a more difficult part of the sector to support, but the Bank Group has done so in other African countries and the payoff could be high in terms of improved working conditions for the poor, as well as risk mitigation with respect to environmental damage.

Forest Management

Liberia contains the largest contiguous forest blocks remaining in West Africa. These forests provide diverse benefits to local communities, including food, medicine, and livelihoods. Before the emergence of conflict, commercial forestry also played a crucial role in the formal economy, accounting for about 20 percent of GDP. However, logging was proceeding at an unsustainable pace while poor governance limited its contribution to society. As the country slipped into civic strife, forest revenues were dissipated through corruption and patronage. Part of the logging money was used to finance conflicts both in Liberia and neighboring countries. In addition, the logging companies seldom paid attention to the concerns of local communities.

In July 2003, the United Nations imposed sanctions on the export of Liberian timber and logs. The measure disrupted the funding of the civil war, leading to the fall of Charles Taylor and the end of conflict. The United Nations then set a number of requirements for the lifting of sanctions, including: the establishment of full control of all forest areas by the government of Liberia; a review all forest concessions in order to set internationally acceptable standards for sustainable forest management; and implementation of good governance in the forest sector.

After the peace agreement, the U.S. State Department launched the "Liberia Forest Initiative" (LFI) to assist the Liberian authorities in meeting the requirements. The LFI included initially a number of US agencies, including the US Forest Service, USAID, and the US Treasury Department, as well as

NGOs such as Conservation International and the Environmental Law Institute. Later, the World Bank Group, the European Commission, the FAO, the IMF, and the World Conservation Union (IUCN) joined the initiative.

WORLD BANK GROUP OBJECTIVES

Early on, the main goal of the World Bank Group in the forest sector was to help lift the United Nations sanctions. The 2007 Interim Strategy Note set an initial goal of "reactivating the forestry sector in a sustainable manner with emphasis on increasing value added." In the 2009 CAS (World Bank 2009b), the World Bank Group paid more attention to the social and environmental impact of interventions, stating: "the objectives were to make the forest sector a source of higher income for the rural population, while ensuring that the benefits are shared equitably; and adequate environmental safeguards are in place to ensure sustainability."

THE OUTCOME

The World Bank Group has been effective in helping the government introduce regulatory and legal reforms that have improved transparency and reintroduced rule of law in the sector. These reforms helped put into place the necessary conditions to lift the United Nations sanctions and restart commercial operations. Support for the nationwide chain-of-custody system that tracks timber and the Liberian Extractive Industries Transparency Initiative has shed light on an otherwise opaque system.

However, little progress has been made toward the main goal of reducing rural poverty for residents living near forest concessions. According to a 2011 Rapid Social Assessment (World Bank 2011c) carried out by the World Bank Group in response to an Inspection Panel request, food insecurity around forest concessions is extremely high— with 94 percent of the sample expressing difficulty in accessing foodstuffs, and with virtually none of the residents living around the concession areas employed in commercial forestry.

In addition, World Bank Group support was unbalanced in favor of commercial goals— and at the expense of community forest management and conservation. It focused on the resumption of large-scale commercial logging, which historically has done little to enhance the livelihoods of local people. This approach was derived in part from faulty analysis. The estimates of timber output and revenue collection were too optimistic. The World Bank Group advice led the government to believe that forest products would yield $108 million in revenues for the period 2007–11 on a timber volume of 3.3 million cubic meters. In reality, only 5 percent of forest concessions reached the production stage while revenue collection was roughly $10 million -- less than one-tenth of projections.

The unwarranted optimism regarding commercial logging produced many unfortunate consequences. First, it encouraged the government to pursue an aggressive program of forest concessions, with contracts awarded to companies that lacked the necessary qualifications or track records. As reported by the independent firm in charge of Liberia's chain-of-custody system, by January 2012, logging companies operating full management concessions owed the government of Liberia $23.7 million in tax arrears. Second, it led the World Bank Group to overlook other key objectives of the government such as building capacity or promoting added value through conversion of round logs and further processing. Third, the approach did not recognize the potential of the informal sector in creating jobs and building skills for local people. Overall, the preoccupation with commercial logging has cost Liberia and the World Bank Group years of opportunity in promoting equitable and sustainable forest management.

Reasonably good progress has been made in relation to the specific milestones stipulated in the CAS. As table 5.5 shows, two out of five milestones have been met after some delays, with some headway on the remaining milestones. However, these results have yet to demonstrate material progress toward the outcomes sought.

The World Bank Group is gradually changing the way it is doing business in the forestry sector. It now recognizes that its reliance on commercial forestry absorbed too much of the limited capacity available in the government, while marginalizing the objectives of conservation and community forestry. In the future, the World Bank Group will need to deepen its engagement in forest-based communities to enhance the pro-poor results it seeks. The Bank will also need to understand that the complex issues of land tenure and customary land rights will have to be untangled to effectively implement sector-wide reforms.

CONTRIBUTION OF THE WORLD BANK GROUP

During the transition period, the World Bank utilized the LICUS Trust Fund to provide technical assistance and policy advice to the Liberian Forest Development Authority. Assistance focused on forestry sector reforms that would support a reconstitution of the commercial forestry industry. From 2006 onward, the World Bank executed a small IDA-funded forest project, the Development Forestry Sector Management Project (DFSMP) (World Bank 2011d)

Table 5.5	Progress Made Against CAS Milestones — Forest Management	
Result Indicator	Actual Result	Progress Made
Two forestry concessions by 2010	Sites approved; not operational	Some progress
Community Rights Law by 2009	Approved two years late	Achieved
Three new protected areas by 2010	One Area declared	Some progress
Set carbon storage by 2009	Done in 2009	Achieved
Framework for land tenure	Work is underway	Some progress
Source: IEG.		

that financed a review of existing timber concessions. The review led to the cancellation of all forest concessions because of "massive non-compliance" in the system. This DFSMP project also contributed to the development of the 2006 Forest Reform Law and the Forest Policy, a Community Rights Law (2009), and the creation of a Strategic Planning Unit in the Forest Development Authority.

The World Bank also utilized funds from the *Program for Forests* (PROFOR) and the, then active, *Forest Law Enforcement and Governance Fund* (FLEG). These funds were used to help put in place a one-of-a kind "chain of custody" system designed to ensure that only legally harvested logs are exported, and that all taxes and fees are collected. The system was established by means of a contract between the government and the Swiss-based Société Générale de Surveillance (SGS). Three medium-sized Global Environment Facility projects have been awarded for forest conservation activities. In addition, carbon finance has been made available through the Forest Carbon Partnership Facility to help Liberia prepare its National Reducing Emissions from Deforestation and Degradation (REDD+) Strategy.

In 2008, the World Bank completed a comprehensive diagnostic of Liberia's land tenure security, land laws, and registration system. This led to the establishment of a Land Commission and the approval of a small Land Rights and Registration project (World Bank 2008b) that is helping to digitalize land records within the National Archives. Although it lacks implementation authority, the Land Commission has proven effective in helping to make policy reforms, including a Moratorium on Public Land Sales. A functioning public land law and a customary land law, which are critically needed to enable policy-makers to make sound resource allocation decisions, are currently being worked out.

A summary of the outcomes and World Bank Group contribution is provided in table 5.6.

RELEVANCE

The relevance of the World Bank support for pro-poor growth in the forestry sector is modest, reflecting in part a severe budget constraint over much of the review period which limited the extent of World Bank Group engagement

Table 5.6	Summary Results of Pillar 3 – Forest Management
Outcome	Contribution of the World Bank Group
Little or no gains have accrued to the poor of the forest regions. Food insecurity around forest concessions is very high and few of the local residents are employed in commercial forestry. Only 5 percent of forestry concessions have reached the production stage since 2007, while revenue collection was 10 percent of the amount projected.	The World Bank Group has supported the government in introducing regulatory reforms that helped lift the United Nations sanctions. Assistance for the Liberian Extractive Industries Transparency Initiative (EITI) and a nationwide chain-of-custody system that tracks timber harvests has increased transparency. However, the outcome in this area has been neither pro-poor, nor supportive of growth.
Source: IEG.	

in this crucial area of the economy. Although the support for the chain-of-custody system has improved governance in the forest sector, the forest concession model that it has supported holds little promise for job creation and inclusive growth. Little attention has been given to community forestry or value addition within the sector —at either the secondary (conversion of round logs) or the tertiary (wood products) levels —which offer local skills development and greater opportunities for poverty alleviation.

The design of World Bank Group support could also have been improved. For example, the 2006 Forest Reform Law that the Bank helped put in place includes: (i) revenue-sharing agreements and; (ii) social agreements, which are to be established through negotiations between logging companies and community representatives. It is well known, however, that this arrangement is highly favorable to logging companies and detrimental to local communities which often lack the necessary skills, information and political support. Experience shows that such agreements produce little more than token benefits to local people.

With respect to the results framework, the milestones and indicators should have been chosen to better track the desired outcomes, as well as the facilitation of monitoring activities. Despite the explicit goals of generating employment for rural people and promoting shared growth, neither result is captured by indicators or reflected in the monitoring and evaluation systems. The only indicator included in the ISN is to award ten forestry contracts, whereas the CAS sets as a production target 1.3 million cubic meters of timber.

The relevance of the World Bank's support in the forestry sector is also undermined by inadequate attention to land tenure security issues in Liberia. Although the AAAs were of high quality, the World Bank has not supported investments to help tackle the issues of land tenure. At the root of the diagnostic is the recognition that the extreme tenure insecurity -- spurred by historical causes and unresolved legal uncertainties— greatly threatens the country's fragile political security.

Investment Climate

The war wreaked havoc on the investment climate. As the preceding chapters show, the cornerstones of the business environment disintegrated, with the destruction of markets, infrastructure, the regulatory framework and economic services. Productive factors, including land and finance, were left paralyzed — incapable of providing necessary services without major overhauls. In addition, skilled professionals and entrepreneurs had fled to safety abroad. Only the most rudimentary of markets and supporting institutions remained.

WORLD BANK GROUP OBJECTIVES

The 2004 Country Re-Engagement Note focused on building the knowledge base and launching institution building activities to achieve quick results. Later, the Interim Strategy Note (World Bank 2007b) envisioned an IFC program as the main mechanism for delivering support to revitalizing the economy. The strategy was to create sustainable institutions that would enhance repayment discipline by: (i) establishing a new and commercially-oriented microfinance institution; and (ii) supporting the Central Bank of Liberia (CBL) in reforming the regulatory regime in the financial sector and in microfinance. In 2009, the Country Assistance Strategy expanded the role of the IFC. According to the CAS, "through its post-conflict initiative, IFC plans to combine advisory, technical assistance and investment operations to introduce innovative ways to mitigate risk, help improve the investment climate and strengthen the financial sector." (World Bank 2009)

THE OUTCOMES

Much was accomplished in establishing an enabling legal and regulatory framework to attract and support private business. Several critical pieces of legislation were enacted during the evaluation period, notably the revised Investment Law, the Commercial Code, and the Commercial Court Bill. Regulations were reformed to reduce the cost of doing business in many areas, such as Starting a Business, Dealing with Construction Permits, and Trading across Borders.[1] A modern business registry was developed that would complete business registration within 48 hours. Between 2007 and 2010, new business registration increased by about 40 percent, thus overshooting the PRS target.[2]

However, many systemic issues remained to be addressed. First, there has been little progress in resolving land disputes and clarifying land titles, despite the establishment of a Land Commission. Second, business facilitation needs greater depth in areas such as indicators in "Registering Property, Protecting Investors, and Enforcing Contracts." Third, formal employment has not helped absorb the vast pool of youths who are unemployed or who are in low-paying work in the informal sector.

In the financial sector, there was an increase in microfinance lending with the entry of Access Bank Liberia, a private bank set up in 2009, in an industry that had been dominated by NGOs. More generally, there was an improvement in financial intermediation: banking deposits and credit to private sector were increasing. With the enactment of the Commercial Court Bill, there was an improvement in the "Strength of Legal Rights Index" in the 2012 *Doing Business* survey. The government is addressing financial market integrity issues with the drafting of anti-money laundering legislation. However, while the ratio of non-performing loans to gross loans in the banking system has recently declined, credit risks remain high (IMF 2011) due in part to inadequate financial infrastructure and weak banking skills, such as in credit assessment and risk management. There has been no change in the "Depth of Credit Information Index,"[3] where Liberia has a very low score, and where there is a lack of an institutional framework for secured lending. These weaknesses increase system vulnerability, constrain efficient allocation of resources, and inhibit development of financial products. While there is an ongoing process in the Central Bank of Liberia to transition to risk-based supervision supported by the IMF (IMF 2011b), there is no systematic program dealing with financial infrastructure and banking skills development.

All of the specific investment climate milestones in the CAS have been met, as indicated in table 5.7. It should be noted, however, that the CAS results framework does not give adequate attention to systemic issues, which continue to constrain growth and investment. Although all of the milestones have been achieved, more progress on the investment climate is needed to make a significant difference to the ultimate outcomes in job creation and poverty reduction.

CONTRIBUTION OF THE WORLD BANK GROUP

The main instrument of the World Bank Group in supporting business legal and regulatory reform was the IFC Advisory Service Liberia Private Sector Development in Post-Conflict Program (Private Sector Development program). It built on the 2007 work done by the Foreign Investment Advisory Service (FIAS). The Mini-Diagnostic of the Investment Climate played a major role in reforming the legal and regulatory framework for business activities. The PSD program began in FY2008 with two main tasks: (i) implementing a survey to identify the barriers to formalization; and (ii) putting into place the basis for a structured dialogue on reforms with both the government and the private sector. Since FY09, the investment climate agenda has expanded. The World Bank Group Enterprise Survey (World Bank 2009a) reconfirmed many of the investment climate issues being addressed. However, the planned Investment Climate Assessment which was part of the program in the FY07 ISN did not materialize, though an investment climate policy note to the government was produced in FY11.

In supporting financial sector development, the World Bank Group initially focused on microfinance. During the ISN period, an IFC Advisory Service

Table 5.7	Progress Made Against CAS Milestones	
Result Indicator	Actual Result	Progress Made
Create Liberian Better Business Forum (LBBF)	LBBF set up in 2007	Achieved
Create one commercial microfinance bank	Access Bank (2009)	Achieved
Identify of barriers to formalization	New registry in place	Achieved
Redrafting Investment Code	New code in 2010	Achieved
Modern business registry operational	Working by 2011	Achieved
Two business-related reforms enacted	Eight reforms implemented	Achieved
Access Bank has 20,000 accounts by 2011	28,000 by 2010	Achieved
Functioning one-stop shop at Customs	One-Stop shop since 2010	Achieved
Source: IEG.		

project conducted a pre-feasibility study on microfinance and recommended revisions to the banking law and related regulations. As a follow-on to the Advisory Service project, IFC invested in a new microfinance bank, the Access Bank Liberia (ABL), in FY09.

Beyond microfinance, the World Bank Group supported the development of the banking system. IFC provided technical assistance and trade finance to several banks, and the World Bank produced knowledge products on the financial sector. IFC accompanied its investment in Access Bank Liberia with technical assistance to help the bank develop loan products and attract deposits. In addition, it provided liquidity support through trade finance lines to the Liberian Bank for Development and Industry (LBDI) and to EcoBank Liberia. These IFC investee banks had a significant share of total banking assets. In FY09, the Financial Sector Reform and Strengthening (FIRST) Initiative led to the production of an internal financial sector diagnostic report, though there was no World Bank Group follow-up in addressing many of the key issues identified in the report. IMF technical assistance in the financial sector focused on strengthening the Central Bank of Liberia, including its banking supervision function and monetary operations. It also focused on developing the national payments system (IMF 2011a).

The World Bank Group's work on the investment climate benefitted from collaboration with many partners, notably the European Union (Customs Code), USAID (Bureau of Customs and one-stop shop), the African Development Bank (trade promotion and support to banks), and the IMF (tax administration and the financial sector).

MIGA has approved one project to support private investment — a FY11 guarantee valued at $142m to a foreign investment in Buchanan Renewables Fuel, Inc. Buchanan Renewables engages in the collection and processing of non-productive rubber trees damaged during the war. A biomass of nearly 60 million tons can be harvested from these trees for export. Buchanan Renewables obtains the trees mainly from the largest concessionaires and plantation owners, where the cost is lower and the yield more attractive. In addition,

Table 5.8	Summary Results of Pillar 3 — Investment Climate
Outcome	Contributing Activities of the World Bank Group
There was a reduction in the cost of doing business mainly in the areas of: starting a business; getting credit; dealing with construction permits; and trading across borders (where Doing Business Surveys show improvement). New business registration increased during 2007–11. The banking system experienced growth in both deposits and private sector credit.	The World Bank Group played a key role in the reforms that reduced the cost of doing business. The IFC-led program was the main instrument in supporting the design and implementation of the reforms, including establishing a mechanism for public-private sector dialogue. The IFC investments in three commercial banks, including the first microfinance bank, contributed to the development of the banking system.
Source: IEG.	

Buchanan Renewables has supported a social enterprise (*"Farmbuilders"*) that brings smallholders into the supply chain. However, there is concern about the effects of the Buchanan Renewables operation on local producers and users of charcoal, including the possibility of higher prices, although the causal linkage has not been established. MIGA has begun looking at this issue as part of its supervision of the environmental and social aspects of the project.

RELEVANCE

The World Bank Group's initial response to Liberia's post-conflict needs in the area of the investment climate was timely, relevant, and based on fast-track analysis of the business environment at a time when country knowledge was deficient due to the Bank's long absence. The PSD program focused mainly on the reduction of the cost of doing business, which helped establish the credibility of the reforms through quick and concrete results. The PSD program also supported critical legislation, which had a longer-term impact. The IFC work on microfinance addressed the lack of access of a large segment of private businesses, and the process introduced innovations in the microfinance market by using a private commercial bank as the funding and delivery mechanism.

However, World Bank Group activities failed to evolve in addressing difficult systemic issues, many of which were identified in various AAAs. The World Bank Group could have used the transition from the ISN to the CAS to review the strategic focus of investment climate work and develop a program that builds on the experience from work in other countries, such as IFC activities in strengthening financial infrastructure, for example, secured transactions, leasing, and credit information, as well as World Bank initiatives on growth corridors in resource-rich countries.

Human Development

In the aftermath of the war, poverty was prevalent and often extreme in nature. Nearly two-thirds of the population lived below the national poverty line, and nearly one-half lived in extreme poverty.[4] No social services or safety nets were available. Life expectancy at birth was 42 years— lower than the average of 45 for fragile and conflict-affected states. Infant mortality was estimated at 157/1000, under-5 mortality at 235/1000, and the maternal mortality ratio was 760 deaths/100,000 births.[5] Health facilities and schools were mostly destroyed. More than half of the functioning health and educational facilities were operated by international relief organizations. Qualified teachers were in critically short supply. Following the 14-year conflict, a lost generation of children and young adults with little or no education emerged, accompanied by many disenfranchised youths and young ex-combatants.

Improving the delivery of basic services (including health and education) was one of the four key pillars of both the iPRS (World Bank 2007b) and the PRS (World Bank 2008c). Noting the high value placed by ordinary Liberians on health and education, the PRS stated: "....Only through sustained increases in income, coupled with access to improved health and education services, can the poorest Liberians gain the foothold to climb out of poverty."

Many partners and NGOs were already active in human development when the Bank reengaged. USAID led in the health sector, providing $60 million of assistance annually, and the United Nations Children's Fund (UNICEF) was the lead partner in education. The European Union, World Health Organization (WHO), UNICEF and Irish AID funded many programs implemented by civil society organizations for the delivery of health services throughout the country. In the education sector, as in social protection, the key partners are UNICEF, the World Food Program (WFP), USAID, and the European Union.

WORLD BANK GROUP OBJECTIVES

Within the World Bank Group, human development is recognized as a crucial element of post-conflict assistance. Education, in particular, is considered a critical element to minimize the likelihood of renewed conflict (see box 5.2). However, reflecting the budget constraints of the Liberia program and the need to be selective, the World Bank Group chose to limit the extent of engagement in human development, except for social protection. The only goal related to human development in the 2009 Country Assistance Strategy was to include access to social protection and social services with special attention to women and children.

In the health sector, the World Bank Group sought to support the 2007 national strategy (National Health Policy and Plan - NHPP) in building a modern, equitable and efficient healthcare system to be managed by Liberians. The NHPP had 4 pillars: basic package of health services; human resources for health; infrastructure development; and support systems. Through an emergency operation in health which came about prior to the PRS and CAS, the Bank's Health Systems Reconstruction Project (HSRP)[6] aimed to: (i) strengthen the policy framework and selected management functions of the Ministry of Health and Social Welfare; and (ii) improve pre-service training and selected components of a basic package of health services. The World Bank Group also sought to develop the tertiary hospital subsector.

In the education sector, the World Bank Group was ambivalent about its role. Sector staff recommended significant engagement in secondary education, but reflecting the presence of many active partners and the potential support of trust-fund resources, the country management unit decided to deploy the limited IDA resources elsewhere. Sector staff was encouraged to carry out AAAs and seek trust fund resources that would assist the government and other partners. This strategy led, among other things, to the preparation of the Basic Education Project (approved in 2011), which assisted in the reconstruction of rural primary school and supported institutional reforms, including the decentralization of personnel management.

THE OUTCOMES

In the health sector, Liberia has successfully moved beyond humanitarian relief and has embarked on the rebuilding of its health system. It is currently implementing the second National Health and Social Welfare Plan and Policy 2011–21 with an emphasis on efficiency and effectiveness. From delivering a basic package of health services in the first plan (2007–10), the Ministry of Health and Social Welfare has now shifted its focus to quality health and social welfare services, to be delivered close to communities in a manner responsive to patient needs, and with management delegated to lower administrative levels. Core functions of the Ministry (planning, research and development) and the tertiary hospital subsector have been strengthened. The Ministry's policy framework and management functions (including monitoring and evaluation, a Health Management Information System, financial management and procurement oversight) are much improved. The Ministry is now the only line agency to receive direct funding from partners, including USAID. This is due in large part to the strength and commitment of the Ministry leadership and good harmonization of partner assistance.

In the education sector, the first comprehensive economic and sector work was completed in 2010 and provided important knowledge on the financing gaps in the system. A sector-wide Education Sector Policy (ESP 2010–20) was developed and replaced the Liberia Primary Education Recovery Program (LPERP) as the blueprint for sector policies.[7] Partner support, however, remained concentrated on primary education, including the $40 million grant from the Education-for-All/Fast Track Initiative partnership program approved in 2011.

In the area of social protection, early interventions have produced positive results, including the rehabilitation of war-torn communities, the mitigation of adverse effects from the food crisis, and the development of institutional capacity at LACE (which implements several community development projects). As indicated in table 5.9, most of the milestones have been achieved or substantially achieved.

Table 5.9	Progress Made against CAS Milestones in Social Protection	
Milestone	**Actual Results**	**Progress Made**
Increased access to social protection and social services in the face of shocks		
Cash-for-work: 17,000 households by 2010	17,000 reached	Achieved
One thousand girls receive training for business	1,250 girls received training	Achieved
Fifty percent of road work contracts use labor-based methods	Thirty percent	Good progress
School-feeding in five counties in 2008/09	Eighty-seven percent achieved	Good progress
Social Services. 25 clinics meet standards	Standards met	Achieved
Twenty schools and 20 health units rebuilt by 2010	Ten school and 5 health units rebuilt	Good progress
Ninety percent of Community Empowerment Project II tasks show local priorities	Sixty-nine percent	Good progress

Sources: Andrews and others 2011. World Bank project reports.

CONTRIBUTION OF THE WORLD BANK GROUP

Overall, IDA committed $39 million (through 4 projects) to social protection, $8.5 million to health, but none to education— although Bank staff were instrumental in obtaining a grant from the "Education-for-All" Fast Track Initiative (EFA/FTI).

In the health sector, much of the World Bank Group's early contribution (2006/7) took place without lending operations. Rather, the Bank's contribution was through engagement in strategic policy dialogue with the Ministry of Health and Social Welfare and USAID on major sector issues such as health financing, and on the implementation plans and strategies of the 2007 National Health Policy that was being finalized. The partners successfully brought in new donor funding to the sector.

Later, the Bank approved an emergency operation in health, the Health System Recovery Project, which was designed as a Sector-Wide Approach, but later restructured into a Specific Investment Loan. The Health System Recovery Project helped strengthen the Ministry's policy framework and management functions (monitoring and evaluation, financial management and procurement oversight), and improved the quality of pre-service training for nurses, doctors and other health workers. These activities complemented those of other donors which focused on the delivery of basic health services.

Among the health-sector studies supported by the World Bank Group were: National Census of Health Workers, An Assessment of Health Training Institutions, and Policy Options to Attract Nurses to Rural Liberia, all of which have helped the Ministry meet their human resource development needs.

In the education sector, the contribution of the World Bank Group was primarily through analytical and advisory services. The Bank led the stand-alone ESW of the education sector (the Liberia Education Country Status Report), and was a key architect of the Education Sector Plan (ESP 2010–20). Later the Bank also became the executor for the $40 million EFA/FTI Basic Education Project.

In the area of social protection, the World Bank Group initially relied on the community-driven approach with positive results, including the rehabilitation of infrastructure in war-torn communities, and the development of institutional capacity at LACE. During the food and financial crises, the Bank helped protect the poor and vulnerable from the shocks through a public works program (PWP) and a program for vulnerable women and children. The public works program provided income support to 17,000 vulnerable households. Based on the success of the PWP, a new project, the Liberia Youth Employment and Skills Project (FY2009), was prepared to scale up this intervention to 49,500 beneficiaries. The program for vulnerable women and children provided food support to 87 percent of its target population, despite logistical problems during the rainy season. More recently, the World Bank Group has contributed to a shift in the government approach toward the development of a social protection system as a replacement for the highly fragmented donor-driven social assistance programs.

A summary of the outcomes and World Bank Group contribution to human development is presented in table 5.10.

Table 5.10	Summary Results of Pillar 3 — Human Development
Outcome	Contribution of the World Bank Group
Objective: Rebuilding health, education and social protection systems	
In the health sector, Liberia has moved beyond emergency relief and has started rebuilding its health system. Core functions of the ministry — policy making, procurement and financial management — have improved, as have some areas of the tertiary hospital subsector.	The World Bank Group's policy advice, technical assistance and a small grant complemented other donor support for basic health services. In addition, Bank assistance, although limited, also addressed institutional needs for the whole sector.
In the education sector, Liberia has completed the development of the Education Sector Plan (ESP) 2010. In addition, a $40 million Education-For-All/Fast Track Initiative grant has been given to implement the basic education parts of the Education Sector Plan.	There was no direct IDA support for education. The World Bank Group was instrumental in securing the $40 million Education-For-All/Fast Track Initiative grant. However, Liberia still needs help in post-basic education, including producing more teachers.
In the area of social protection, early interventions produced positive results, including capacity development at the Liberia Agency for Community Empowerment, and community projects. Access to food improved during the recent food and financial crises.	The World Bank Group helped strengthen social protection through community empowerment projects (Community Empowerment Projects I and II) and supplemental funding for food security. Today, the Bank and UNICEF are supporting the development of a National Social Protection System.
Source: IEG.	

Despite limited engagement, the assistance of the World Bank has been of substantial relevance, particularly in health and social protection. By and large, the interventions were essential, timely and well-aligned with government priorities. The contribution addressed sector-wide constraints in health and helped set the strategy for social protection.

In the education sector, however, the relevance of World Bank assistance was modest. A potentially valuable contribution to the strategically important secondary education field was bypassed.[8] With an unprecedented scarcity of skilled workers— especially teachers, both in the private sector and in the government, and the limited support of both the government and other partners,[9] the case for Bank involvement was evident. Nonetheless, the World Bank Group — which was operating under a tight budget at the time — chose not to commit IDA resources to support secondary education. Instead, it conducted analytical work and helped obtain trust fund resources (EFA/FTI), which were required by charter to support primary education. As a result, a valuable opportunity and many years of time were lost to make a difference in the lives of the "lost generation" (of young people with little or no education) and to advance the World Bank's own capacity building agenda.

Overall Assessment of the Pro-Poor Growth Agenda

The outcomes of this initial phase of the pro-poor growth agenda have not yet reached the "satisfactory" threshold. There have been modest results in agriculture and forestry. Somewhat more progress has been made in the investment climate, as well as in two other areas where engagement has been limited — mining and human development. However, a good start has been made and lessons have been learned to help fortify the next phase of this important agenda. In the future, the World Bank Group will have an opportunity to develop a truly pro-poor growth strategy, that is, one that integrates natural resources with broader private sector development— and mitigates the "enclave" effects of mining and commercial logging operations. It would be appropriate to review and reconsider the "concession models" that have been applied in the past, and to integrate the role and needs of indigenous local communities. Such a strategic framework would be more pro-poor and add considerable value to a wide range of Bank interventions.

Risk Development Outcomes

Because the Bank's agenda of supporting pro-poor growth had a late start and had not addressed many of the fundamental issues, the risk to sustainability is high. Although the sequencing adopted by the Bank is defensible, it is necessary to recognize the fragility of the results to date. Most of the results achieved so far pertain to policy reforms and technical assistance, which will take time to influence behavior and change perceptions. At this stage, the results are fragile and vulnerable to dissipation.

Further, the rural poor and forest-based communities, who are eager to make up for the years of deprivation during the war, have yet to see tangible results. In addition, much more progress is needed in creating educational or employment opportunities for youths and members of the "lost generation." Perhaps the most important factor that could help maintain the momentum would be active and robust consultations between businesses and public officials. The private sector, however, still lacks the depth and diversity needed to support a productive policy dialogue.

Notes

1. Doing Business Reports, 2008–12. World Bank.

2. Annex 1, Joint Country Assistance Strategy for Republic of Liberia for the Period FY2009–11, World Bank.

3. Doing Business 2008–12, World Bank.

4. Based on national definition of poverty, as indicated in the 2008 Poverty Reduction Strategy Paper.

5. WHO, World Health Statistics, 2004.

6. Originally designed as a SWAP, the project was restructured as a Single Investment Loan, with some targets scaled back and areas of policy support redefined.

7. The ESP noted weak management and capacity in the sector, as well as a lack of resources to meet the increasing public expectations on education.

8. The crucial role of upper level and general secondary education is in contributing to the needs of job markets, and is highlighted in: "Expanding Opportunities and Building Competencies for Young People: A New Agenda for Secondary Education," Education Policy Paper, the World Bank, 2005.

9. The national budget allocated 29 percent of expenditures to primary education and only 13 percent to secondary education. In addition, virtually all partner assistance has been directed to primary education.

References

Andrews, C., P. Backiny-Yetna, E. Garin, E. Weedon, Q. Wodon, and G. Zampalione. 2011. "Liberia's Cash for Work Temporary Employment Project: Responding to Crisis in Low Income, Fragile Countries". Social Protection Working Paper Series No 1114; July 2011. World Bank: Washington, DC.

Blair, R., C. Blattman, A. Hartman. 2011. "Patterns of Conflict and Cooperation in Liberia. Results from a Longitudinal Study." *Innovations for Poverty Actions*. Yale University.

International Monetary Fund. 2011a. "Liberia-Seventh Review Under the Extended Credit Facility Arrangement." IMF Country Report No. 11/345. Washington, DC: International Monetary Fund.

————. 2011b. "Liberia: Sixth Review Under the Three Year Arrangement Under the Extended Credit Facility." Request for Extension of the Arrangement, and Augmentation of Access - Staff Report; Staff Supplement; Press Release on the Executive Board Discussion; and Statement by the Executive Director for Liberia. Washington, DC: International Monetary Fund.

Sawyer, A. 2009. "Land Governance Challenges: The case of Liberia." Presentation prepared for ARD Week 2009. March 2, 2009. Washington, DC: World Bank.

World Bank. 2011a. *Ghana - West Africa Regional Fisheries Program Project.* Washington D.C.: World Bank.

————. 2011b. "Project Appraisal Document for Proposed IDA Grants in the Amount Equal to US$8 Million to the Republic of Liberia for the 3rd Series of Projects Under the First Phase of the West Africa Agricultural Productivity Program (WAAPP-1C)." Report No. 58328-AFR. February 2011. Washington, DC: World Bank.

————. 2011c. "Rapid Social Assessment." World Bank: Washington, DC.

————. 2011d. "Restructuring paper on a Proposed Project Restructuring of the Development Forestry Sector Management Project P104287/TF057090 (Board Date September 6, 2006) to the Republic of Liberia." Report No. 63061. June 30, 2011. Washington, DC: World Bank.

————. 2009a. *Enterprise Surveys: Liberia Country Profile.* Washington, D.C.: World Bank and International Finance Corporation.

————. 2009b. "International Development Association, International Finance Corporation and African Development Fund Joint Country Assistance Strategy for the Republic of Liberia for the Period FY09-11". Report No. 47928-LR. Washington, DC: The World Bank and the African Development Bank.

————. 2008a. "Emergency Project Paper for an IDA Grant in the Amount of SDR 6.7 Million (UUS$ 11.0 Million Equivalent) to the Republic of Liberia for an Economic Governance and Institutional Reform Project". Report No. 42836-LR. April 29, 2008. Washington, DC: World Bank.

————. 2008b. *Liberia Insecurity of Land Tenure and Land Law.* Report No. 46134-LR. October 22, 2008. Washington, DC: World Bank.

————. 2008c. *Lift Liberia: A Poverty Reduction Strategy.* World Bank: Washington, DC.

————. 2007a. "Emergency Project Paper on a Proposed Pre-Arrears Clearance Grant in the Amount of SDR 24.30 Million (US$37.0 Million Equivalent) to the Republic of Liberia for an Agriculture and Infrastructure Development Project." July 17, 2007. Report 39163-LR. Washington, DC: World Bank.

———. 2007b. "International Development Association and African Development Fund Joint Interim Strategy Note for the Republic of Liberia. " June 14, 2007. Report No. 39821. Washington, DC: World Bank and African Development Bank.

———. 2005a. "Expanding Opportunities and Building Competencies for Young People: A new Agenda for Secondary Education." Education Policy Paper. Washington, D.C.: World Bank.

———. 2005b. *Reshaping the Future: Education and Post Conflict Reconstruction.* Washington, D.C.: World Bank.

Chapter 6

Cross-Cutting Themes: Capacity Building, Gender, and the Environment

The cross-cutting themes (CCTs), which include capacity building, gender and environmental sustainability, are designated as such because they are multi-sector issues in which the efforts of individual sectors need to be combined in a holistic framework if they are to be tackled effectively. In each of these areas, there is a set of core activities with specific lending and AAAs designed to support them. In the case of capacity building, there are substantial programs of support for institution building in public financial management and governance. Regarding gender, there is analytic work and the Economic Empowerment of Adolescent Girls Project (EPAG). As for environmental sustainability, there are biodiversity conservation projects with GEF support. In addition, the intention is to go beyond these core programs and encompass sector-based programs in an integrated results framework

Effective World Bank Group support for CCTs requires planning, capacity building and monitoring. First, there is a need for analytic work in the preparation of a strategy. Second, the Bank needs to prioritize its own work in the area, based on its comparative advantage and the support of other partners. This requires a coherent mapping of the needs against the array of World Bank Group and partner programs. Third, there is a need to support training and institution building to promote implementation. Fourth, monitoring and evaluation are needed to measure progress. Although some elements of this approach are present in the three CCTs (for example, national strategies in capacity building and effective monitoring and evaluation of the EPAG), these do not add up to a coherent, well-integrated approach.

The CCTs were designated as such in World Bank Group strategic documents because of their importance to Liberia, and because the normal structures of government departments and Bank objectives do not allow for easy mapping into the pillars. IEG finds, however, that the designation has not served its purpose. The thematic vision is not well defined. The sector thematic programs are not integrated into that vision; rather, they are ad hoc and lack serious planning and monitoring dimensions.

Capacity-Building

Liberia's civil service was devastated by the civil war. Institutional and public administration capacities were left in a state of extreme degradation. Public services and facilities throughout the country had collapsed. Qualified staff had abandoned their posts during the war, and remaining staff were either older civil servants or individuals hired during the civil war with questionable qualifications. Staff did not know how to carry out basic functions nor did they keep regular hours. In addition, they suffered from low wages, irregular payments, lack of equipment and no training. There was little chance for building capacity.

WORLD BANK GROUP OBJECTIVES

The World Bank Group's early strategy frameworks recognized that the country's civil service would have to be completely rebuilt (National Transitional

Government of Liberia 2004; World Bank 2004a). (See box 3.1 in chapter 3 for a definition of capacity building and the Bank's approach). The assistance strategies (CAS [World Bank 2009a], ISN [World Bank 2007b] and CRN [World Bank 2004a]), all identified capacity building as a crosscutting objective of the Bank's work. The 2004 Country Re-engagement Note focused on "Technical assistance and capacity building efforts to assist with the establishment and operation of a strong and transparent mechanism for coordination and oversight." Early capacity building efforts made use of AAA and Trust Fund resources. The planned AAA included: institution building and governance reform through a Public Expenditure Management and Fiduciary Accountability Review (PEMFAR) (World Bank 2009b).

The 2007 Joint Interim Strategy Note (World Bank 2007b) provided a detailed program for achieving its capacity building objectives, including:

- Public sector capacity building efforts through the Economic Governance and Institutional Reform Project (EGIRP) (World Bank 2008a) with a series of AAA activities;

- Re-establishing training centers and programs, through support from the Global Distance Learning Center, the World Bank Institute, a Judicial Reform Project, a Civil Service Reform Project and partnerships with other development partners;

- Strengthening the Liberia Institute for Public Administration ;

- Supporting the Senior Executive Service program;

- Strengthening the capacity of the judicial functions in Monrovia and clearing case backlogs through a Judicial Service Reform Project ;

- Providing capacity building support for human resource management and leadership development through a Civil Service Reform Project; and

- Strengthening the capacity of the Liberian Agency for Community Empowerment.

The Joint Country Assistance Strategy for FY2009–11 (World Bank 2009a) deepened the capacity building efforts. Planned activities included: (i) using the Senior Executive Service Program to bring qualified Liberians into management of the civil service; (ii) strengthening the Liberian Institute for Public Administration to train mid-level civil servants; (iii) strengthening the capacity of the Financial Management Training School to train accountants to staff key ministries; and (iv) capacity building in other areas of service delivery. The CAS also planned to build public implementation capacity for large infrastructure projects and to encourage private sector development.

The results framework of World Bank Group interventions also became clearer in the CAS, but there was a large difference across areas of engagement. Core activities such as support for financial management and accountability generally provided well-defined programs with specific targets to be achieved. For example, public financial management indicators included: establishing and using new fiduciary controls in spending; hiring and training of new civil servants; and putting into place a biometric system for identifying public servants. However, the design of sector programs was less well calibrated. Sector-specific indicators for capacity building are often missing or process-driven, with few measurable indicators. In health services, indicators were available although they pertained mainly to training programs. Indicators for the private sector related to increases in employment.

THE OUTCOMES

As discussed in greater detail in chapter 3, the progress made in strengthening human resource capacity in the civil service, information systems for planning and budgeting, and financial management and oversight and regulatory institutions is a significant achievement of the Liberia program. One particularly interesting initiative, the Financial Management School, is noted in box 6.1.

By and large, the Bank's sector-level capacity building efforts do not reflect a structured approach that is adequate to meet the needs. The achievements in building capacity at the sector level thus far are modest. It is true that other partners are often engaged in capacity building, but this is also the case for the core functions where the Bank has added value by providing coherence to these efforts and ensuring that no key institutions are left out. In each sector program, World Bank Group staff need to take a broader view beyond the needs of a specific project.

Box 6.1.	The Financial Management School

The program for Financial Management Training is a unique capacity-building model that could well be replicated in other fragile states.

In 2007, the World Bank Group provided a grant to support Liberia's Public Financial Management Capacity Building Technical Assistance project, which assisted the Ministry of Finance in establishing the Liberian Institute of Financial Management (LIFM) as a unit within the ministry. The plan was to offer short-term courses to ministry staff and a two-year program in financial management with the objective of graduating 30 students selected annually through competitive examination. The grant paid for staffing, trainee stipends, operating costs, the facility, equipment, training materials and a website.

The financial management school was established to attract high-performing Liberians into the civil service. The program is linked with the University of Liberia, and students receive an MBA after successful completion of the program. Participants sign a contract to work in government for four years. They receive a new assignment after two years. To date, three groups of participants have completed the course with 82 participants working in the Ministry of Finance as well as in other line ministries.

Source: IEG.

To develop the capacity of the core public sector agencies, the World Bank Group has provided an integrated package, a comprehensive strategy, and training and logistics. This support has materialized through many years of analytical and advisory activities, four development policy operations (Reengagement and Reform Support Programs), technical assistance projects (notably the Economic Governance and Institutional Reform Program and Senior Executive Services), as well as multiple small grants for special purpose agencies.

At the sector level, however, the World Bank Group's efforts are largely ad hoc and not part of a longer-term strategy for institutional capacity building. Thus far, transport is the only sector in which the Bank has supported the development of a detailed sector strategy that could provide a framework for capacity building efforts. Among sector programs, the most frequent Bank intervention to build capacity has been training. The Agriculture and Infrastructure Development Project (World Bank 2007a) provided technical assistance to entities in government responsible for transport and infrastructure capacity building, that is, training of trainers. World Bank Group AAAs provided support to the Liberia Forestry Initiative including forestry training programs. The Health Systems Reconstruction Project has provided a large component of technical assistance and training activities to be given to Ministry of Health and Social Welfare's procurement unit. The Community Empowerment Projects I (World Bank 2005) and II (World Bank 2007c) (including additional financing) provided funding for communities and partnering NGOs to organize hands-on training based on needs.

The recent Youth Employment and Skills (YES) project (World Bank 2010a) is an important initiative with strong implications for basic service delivery and private sector development. The World Bank Group's decision not to engage in general secondary education left a large void. Secondary schools would have helped to keep a segment of idle youths off of the streets. More importantly, such schooling would have helped to develop a better trained workforce, including teachers. The YES project will provide support for the Technical and Vocational Education and Training system, which serves the needs of the private sector.

A summary of the outcomes and World Bank Group contribution is presented in table 6.1.

Table 6.1	Summary Results — Capacity Building
Outcome	Contribution of the World Bank Group
Capacity development in the civil service, and budgeting, financial management and oversight institutions has been impressive. However, the achievements in building capacity at the sector level thus far are modest.	The Bank has provided an integrated package, with strategy, training and logistics to build the capacity of the core public sector agencies. At the sector level, the efforts are largely ad hoc and not part of a strategic vision.
Source: IEG.	

There is scope for improving the relevance of capacity development among sector programs. As has been done with capacity development among the core fiscal agencies, there is a need for sector units to develop a more strategic vision and to provide a more systematic package of support, including analytical work and technical assistance, followed by the monitoring of results.

Gender

Women have played a major role in the economy before, during and after the war, accounting for 60 percent of agricultural output, as well as much of the food processing and cash crops. They carry out 80 percent of trading in rural areas and help link rural and urban markets through informal networks (World Bank 2007d). Despite their contribution, women face numerous disadvantages, including limited access to farm inputs and services (land, credit, training and technology). Women are also poorer than men and have a higher illiteracy rate (59 percent for women versus 37 percent for men). They are also exposed to other types of insecurity, including gender-based violence (GBV), sexual exploitation, human immunodeficiency virus/ acquired immune deficiency syndrome (HIV/AIDS), and so on—especially among young girls.

WORLD BANK GROUP OBJECTIVES

Gender was not mentioned in the initial strategy (World Bank 2004a). The 2007 ISN (World Bank 2007b) introduced gender as a cross-cutting theme and planned to provide technical and advisory assistance to the Ministry of Gender and Development. The 2009 CAS (World Bank 2009a) included a gender specific objective to be supported by operations, namely "to promote gender equality and women's economic empowerment wherever such opportunities arise." Gender was mentioned throughout the CAS and in the analysis of several sectors, such as health and public financial management. Operationally, the portfolio included stand-alone gender projects, such as the Economic Empowerment of Adolescent Girls (EPAG), the United Nations Development Fund for Women (UNIFEM) Results-Based Initiative, and the Food Support Project for Vulnerable Women and Children.

The CAS results framework had one gender specific indicator relating to the EPAG project: "1000 adolescent girls in the Monrovia area have received training relevant for business employment by 2010." To pursue these goals, the World Bank Group collaborated with a variety of private sector and official partners to promote gender equality, including private foundations, such as NIKE, bilateral agencies such as Denmark's DANIDA, and the United Nations system (International Labor Organization (ILO), United Nations Development Programme (UNDP), United Nations Educational, Scientific and Cultural Organization (UNESCO), UNIFEM, United Nation Office of Project Services (UNOPS), and UNMIL).

The Outcome

Although the 2009 CAS objectives included gender equality in a broad sense, the design of assistance focused narrowly on women's economic empowerment, both in projects (EPAG and the Results Base Initiative) and in AAAs (gender needs assessment). In addition, both the ISN and CAS identified GBV as a serious problem affecting women and girls, but no assistance was provided. Without alleviating the threat of physical assaults, the objective of women's economic empowerment has been compromised.

The EPAG project is currently under implementation, but preliminary results are positive. The CAS milestone of training 1000 adolescent girls has been met and surpassed, with 2408 participants completing the program by 2011. The project has increased employment among participants and improved other behavioral indicators. The program, however, is costly and beneficiaries are mostly from somewhat better-off families, rather than the poor.

Contribution of the World Bank Group

AAAs have been an important part of the gender work. The Bank provided technical advice to the government and other partners to integrate women's economic empowerment in the PRS. The analysis focused on understanding the constraints of women's economic empowerment. Four areas were given priority: poverty diagnostics; food and agriculture; commerce; and employment. Technical support was also provided for monitoring and evaluation. A key piece of analytical work is the Gender Needs Assessment, jointly produced with the Ministry of Gender and Development. However, the World Bank Group needs to make additional efforts to engage line ministries responsible for sector-specific gender mainstreaming.

The main gender project is the Economic Empowerment of Adolescent Girls (EPAG). The EPAG is a three-year pilot project supported by the NIKE foundation and the government of Denmark, with the World Bank Group serving as executor. EPAG's objective is to improve employment and increase incomes for adolescent girls and young women aged 16-24 in the Greater Monrovia area. Participants receive six months of training in business development skills, job skills and life skills, with additional support to find jobs or start new businesses.

The mainstreaming of gender in sector programs has begun, but remains uneven. Of the 41 sector projects, only nine had gender-based indicators. This has changed since July 2009, as new IDA projects are required to have information on beneficiaries disaggregated by gender. Of the ten IDA projects approved since then, 70 percent provide the requisite information.

Table 6.2 presents a summary of outcomes and World Bank Group contributions on gender.

Relevance

The relevance of World Bank Group assistance on gender issues has been modest. It would have been enhanced by greater efforts to tackle the systemic

Table 6.2	Summary Results – Gender Equality
Outcome	Contribution of the World Bank Group
The World Bank Group's AAA and lending operations informed the gender policy in Liberia. The Economic Empowerment of Adolescent Girls (EPAG) project is showing positive results. However, Bank assistance focused only on women's economic empowerment and did not address pressing issues such as gender gaps in education, health and, most notably, gender-based violence.	The World Bank Group provided technical support to the Ministry of Gender, including the integration of gender issues in the Poverty Reduction Strategy. The EPAG project has assisted high school graduates in improving their readiness for the job market or in starting a business.
Source: IEG.	

issues that hinder the achievement of its objectives, including the gender-based violence and gender disparities in health and education. As with the capacity development agenda, a more comprehensive package of assistance, including analytical work focusing on the constraints, and the necessary technical assistance would have been warranted.

Environmental Sustainability

Environmental sustainability covers numerous aspects of natural resource management, as well as pollution control and environmental safeguards. The CAS characterizes the challenges as follows: "Liberia retains an important area of the endangered Guinean Forest Ecosystem, while its coastal waters and uplands are rich sources of biodiversity. Its abundant natural resources have enormous economic potential, making the sustainability of these resources a primary issue." (World Bank 2009a).

WORLD BANK GROUP OBJECTIVES

The 2004 Country Re-engagement Note (World Bank 2004) focused on reform and reactivation of forest management. It noted that a proposal for the Global Environment Facility was under preparation to "re-establish management of Sapo National Park, a prime biodiversity resource and protected area." The 2007 ISN emphasizes the environmental and social risks, observing that "given the strategic emphasis on new construction of infrastructure and the mining sector, the government's ability to address environmental and social impacts is a concern." To mitigate this risk, "the World Bank Group will work to build planning and management capacity in key line ministries and the Environment Protection Agency (EPA)."

The 2009 CAS specifically identifies environmental sustainability as a cross-cutting theme, stating: "Initiatives to address gender and environmental sustainability are integrated throughout the strategy." In addition, it stated that:

"Both the World Bank Group and African Development Bank are providing a range of support for Liberia's implementation of the Extractive Industries

Transparency Initiative (EITI),[1] to enable Liberia to continue its strong progress toward EITI compliance. Taking the work one step further, the World Bank Group will support a scoping study of the EITI ++ Initiative," a broader approach which brings in the full value chain of natural resource management.

THE OUTCOME

Since 2004, environmental sustainability has received attention in Bank assistance through operational programs and designation in the Joint Country Assistance Strategy as a "cross-cutting" theme. In practice, however, this assistance has lacked a holistic and nationally-focused strategic approach. The CAS indicated that the World Bank Group would provide capacity building assistance to the EPA and other agencies. However, with the exception of the Forestry Development Agency, the support to date has been modest and uncoordinated. No analysis of the country's environmental priorities has been undertaken, nor has the Bank carried out a comprehensive institutional assessment of the EPA to determine the requirements needed to be able to effectively perform environmental protection functions.

The World Bank Group has provided reasonably good support for biodiversity conservation, but very little else. A series of biodiversity projects have been carried out with GEF support. The one closed GEF-supported medium-size project for Sapo National Park was rated Moderately Satisfactory, although the longer-term sustainability of its outcomes was identified as a concern. The second project has experienced implementation difficulties, and the third is just getting underway early in 2012. The combined resources to be made available under the latter two projects would appear to be insufficient to achieve their ambitious, albeit worthy objectives. The World Bank Group's effectiveness on environmental sustainability, however, has been less impressive, due to the piecemeal approach and limited assistance to the EPA.

The reliance on GEF resources means that Bank support for the environment in Liberia is being driven more by global than by national priorities. Moreover, local priorities are not clearly defined and earlier analytical work supported initially by the United Nations Environment Programme (UNEP) and subsequently by the UNDP needs to be updated and complemented with economic and institutional analysis together with broad stakeholder participation. Undertaking a participatory Country Environmental Assessment (CEA) in the years ahead could significantly improve the situation in this regard. The priorities identified are likely to include the need to address environment-related health concerns associated with persistent water and indoor air pollution, as well as to more effectively deal with an above average deforestation rate. Accordingly, even though environmental sustainability was explicitly identified as a cross-cutting theme in the 2009 CAS, actual World Bank Group interventions have been limited. There has been no clear vision, and the Bank's interventions were essentially confined to biodiversity and safeguards policies. A much more holistic and strategic approach is needed if the World Bank Group is to be more effective in addressing this important CAS theme in the future.

CONTRIBUTION OF THE WORLD BANK GROUP

In terms of analytical work, the World Bank Group undertook two studies: a Strategic Environmental Assessment for the forestry sector, not published until 2010 (World Bank 2010b), and a Strategic Environmental and Social Assessment for the Mineral Sector in the Mano River Union countries including Liberia, completed in March 2010 (World Bank 2010c). However, a broad Country Environmental Analysis or environmental institutional analysis has not yet been conducted. This is a shortcoming in a country so vitally dependent on its natural resources.

In terms of financial assistance, three small GEF biodiversity projects and one forestry sector project were approved:

- The development of the Forestry Sector Project, for which a US$2.0 million grant was approved in September 2006 (World Bank 2006);

- The GEF MSP for Establishment of Protected Areas, for which a US$ 800,000 grant was approved in May 2008 (World Bank 2008b); and

- The GEF MSP for Protected Areas Network II (World Bank 2011), for which a US$ 1 million grant was approved in March 2011.

- The GEF Medium-size Project (MSP) for National Park (World Bank 2004b), for which a US$1 million grant was approved in September 2004;

As indicated, one implication of these GEF grants has been to skew the program toward the global biodiversity agenda, rather than more systematically tackling Liberia's own pressing local environmental and environment-related capacity building needs.

Table 6.3 presents a summary of the outcomes and the World Bank Group contribution.

RELEVANCE

Other than with respect to biodiversity conservation and forest management, the objectives of World Bank Group assistance were essentially defensive, that is to guard against potential adverse environmental (and social) impacts of other Bank-financed, especially infrastructure, projects. Bank interventions in support of natural resource management (NRM) and environmental

Table 6.3	Summary Results — Environmental Sustainability
Outcome	Contribution of the World Bank Group
Little progress has been made due to the limited engagement of the World Bank Group. Weaknesses in environmental management and national institutions persist.	The World Bank Group carried out analytical work on environmental and mining regulations. Support to the Environmental Protection Agency has been provided, but on a modest scale.
Source: IEG.	

sustainability to date, however, have lacked a broader vision and framework, although recent sector work on NRM has been more promising in this regard. Overall, the relevance of Bank assistance on environmental sustainability was modest.

Note

1. According to the CAS, "this initiative supports governance in resource-rich countries through the verification and publication of company payments and government revenues from oil, gas, and mining."

References

National Transitional Government of Liberia. 2004. "Results-Focused Transition Framework Progress Review Report." Report No. 30049. September 2004. World Bank: Washington, DC.

World Bank. 2011. *Liberia Expansion of Protected Areas Network- II*. Project ID P114580. Washington, D.C.: World Bank.

———. 2010a. *Liberia Youth Employment and Skills Project*. Washington, D.C.: World Bank.

———. 2010b. "Strategic Environmental Assessment of the Liberian Forestry Sector: A Strategic Environmental Assessment for Implementation of the 3 Cs of the Forest Reform Law of 2006." Washington, D.C.: World Bank.

———. 2010c. "West Africa Mineral Sector Strategic Assessment: An Environmental and Social Strategic Assessment for the Development of the Mineral Sector in the Mano River Union." Report No. 53738-AFR-West Africa. Washington, D.C.: World Bank.

———. 2009a. "International Development Association, International Finance Corporation, and African Development Fund Joint Country Assistance Strategy for the Republic of Liberia for the Period FY09–11." Report No. 47928-LR. Washington, D.C.: World Bank and African Development Fund.

———. 2009b. "Liberia 2008 Public Expenditure Management and Financial Accountability Review." Report No. 43282-LR. Co-produced with the Government of Liberia, the African Development Bank, International Monetary Fund, United Nations Development Programme, U.K.'s Department for International Development, and the Swedish National Auditing Office. Washington, D.C.:World Bank.

———. 2008a. "Emergency Project Paper for an IDA Grant in the Amount of SDR 6.7 Million (US$ 11.0 Million Equivalent) to the Republic of Liberia for an Economic Governance and Institutional Reform Project." Report No. 42836-LR. Washington, D.C.: World Bank.

————. 2008b. *Liberia Establishment of Protected Areas Network I.* Project ID P105830. Washington, D.C.: World Bank.

————. 2007a. "Emergency Project Paper on a Proposed Pre-Arrears Clearance Grant in the Amount of SDR 24.30 Million (US$37.0 Million Equivalent) to the Republic of Liberia for an Agriculture and Infrastructure Development Project." Report NO. 39163-LR. Washington, D.C.: World Bank.

————. 2007b. "International Development Association and African Development Fund Joint Interim Strategy Note for the Republic of Liberia." Report No. 39821. Washington, D.C.: World Bank and African Development Fund.

————. 2007c. *Liberia – Community Empowerment II Project.* Project ID: P105683. Washington, D.C.: World Bank.

————. 2007d. *Liberia: Toward Women's Economic Empowerment: A Gender Needs Assessment.* Report prepared by the World Bank's Gender and Development Group in collaboration with the Liberian Ministry of Gender and Development. Washington, D.C.: World Bank.

————. 2006. *Liberia Forestry Sector Project.* Project ID P104287. Washington, D.C.: World Bank.

————. 2005. *Liberia- Community Empowerment I Project.* Project ID: P098266. Washington, D.C.: World Bank.

————. 2004a. "Liberia – Country Reengagement Note." Report No. 28387. Washington, D.C.: World Bank.

————. 2004b. *Liberia Medium-Size Project for Sapo National Park.* Project ID P104229. Washington, D.C.: World Bank.

Chapter 7

Strengthening Program Implementation

There is a perception among several stakeholder groups—country team members, development partners, and government counterparts—that implementation of projects financed and/or administered by the Bank Group is slow and requires stronger support. That sense applies specifically to the Bank, and particularly to Bank-supported infrastructure projects. Since 2011, several government officials have lamented what they consider to be insufficient responsiveness on the part of Bank task teams. Failure to strengthen implementation support, many argue, will pose reputational risks for the Bank.

This chapter briefly reviews some of the Bank's organizational arrangements that are seen to underlie the weaknesses in implementation support. Although the country team may not be in a position to deal systematically with these issues, it is nonetheless essential to find pragmatic, if ad-hoc, ways around them. This chapter reviews certain guidelines of the World Bank Group for engaging in fragile and conflict-affected states[1] that, if observed consistently, would strengthen implementation support and indeed make for a stronger program more generally. This chapter refers to the organizational framework of the World Bank—and not that of IFC or MIGA.

Perceived Constraints on Bank Implementation Support

Administrative budget limitations. Although the Liberia program has benefited from provisions for enhanced IDA support to FCSs from IDA-13 (FY2003–05) onwards, the administrative budget for the country program is widely viewed as insufficient relative to needs. Barring the possibility of significant increases by the Africa Region of the administrative budget for Liberia—presumably at the expense of other needs within the Region—given the flat budget environment, the only way of mobilizing additional resources for the program is through trust fund monies. As discussed in chapter 2, trust funds accounted for an average of 54 percent of administrative budgets during the review period, and over two-thirds in the first four years. However, reliance on trust funds raises new issues. First, staff need to devote additional time and effort to obtain funding and comply with trust fund rules. Second, trust funds designate specific priority areas, which may or may not match the priorities of the country. In cases where the match is imperfect, the Bank may not be able to offer the most appropriate form of assistance.

Staffing and incentives. Shortcomings in implementation support are typically attributed, at least in part, to the difficulty of getting sufficient input in-country from staff with the right expertise and experience. In turn, this difficulty can be traced to various aspects of staffing and incentives. One aspect concerns staffing presently on the ground in Monrovia, where on average the 13 staff members have a relatively short period of experience in the Bank (see table 7.1). In addition, there is a total absence of staff covering crucial areas such as infrastructure. A second aspect has to do with the difficulty of mobilizing Bank staff with the requisite experience to deploy in-country. It is a non-family duty station where the work is demanding and conditions on the ground still relatively unattractive. In addition, hardship

Table 7.1	World Bank Staff in the Liberia Office during FY2011	
Title	Sector Mapping	Years in Bank
Transport Engineer	SDN - TRAN	4.2
Economist	PREM - PREM	9.3
Senior Natural Resources Management Specialist	SDN - ARD	9.3
Procurement Specialist	-	0.8
Operations Officer	-	5.4
Financial Management Specialist	OPCS - FM	1.8
Junior Professional Officer	-	0.9
Senior Economist	PREM - EPOL	9.8
Junior Professional Officer	SDN - ARD	0.3
Senior Operations Officer	OPCS - CSP	6.8
Public Sector Specialist	PREM - PSM	1.2
Country Manager	OPCS - CSP	26.4
Communications Associate	-	0.4

Source: World Bank Human Resources database.
Note: ARD = Agriculture and Rural Development; CSP = Country Services Panel; EPOL = Economic Policy; OPCS = Operations Policy and Country Services; PREM = Poverty Reduction and Economic Management; PSM = Public Sector Management; SDN = Social Development Network; TRAN = Transport.

post rest and relaxation entitlements have now been discontinued. A third aspect has to do with the reportedly unreasonable workloads and travel schedules of Washington- or hub-based sector staff, especially those known for the high quality of their work. Anecdotes abound of staff handling inordinate workloads, such as managing or supporting projects in Liberia as well as in several other countries, and stretched to the limit by travel schedules. And finally, turnover among key staff in the country team—perhaps in part owing to the demands of the work—has been high, affecting task team or cluster leaders for infrastructure, land tenure, forest development, education, health, and agriculture.

Managerial oversight. Just as importantly, the Liberia program appears to face stiff competition for management attention. In sector units, where project management is typically lodged, the large span of control of sector managers means that, besides the dearth of attention that sector staff can devote to activities in Liberia, management oversight of their work is also lacking. On the country side of the matrix, the dedicated Country Manager notwithstanding, the Country Director position covers three countries (the other two being Ghana and Sierra Leone). In an evaluation of Bank support to fragile states, IEG noted "the uneven attention of country directors, especially if they are also covering a larger, more "successful", or higher profile country." (Independent Evaluation Group 2006) In the best of circumstances, the Country Director's attention to Liberia faces competition from Ghana (where the Country Director resides), a high-profile country that requires close attention, as well as from Sierra Leone, a larger fragile, post-conflict economy with its own special needs. Beyond this organizational constraint, the Country Director position was vacant from June 2011 to March 2012.

Specific Areas for Attention

In addition to managing the constraints to ensure that implementation support does not falter, there are specific tenets of the Bank's approach to FCS,[2] which, if adequately mainstreamed into the work program in Liberia, would help buttress its overall quality.

The first tenet involves underpinning strategies and operations with socio-political analysis. A key tenet of the Bank's approach in FCS is an adequate understanding of conditions likely to impact its program. This can be achieved through socio-political analysis (World Bank 2002). The rationale was clear and is certainly relevant in Liberia: knowledge of social relations and dynamics helps the Bank in designing and implementing policies and programs to further development goals. However, despite the considerable knowledge work that has been carried out on Liberia, little of this has involved socio-political analysis.[3] This may reflect the resource constraints and heavy workload, as well as the large knowledge gap given the Bank's 20-year absence.

In certain key areas, the usefulness of relevant socio-political analysis has become clear, at least in hindsight. In forest management, for instance, a study of inclusive growth opportunities that analyzed the interests, capacity and aspirations of forest-based communities, as well as their customary land rights, might have helped to foresee the strong local resistance to some of the commercial logging practices, which later led to a formal complaint filed with the Inspection Panel.[4] Similarly, Bank support in strengthening the investment climate, which is significantly influenced by the insecurity of land tenure, could usefully have been guided by a study of how traditional tribal relations and customary land rights restrict the application of modern laws.

Despite the absence of socio-political analysis to guide decision-making, the Bank staff intuition proved sound in key components of the program. For instance, the Bank's judgment that, together with security partners, it would overcome the opposition of transitional political leaders to the fiduciary safeguard arrangements under the Governance and Economic Management Assistance Program in 2005 proved well-founded. In another case, the Bank correctly judged the elected government's political will to challenge the vested interests at the port of Monrovia. Despite the objections of the existing port management, the Bank escalated the case for reforms to the political leadership in Liberia and its own top management. Ultimately, the case for port reforms prevailed.

The second tenet involved specifying and monitoring results. The Bank's approach to FCS underscores the need for the country program and individual interventions to be underpinned by a realistic results framework. Monitoring should also be based on indicators that can track progress (World Bank 2002).

However, the implementation experience in Liberia shows that this is easier said than done. Results frameworks exhibit shortcomings in several respects. In some cases, such as forest management, there is an insufficient link between the goal—better livelihoods for rural inhabitants—and the associated indicator, the tonnage of timber production. In the CAS results framework, many of the results targeted were over-ambitious. For example, the rollout of the management information system under the Integrated Financial Management Information System project was projected to be faster than elsewhere in Africa. Regarding civil service reform, the schedule for a biometric registry did not anticipate the logistical difficulties of including civil servants located outside the capital.

Rigorous monitoring of results—and the activities that are intended to generate them—also received insufficient attention. Implementation of most projects outside of budget support operations has been behind schedule, and has had closing dates extended. During the eight years under review, only one country portfolio performance review was conducted, when annual reviews should be the norm.[5] Implementation Status and Results reports are prepared by task teams with reasonable regularity, but they often require greater candor. Most task managers are concerned that ratings below moderately satisfactory (MS) could stigmatize the project and give rise to negative perceptions concerning their own performance. Yet without regular tracking of progress and due recognition of problems when they arise, it is difficult to ensure prompt corrective action (see box 7.1).

A third tenet involves developing adequate capacity for public procurement. Although the Bank's strategies on Liberia have highlighted the importance of procurement-related capacity building, little guidance for staff is available. Actual support for the national system has been surprisingly modest. Comprehensive procurement reforms and capacity development have not been consistently pursued, with support being given on a project-specific basis. In addition, there has not been a system-wide vision or integration of similar support across the public sector. There were also no procurement specialists assigned to the country office until early 2011. As a result, procurement practice and capacity development vary considerably across different areas of Bank engagement, with significant delays in results in some areas, especially with respect to infrastructure projects.

The overall management of public procurement in Liberia rests with the newly-established Public Procurement and Concessions Commission (PPCC). The PPCC is in need of support to help develop its capacity. Even though procurement-related delays appear to be lower than elsewhere in Africa, it is due largely to the service of temporary consultants, rather than regular staff. In addition to procurement, the lack of contract management is very acute and needs to be enforced as much as possible.

Procurement is only one aspect of proper contract management. It should be considered in light of demand and possibilities of the market to deliver. The need for capacity development extends also to the domestic contractor industry, which can also benefit from appropriate procurement arrangements. Whereas

The short answer: Nobody knows. The Bank does not have a system that can give a clear answer to this simple but important question. What we do know, however, is surprising. First, contrary to general perceptions, the procurement process in Liberia is substantially faster than the average for the Africa Region. Second, procurement staff do not appear to be the bottleneck, as they account for significantly less processing time than do task team leaders.

The findings are based on an IEG review of recent procurement transactions under all active Bank-supported projects in Liberia, as recorded by the Procurement Tracking System. On average, a request for no-objection in Liberia takes 50 days to process—31 days on the part of the Bank and 19 on the part of the client. In comparison, the average for the Africa Region is 95 days (54 days on the Bank's part and 41 on the client's). These figures however, cover only the time it takes to complete a procurement transaction, for example, from initiation to contract signature.

A more accurate picture emerges when the "down time" between steps is included. By this metric, it takes about six months (181 days) on average to get a contract approved in Liberia. This is much better than the average of more than a year (387 days) for the Africa Region as a whole. It is important to note, however, that procurement transactions in Liberia are largely handled by project management units—not by the regular government system, which is being rebuilt, but is not yet complete. This may also to be true in many countries within the region. However, the reliance on external help in a parallel system may be greater than average in Liberia.

In addition, the perception that delays are mainly attributable to procurement staff is not supported by the data. When the Bank has procurement responsibility, the Task Team Leader who deals with technical issues accounts for about two-thirds of the time, with procurement staff who handle more procedural matters accounting for the remaining one-third.

Source: IEG.

the major infrastructure projects, roads in particular, require well organized, financially solid and technically capable contractors, the local underdeveloped industry needs to handle smaller projects so as to build their capacity and ability to plan and implement. Smaller projects, such as maintenance and smaller physical works, could be specifically designed. Indeed, there is discussion among development partners on how to introduce these.

However, as mentioned, the major projects requiring skills and expertise will be carried out through international competitive bidding (ICB), for example through output and performance-based road contracting (OPRC). This will also benefit smaller local contractors providing them with basic needs to increase their profit margins and do smaller works. The longer projects, such as OPRC for 10 years, provide an excellent opportunity for such developments. Finally, opportunities to involve civil society in monitoring public procurement could usefully be explored in order to help strengthen governance and curb corruption.

Notes

1. Among the key documents detailing recommended practice in supporting FCSs are: the 2002 LICUS Task Force Report, the 2005 Fragile States Report, and the 2011 World Development Report on Conflict, Security and Development.

2. As set out in the 2002 Report of the Task Force on Fragile States and reaffirmed in 2005.

3. Among the socio-political analysis conducted were the following reports: The World Bank, Community Cohesion in Liberia, 2005; and World Bank, the Political Economy of War and Peace in Liberia, 2010. Both were of sound analytical quality and the former had an impact on the design of community empowerment projects.

4. The Bank's Inspection Panel, however, decided after a review not to conduct a full inspection.

5. The results of this portfolio review, however, were not made available online.

References

Independent Evaluation Group. 2006. *Engaging with Fragile States, An IEG Review of World Bank Support to Low-Income Countries Under Stress*. World Bank: Washington, D.C.

World Bank. 2011. *World Development Report 2011: Conflict, Security and Development*. Washington, D.C.: World Bank.

———. 2010. "Political Economy of War and Peace in Liberia." Washington, D.C.: World Bank.

———. 2005a. "Community Cohesion in Liberia: A Post-War Rapid Social Assessment." Social Development Papers: Conflict Prevention and Reconstruction. Paper No. 21. Washington, D.C.: World Bank.

———. 2005b. *Fragile States: Good Practices in Country Assistance Strategies*. Report No. 34790. Washington, D.C.: World Bank.

———. 2002. "World Bank Group Work in Low-Income Countries Under Stress: A Task Force Report." Washington, D.C.: World Bank.

Chapter 8

Overall Assessment

Liberia has provided an unusual stage for the World Bank Group, presenting at once the formidable challenge of starting from the total ruins of war, combined with the unique opportunity of working with a highly committed partner with a clear vision.

Liberia has moved from a state of complete disarray to one with a solid foundation. It is now well positioned to advance the goal of building an inclusive and prosperous nation. Although not everything has proceeded as quickly as hoped, substantial progress has been made. Key institutions have been built. The main transport facilities in and around the capital city are functional. Basic urban services are reaching more people, and hospitals, schools, and universities are operating. The capacity of the public sector has been strengthened, and governance indicators are improving. The debilitating burden of debt has also been eliminated.

Although the government deserves most of the credit, this success would not have been possible without development and security partners. The Bank has been an important part of the effort, through its analytic work that has provided a solid grounding for the efforts of the government and development partners. The Bank also contributed to the support for public finance and institution building, particularly of fiduciary agencies. In addition, the Bank gave support to rebuilding Liberian infrastructure. Although the Bank has not been a major player in human development and the productive sectors, its activities have helped other partners lay a foundation for future support.

Relevance

The program of assistance has been both timely and well aligned with country goals. The objectives are generally of high or substantial relevance, although the design of many interventions requires better calibration for tracking results, and the targets often need to be less ambitious. In addition, with the benefit of hindsight, it is now clear that more mileage would have been achieved with a reallocation of resources across the pillars. In particular, greater effort in some areas, including addressing the land tenure issues and meeting the needs in human development (both contained in pillar 3), would have been warranted.

Relevance of the three pillars. Regarding pillar 1 -- rebuilding core state functions, both the strategic approach and level of engagement have been relevant. Apart from the period of the Transitional Government, there has been exceptionally strong ownership. The design, which entails diverse modalities and a shift toward more budget support, is appropriate— although the complexity of some elements, including the new information system and medium-term expenditure framework, may have stretched the capacity. In addition, some of the principal milestones appear to be over-ambitious and have not been achieved within the stated time frame.

In rehabilitating infrastructure, early interventions were well aligned and timely. The World Bank Group was also responsive in meeting evolving needs by restructuring the projects or seeking supplemental funds. Many of the projects include labor-intensive components and measures to involve private sector participation. But project design has not adequately allowed for the evolving conditions on the ground and shifts in government priorities. This has led to delays across the board in facilitating pro-poor growth.

The objectives are uniformly of high relevance across a broad spectrum of interventions. However, resource constraints have delayed – and limited the level of – the engagement in agriculture, health and education. In addition, a greater focus on achieving pro-poor results would have been desirable with regard to forestry and mining. The support for the investment climate should have been more strategic and addressed systemic issues such as land tenure and growth strategy. These two issues were extensively analyzed and discussed in the few socio-political studies commissioned during the review period (World Bank 2005, 2010). The findings of these studies also informed some of the projects, but were not adequately reflected in the strategic approach.

Among the cross-cutting themes —capacity-building, gender equality and environmental sustainability— the objectives are largely relevant, although the support for gender is narrowly confined to economic empowerment. In the design, a strategic vision is needed in most cases to guide the mainstreaming of the themes into sector programs.

Relevance of the program. Although the evaluation is in broad agreement with this approach, there are two significant areas that appear to have received inadequate attention. One is a long-term program to systematically capture natural resource rents and convert them to service delivery. The second is a concerted effort to tackle unemployment or under-employment, especially among young people.

An analysis of Liberia's history gives ample evidence of the role that rents derived from control of its natural resources has played in bringing about inequality and political instability. In the long run, it is essential that Liberia develops a system of natural resource management that ensures equitable distribution of the benefits. An example of such a system is the integrated framework of "value chain" in natural resource management, which has been found constructive in Bank assistance to many resource-based economies, including Ghana, Laos and Mongolia (Barma and others 2011). Box 8.1 shows a simplified and condensed version of this approach.

A second area that calls for more attention is employment. The Bank analyzed employment during the evaluation period, and found that it was much lower than had been previously thought. Underemployment and unpaid or low-paid informal employment are estimated to constitute between 20 and 30 percent of the total employment rate. However, almost all those who work outside the small formal sector earn incomes that fall below the poverty line. The problem is particularly serious for youth. In Monrovia, for example, much of the employment consists of pushing small wheelbarrows in the market or selling a few items on the roadside. The capacity to steadily expand employment opportunities to absorb these youth, who include a large number of ex-combatants, is key to Liberia's political stability.

Efficacy

Considerable progress has been made, but it is uneven across the pillars— ranging from substantial in some areas to negligible in others. In rebuilding core state functions, the achievements have been impressive, although the indicators used do not fully reflect them.[1] Public financial management has been significantly strengthened, and the professionalization of the civil service is well underway. There has been steady progress in governance generally, but progress has been slow on judicial reform issues. Regarding rehabilitating infrastructure, solid improvements have been made in transport, waste management and power, while in telecommunications access to broadband networks should soon be possible. More progress is needed, however, on water reform. In addition, the limited capacity in the Infrastructure Implementation Unit (Ministry of Public Works), has delayed projects supported by many development partners, and needs urgent corrective action.

In facilitating pro-poor growth, the results have so far been modest in key areas, such as agriculture, forestry, and education— reflecting a late start in many areas. There are exceptions, however, including the lifting of sanctions on timber and diamonds, community empowerment, the Liberia Extractive Industries Transparency Initiative, and the administrative reforms to reduce transactions costs for businesses.

Among the three cross-cutting themes, progress achieved has been modest for capacity building (except with respect to core state functions), for gender (except for the Adolescent Girls Initiative) and for environmental sustainability.

IFC and MIGA Additionality. The IFC approved four investments, and MIGA approved one guarantee during the review period. The focus of IFC investments was on the financial and agriculture sectors. IFC additionality in the Salala Rubber Company investment was mainly in: (i) providing long-term funding which the company had difficulty securing: (ii) providing political comfort; and (iii) assisting the company in developing social and environment best practices. IFC investment in Access Bank Liberia was accompanied by technical assistance which enabled the bank to develop good practices in microfinance. IFC provided trade finance to two banks (Liberian Bank for Development and Investment and EcoBank) at a time when international banks required 100 percent cash backing due to high country risk. The IFC guarantees allowed the cash holdings of these banks to be used for further lending. IFC additionality is rated satisfactory.

MIGA provided a political risk guarantee to a foreign investor valued at US$142.2 million to support an investment in renewable energy. The guarantee, issued in December 2010, has supported the collection and processing of non-productive rubber trees in Liberia. This operation has created new jobs and generated more

Box 8.1. Turning Resource Wealth into Development: Liberia's Central Challenge

In order to build an inclusive society while preventing a recurrence of "growth without development," Liberia will need to convert natural resources into physical and social capital through service delivery. The key challenge is to keep enhancing governance and institutional capacity to match the expanding impact of natural resources. The "value chain" approach highlights what is needed to meet this challenge.[a] It serves as an organizing framework for public sector management strategies and programs. The general process has the following five steps:

Setting policy and institutional framework	Deciding to extract	Getting a good deal	Managing volatile revenue	Investing in development

1. Setting the policy and institutional framework: The first step is to clarify national objectives and strategies for managing natural resources, including the roles of key government actors involved in the regulation and management of resources.

2. Deciding to extract: A key decision faced by the government is if and when to begin extracting natural resources and converting them into monetary benefits. During this stage, governments may take the opportunity to get prior informed consent from the local communities and conduct social and environmental assessments.

3. Getting a good deal: With a decision to extract, the government must decide on a framework for awarding rights to explore and extract. It must also establish the legal and financial terms. Developing countries are often at a disadvantage when negotiating with multinational companies. Expert advice is often necessary. When the extraction begins, it is essential to ensure revenue transparency, which Liberia is well placed to do, thanks to the progress made under the Extractive Industries Transparency Initiative.

4. Managing volatile resources: Since resources may be depleted and their prices fluctuate significantly, this stage requires deciding how much to save and how much to spend to mitigate disruptions in the flow of revenue. Some countries use special instruments, such as natural resource funds or stabilization funds to absorb the shocks.

5. Investing for sustainable development: To develop human capital and build a cohesive society, the government will need to spend the resource revenue wisely. Apart from good public financial management and a professional civil service, Liberia will also need systematic monitoring of expenditure programs by independent organizations and civil society.

Source: Based on Collier 2005.

a. The discussion in this Box is based on P. Collier, "The Bottom Billion," Oxford University Press, 2005.

foreign exchange from a resource that has no alternative commercial use. The new business has also set up a social enterprise designed to bring smallholders into the supply chain. Although it is too early to discern the outcome, MIGA's additionality is provisionally rated satisfactory.

Table 8.1 provides a summary of the ratings by pillar, taking into account both the relevance and efficiency of the program. More detailed ratings and assessments are presented in appendix A.

Table 8.1	Overall Assessment of Program Outcomes	
Relevance	Efficacy	Overall Rating
Rebuilding core state functions		
The relevance of objectives is high, except for judicial reform. The design of interventions, however, needs better indicators for tracking progress and more attainable targets.	Progress has been impressive on core functions and institutional capacity development, but modest among line ministries. Reform of the civil service is well advanced, and corruption has diminished.	Moderately Satisfactory
Rehabilitating infrastructure		
Early World Bank Group interventions were well aligned, timely and responsive to changing needs. But the project design has grown more complex and responsiveness has receded of late.	Solid gains have been made in transport, waste management and power, but have yet to materialize on water reforms. Implementation support needs to be reinvigorated.	Moderately Satisfactory
Facilitating pro-poor growth		
The objectives are well aligned, but the engagement was modest and not timely due to budget constraints. In some areas, the design needs to be more pro-poor.	Progress has been modest generally, except on administrative reforms, social protection and on the extractive industries transparency initiative (EITI).	Moderately Unsatisfactory
Cross-cutting themes		
The objectives are of substantial relevance, but sector-level interventions need a strategic vision and a strong results framework.	The results have been modest on gender, environmental sustainability, and on sector-level capacity building. But analytic and advisory activities (AAAs) have been appreciated.	Moderately Unsatisfactory
Overall outcomes		
The relevance is substantial, with exceptions.	Efficacy is substantial in some areas, but modest elsewhere.	Moderately Satisfactory
Source: IEG.		

Lessons from the Liberia Program

The Liberia program has been distinctive in many ways. First, the initial conditions of total collapse and disarray were seldom seen among Bank member countries. Second, since 2006, the government has shown exceptional ownership of the assistance program. These factors have led the World Bank Group to tackle a wide range of very difficult issues – often with good results. As a by-product, many lessons could be gleaned from this experience, including:

- In developing the capacity of public sector agencies in FCSs, an integrated package of policy advice, financial and technical assistance as well as logistical support, can help deliver results. This is illustrated by the assistance on public financial management, with the package of economic and sector work, technical assistance projects, budget support, as well as provision of consultants and professional staff on contract, training and facilities.

- In FCSs, unemployment is likely to be pervasive. It often constitutes a major risk factor for peace and stability. It may be helpful to integrate explicit job creation objectives in the assistance program. In Liberia, job creation took on an increasingly larger role over time in World Bank Group assistance. Early projects sometimes needed funding supplements or were restructured for this purpose. This resulted in delayed project completion.

- In supporting infrastructure, a prioritized programmatic approach, perhaps with an Adaptable Programmatic Loan, may provide more scope for efficiency gains compared to a series of individual investment projects. With a flexible program in place, the World Bank Group is better equipped to respond to unexpected changes, such as the collapse of a bridge or a shift in government priorities, which have occurred from time to time in Liberia.

- Partnerships with the private sector (foreign or domestic) can help address major issues, such as shortages of capital, management and skills. In Liberia, the experience with the landlord port, where a private operator handles commercial services, and the power sector, where a private firm operates under a management contract, has been very positive. The government is now expanding the scope of public-private partnerships (PPPs).

- In supporting private sector development, rapid response and quick results can enhance the World Bank Group's credibility. This is illustrated in the case of IFC assistance in improving, among other things, public-private sector dialogue and the business registry. This has generated goodwill and publicity for the World Bank Group. In pursuing quick results, however, the World Bank Group should not overlook analytical work and fundamental issues.

- When the needs of the World Bank Group's intended beneficiaries in FCSs (such as the rural poor) are not explicitly assessed and documented, perhaps through economic and sector work, the resulting interventions may not be compatible with the desired outcomes. This is illustrated by the experience of the forest sector in Liberia. The intended beneficiaries were the residents of the regions where timber concessions were being granted, but the residents' needs and capacity, including their ability to make a deal and monitor the actions of logging companies, were not adequately taken into account. As a result, little gains accrued to the intended beneficiaries.

- In the development of procurement capacity for public sector agencies, which often requires total rebuilding from the ground up, it can help to start with a system-wide vision, rather than ad-hoc, project-by-project assistance. Procurement capacity should be considered as an integral part of public financial management, and is needed across public services. In Liberia, procurement capacity development did not benefit from such a holistic perspective, and the results have been uneven across agencies and functions.

Recommendations

During the next CAS period (2012– 2015), Liberia will face new and different challenges. The shift from emergency assistance to long-term development will continue, as the government takes on bolder reform programs during its second term. In addition, to the extent that the global economy recovers and commodity prices rise, foreign direct investment in Liberia may grow while bottlenecks in finance, infrastructure and human resources are progressively removed, and Liberian economy will continue to gain strength.

However, the expected withdrawal of UNMIL could act as a strong head wind in slowing growth unless the withdrawal process is carefully phased or is offset by private-sector initiatives. The new CAS should anticipate these future challenges while positioning the institution to take advantage of new possibilities. Among the key considerations are:

The growth agenda. The World Bank Group can help the government and other partners develop a new strategic framework for growth with the following characteristics:

- It is explicitly pro-poor and inclusive, taking into account the needs and circumstances of intended beneficiaries based on careful socio-political assessments. The pro-poor focus would be enhanced by integrating the role of indigenous communities and civil society in the design of inter-ventions.

- It reexamines the "concession model" that has been traditionally applied in mining, forestry and plantations. A key question is to what extent such concessions are pro-poor when they often involve pitting local com-munities, with limited capacity, against operators who are far more so-phisticated.

- It focuses on job creation and employment, especially for youth. Although job schemes under social protection will remain important, ultimately most of the jobs will need to be created in the private sector. Measures to enhance the investment climate may be an essential element of the strategy.

- It addresses systemic issues such as land tenure, access to credit and skill development to meet the demands of private businesses. This effort would be facilitated by supporting post-primary education, which would alleviate the shortages of teachers while expanding the scale and quality of education.

Sharing the wealth of natural resources. The government will increasingly face the challenge of matching the quality of governance with the expanding impact of natural resources. The World Bank Group can assist the government in the development of an integrated regime for natural resource management based on the "value chain" approach. It can serve as an organizing framework for improving transparency at each of the key decisions points. The general process is as follows:

- Setting objectives, policy and the institutional framework;

- Deciding to extract based on policy and consultations with stakeholders;

- Getting a good deal from investors through a competitive bidding process and favorable agreements. In addition, it is essential to ensure the transparency of revenue flow, which Liberia is well placed to do—thanks to the progress made under the Extractive Industries Transparency Initiative;

- Managing volatile revenue to smooth out spending and minimize disruptions in the funding of essential programs -- often by saving for future difficult downturns; and

- Ensuring that the benefits are distributed equitably while social and environmental safeguards are observed.

Strengthening implementation support. To counteract the perception among partners of a slowdown in its assistance program, the World Bank Group may wish to consider the following:

- Formally empowering the Liberia Country Manager to make critical decisions on the country program. This would be coupled with holding the Country Manager accountable for tracking results and country portfolio performance, in light the Country Director's responsibility for multiple country programs.

- Designating a person (or persons) to serve as a focal point on each of the cross-cutting themes (capacity building, gender, and environment), with the responsibility for providing guidelines to sector staff and monitoring progress.

- Developing a strategic vision for procurement capacity enhancement as an integral part of public financial management. In the short-term, this effort would need the support of a team of specialists to provide day-to-day procurement services and develop local capacity, possibly through private-public partnerships or management contracts similar to that of the Manitoba Hydro contract.

There is an urgent need to reinvigorate the capacity of the Infrastructure Implementation Unit (IIU) at the Ministry of Public Works. In particular, the technical assistance for procurement of an international firm (under the Roads Asset Management Project) should be quickly restored, along with the resumption of recruitment of qualified staff as mandated by the IIU's implementation framework.

Note

1. For example, the CAS framework does not capture the contributions of key institutions, such as the Governance Commissions and the Liberia Reconstruction and Development Committee.

References

Barma, Naazneen, K. Kaiser, T. Minh Le, and L. VI Uela. "Rents to Riches? The Political Economy of Natural Resource-Led Development." 2011. Washington, DC: The World Bank.

Collier, P. 2005. "The Bottom Billion. Why the Poorest Countries are Failing and What Can Be Done About It." Oxford: Oxford University Press.

World Bank. 2010. *The Political Economy of War and Peace in Liberia.* World Bank: Washington, DC.

———. 2005. "Community Cohesion in Liberia: A Post-War Rapid Social Assessment." Social Development Papers: Conflict Prevention and Reconstruction. Paper No. 21. Washington, D.C.: World Bank.

Appendix A
Ratings and Overall Program Assessment

This summary table is derived from the assessments presented in chapters 3–6 and the achievements against the stipulated milestones as provided in appendix B.

Objectives	Outcomes	World Bank Group Contributions	Rating
Pillar One Objective: Rebuilding Core State Functions			Moderately Satisfactory
Fiscal policy and financial management: To put in place fundamental public financial management and procurement systems.	Significant progress has been made. From a chaotic beginning (2006), the budget is now prepared on time, published and cast in a medium-term context. Revenue collections rose from $85 million to $275 million in four years. Public spending has grown from 11 percent of gross domestic product (GDP) to 30 percent with improved controls. However, the capacity in sector ministries remains weak, especially in the crucial procurement function. The reliance on a parallel system (project management units and consultants) remains high.	This is a key area of support for the World Bank Group, the United Nations Development Programme and the U.K.'s Department for International Development. Assistance is provided through a comprehensive package of policy advice, technical assistance and budget support. Key operations are: the series of four Re-engagement and Reform Support Programs (RRSP) (World Bank 2004, 2009a, 2010, 2011a) and the Economic Governance and Institutional Reform Project (EGIRP) (World Bank 2008). The World Bank Group has also conducted a variety of economic and sector work, including the 2009 Public Expenditure Management and Financial Accountability Review (World Bank 2009).	Moderately Satisfactory
Comprehensive civil service reform: To put in place a reformed civil service with appropriate staffing, compensation and capacity.	Civil service reform (CSR) is ongoing, with good progress. The CSR strategy has been completed, and implementation is underway. Restructuring has taken place in nine ministries and the Civil Service Agency, resulting in a reduction of employees by 11,000 in four years, including the removal of ghost workers. The work on linking biometric IDs to the human resource information system has yet to be completed. Paying for the cost of the Senior Executive Service remains a challenge.	World Bank Group support was provided through the Senior Executive Service which helped with the recruitment of qualified individuals from abroad. The Bank also provided a variety of grant support to capacity development programs for civil servants. The EGIRP supported the implementation of the biometric system.	Moderately Satisfactory
Improving governance and the rule of law: To establish a reformed judicial system, including courts, corrections, and administration.	Some progress has been made. The Governance Commission has provided a mechanism for progressive and ongoing reforms. The General Audit Commission has enhanced financial discipline. Large-scale corruption has diminished, but petty corruption remains common. Progress on judicial reforms and court administration remains modest.	The World Bank Group was a key party in introducing the Governance and Economic Management Assistance Program in 2005, which limited the scope for state capture. Further assistance was provided through a series of grants to support the Governance Commission and the agencies it created to improve transparency. However, the initial grant for judicial reform had a limited impact. The World Bank Group did not follow up on this until recently.	Moderately Unsatisfactory

Objectives	Outcomes	World Bank Group Contributions	Rating
Pillar Two Objective: Rehabilitating Infrastructure			Moderately Satisfactory
Transport: Rehabilitating the transport network and institutions.	Roads. Early road projects helped restore functionality to the main routes and created temporary employment. Later, many small sub-projects assisted in the movement of farm products and replaced key bridge crossings. Most projects experienced delays or cost overruns. The National Transport Policy and Strategy is in place, but the Infrastructure Implementation Unit remains weak. Maintenance now gets more attention, but sustainability has yet to be achieved.	The World Bank Group assisted the Ministry of Public Works in expanding the stable portion of the network. The World Bank Group also urged the government to consider a Road Fund as an essential element in securing a sustainable stream of funding for maintenance needs within 5 years. The Output and Performance –Based Road Contract project would likely have benefited from a simpler and less ambitious design. It was probably premature given the level of local capacity.	Moderately Satisfactory
	Ports. The Monrovia port became a "landlord port, "with the government serving as regulator and a private firm providing commercial services. A major dredging operation was completed, as were improvements of terminal facilities and safety procedures.	The World Bank Group supported the government's transformation of the port sector through technical assistance to develop a strategic framework and build capacity. The World Bank Group provided excellent technical advice based on its experiences globally with similar port operations.	
Energy: Restoring critical infrastructure on an emergency basis.	Private management was brought into the power sector. A management contract was awarded in mid-2011 to an international firm. An electricity connection program has begun.	The International Finance Corporation (IFC) provided technical assistance on using a management contract to run the electricity corporation for five years. The World Bank Group has assisted Liberia in making plans for sustainability, and in introducing a national energy policy.	Satisfactory
Water and Sanitation: Restoring critical services on an emergency basis.	The urban projects which covered basic urban services in Monrovia have made good progress, except for the water projects and water sector reforms. The solid waste project has exceeded targets in some areas.	The World Bank Group supported multiple interventions including a one-time major clean-up in Monrovia. The World Bank Group's new urban sanitation project has now expanded access to the solid waste collection service through technical assistance to the Monrovia City Corporation.	Moderately Satisfactory
Telecommunications: Reducing the cost of telecommunications services.	The West African Regional Communications Project (World Bank 2011b) was to connect with the international fiber-optic network and reduce costs. A new submarine cable has now "landed" and the link to the local system is to be completed by September 2012.	The project was prepared as a grant. However, with the approval in January 2011 after the debt relief, the finance terms were amended to a credit (with required repayment), thus delaying effectiveness. This unfavorable change for the client should have been averted.	Not evaluable

Objectives	Outcomes	World Bank Group Contributions	Rating
Pillar Three Objective: Facilitating Pro-Poor Growth			**Moderately Unsatisfactory**
Agriculture and fisheries	Expected improvements in food and tree crop output and productivity have been delayed. World Bank Group investment support has been ineffective due to procurement and institutional problems. However, a new fishery project shows promise.	The World Bank Group's main contributions have been analytical work carried out with the Food and Agriculture Organization and the International Fund for Agricultural Development, including policy and technical support to the Ministry of Agriculture for smallholders, coastal fisheries and land tenure issues.	Moderately Unsatisfactory
Mining	Iron ore exports resumed late in 2011 at a level below the Country Assistance Strategy target. New large-scale mining concessions show good prospects. Greater attention is still needed to artisanal mining which generates higher employment.	World Bank Group support to the Extractive Industries Transparency Initiative (EITI) process has been positive, as has its assistance to reform legislation and the regulatory regime in the mining sector, including concession arrangements. Efforts to improve harmonization in mining among Manu River Union countries have yet to show results.	Moderately Satisfactory
Forest management	Residents of the regions near forest concessions have seen little benefit from Bank assistance. Food insecurity is very high and virtually none of the local residents are employed in commercial forestry. Only five percent of forestry concessions have reached the production stage since 2007, while revenue collection was 10 percent of projections.	The World Bank Group has been effective in helping the government introduce regulatory reforms that helped lift the United Nations sanctions. Support for the Liberian EITI and a nationwide chain-of-custody system that tracks timber harvests have increased transparency. However, the World Bank Group's assistance has been neither pro-poor nor supportive of growth.	Moderately Unsatisfactory
Investment climate	There was a reduction in the cost of doing business mainly in the areas of starting a business, obtaining credit, dealing with construction permits, and trading across borders. These are areas where Doing Business Surveys show improvement. New business registration increased during 2007–11. The banking system experienced growth in both deposits and private sector credit.	The World Bank Group played a key role in the reforms that reduced the cost of doing business. The IFC-led program was the main instrument in supporting the design and implementation of the reforms, including public-private sector dialogue. The IFC investments in three commercial banks, including the first microfinance bank, contributed to the banking system.	Moderately Satisfactory
Human development	In the health sector, Liberia has moved beyond emergency relief and has started to rebuild its health system. Core functions of the ministry — policy making, procurement, and financial management — have improved, as have some areas of the tertiary hospital subsector.	The World Bank Group's policy advice and technical assistance addressed the institutional needs (financing and human resource) for the sector and complemented other partner support, which mainly covered basic services.	Moderately Satisfactory

Objectives	Outcomes	World Bank Group Contributions	Rating
	In the education sector, Liberia completed its first Sector Plan implementation and won a $40 million Education-For-All/Fast Track Initiative (EFA/FTI) grant for primary education. However, much remains to be done to re-build Liberia's education system.	The World Bank Group drew on trust funds for its support and helped secure the EFA/FTI grant. It has yet to help rebuild the sec-tor, including expanding post-basic educa-tion and institutional development.	
	Regarding social protection, early interventions produced positive results, including capacity development at the Liberia Agency for Community Empowerment (LACE) and com-munity projects. Access to food improved during the recent food crises.	The World Bank Group helped strengthen social protection (including the capacity of the community organizer LACE through community-driven projects (Community Empowerment Projects I and II (World Bank 2005, 2007), and supplemental funding for food security. Today, it is supporting the development of a National Social Protection System.	
Thematic Objectives: Capacity Building, Gender Equality and Environmental Sustainability			Moderately Unsatisfactory
Capacity building	Capacity development in the civil service, including budget-ing, financial management, and the oversight of institutions has been significant. However, the achievements in building capac-ity at the sector level thus far have been modest.	The World Bank Group has provided an integrated package, encompassing strategy, training and logistics to develop the capac-ity of the core public sector agencies. At the sector level, the efforts are largely ad hoc and not part of a strategic vision.	Moderately Satisfactory
Gender equality	The World Bank Group's Analytic and Advisory Activities and lending operations informed gender policy in Liberia. The Economic Empowerment of Adolescent Girls (EPAG) project is showing positive results. However, the assistance focused only on women's economic em-powerment and did not address pressing issues, such as gender gaps in education, health and, most notably, gender-based violence.	The World Bank Group provided technical support to the Ministry of Gender, includ-ing the integration of gender issues in the Poverty Reduction Strategy. The EPAG project has assisted high-school graduates to enter the job market or to start a business.	Moderately Unsatisfactory
Environmental sustainability	Little progress has been made due to limited World Bank Group engagement. Weaknesses in environmental management and institutions persist.	The World Bank Group carried out analytical work on the environment and mining regula-tions. Support to Environmental Protection Agency has been provided, but on a modest scale.	Moderately Unsatisfactory
Summary of Ratings:			
Pillar One: Moderately Satisfactory			
Pillar Two: Moderately Satisfactory			
Pillar Three: Moderately Unsatisfactory			
Thematic Outcome Rating: Moderately Unsatisfactory			
Overall Outcome Rating: Moderately Satisfactory			

References

World Bank. 2011a. "International Development Association Program Document on a Proposed Credit in the Amount of SDR 3.2 Million (US$5 Million Equivalent) to the Republic of Liberia for the Fourth Reengagement and Reform Support Program." Report No. P123196. September 6, 2011. Washington, DC: World Bank.

——. 2011b. "Resettlement Plan". West Africa Communications Infrastructure Programme (WARCIP) in the Gambia. ACE Submarine Cable Project. Report No. RP1149. Washington, DC: World Bank.

——. 2010. "International Development Association Program Document for the Third Re-engagement and Reform Support Program in the Amount of SDR 7.5 Million (US$11 Million Equivalent) including SDR 4.1 Million in Pilot CRW Resources (US$ 6.0 Million Equivalent) to the Republic of Liberia." Report No. 54493-LR. September 13, 2010. Washington, DC: World Bank.

——. 2009a. "International Development Association Program Document for the Second Re-engagement And Reform Support Program in the Amount of SDR 2.7 Million (US$4 Million Equivalent) to the Republic of Liberia." Report No. P46508-LR. April 28, 2009. Washington, DC: World Bank.

——. 2009b. "Liberia 2008 Public Expenditure Management and Financial Accountability Review." Report No. 43282-LR. Co-produced with the Government of Liberia, the Africa Development Bank, International Monetary Fund, United National Development Programme, Department for International Development, and Swedish National Auditing Office. June 2009. Washington, DC: World Bank.

——. 2008. "Emergency Project Paper for an IDA Grant in the Amount of SDR 6.7 Million (UUS$ 11.0 Million Equivalent) to the Republic of Liberia for an Economic Governance and Institutional Reform Project". Report No. 42836-LR. April 29, 2008. Washington, DC: World Bank.

——. 2007. *Liberia - Community Empowerment II Project.* Washington, D.C.: World Bank.

——. 2005. *Liberia- Community Empowerment I Project.* Washington, D.C.: World Bank.

——. 2004. "Liberia - Country Re-engagement Note. "Report No. 28387. Washington, D.C.: World Bank.

Appendix B
Progress Made under CAS Milestones

Objective / Result Indicator	Actual Results (as of 12/20/11)	Progress Made
Pillar I: Rebuilding Core State Functions		
1. Improved efficiency of budget preparation and execution and enhanced revenue administration		
Budgeting. Eighty percent of vouchers can be approved and paid by the Ministry of Finance by 2009 (compared to 60 percent in 2006).	One hundred percent in 2010	Achieved
Quarterly expenditure reports posted within 6 weeks by 2009 (compared to 3 months after in 2007).	The Quarterly report is published in 45 days	Achieved
Three modules of the Integrated Financial Management Information System (IFMIS) system operational by 2011.	First module expected in 2012	Some progress
Less than 20 percent of procurement on less competitive methods without justification by 2010 (80 percent in 2008).	68.3 percent in 2010	Some progress
General Auditing Commission audits five ministries for Parliament by 2009.	Twenty-two audits in 2009	Achieved
Internal audits produced for 3 key ministries by 2009.	Decision taken to set up internal audits	Some progress
Budget linked to medium-term framework by 2010.	Medium-Term Expenditure Framework established, but lined to budget.	Some progress
Tax Administration. New Integrated Tax Administration System (ITAS) operational by 2010.	ITAS started in Oct 2010	Achieved
Tax administration. Risk management systems implemented and post audit systems enhanced by 2010.	- /	No progress
2. Increased professionalization and human resource management of the civil service		
Professionalization. Senior Executive Service (SES) Scheme has recruited 70 percent staff by 2009.	Ninety-seven percent of staff at post	Achieved
Three ministries implement restructuring plans based on new mandates, organizational structures and staffing plans.	One agency implemented	Some progress
Civil Service Reform (CSR) Strategy in place by 2009.	CSR Strategy approved	Achieved
Development of a plan for Liberia Institute of Public Administration (LIPA) training delivery by early 2009, and 25 staff trained by 2010.	No training plan and no training	No progress
Performance evaluation based on merit is designed and linked to compensation and promotion systems by 2011.	System is being designed	Some progress
Human Resource Management of Civil Service. Personnel records maintained with matching payroll records.	Records created with matching on-going	Good progress
Personnel file includes biometric information for 100 percent of employees.	Biometric ID for 45 percent of personnel	Good progress
Rationalization of civil service grades and development of a well-defined salary structure.	Re-grading done; new pay approved	Achieved
Retirement age and rules are fully enforced.	Fully implemented	Achieved

Objective / Result Indicator	Actual Results (as of 12/20/11)	Progress Made
Pillar II: Rehabilitating Infrastructure		
3. Improved access to key infrastructure services		
Transport. Cotton Tree – Buchanan road corridor by 2010; Monrovia - Ganta corridor under Output and Performance-Based Road Contract (OPRC) by end 2011.	Cotton Tree - Bokay Town complete. Bokay - Town to Buchanan procured. Monrovia - Ganta bids invited 12/2010;	Good progress
Draft legislation on Road Authority and Road Maintenance Fund by 2011.	In preparation	Some progress
Twenty-four kms of Monrovia roads resurfaced.	Twenty-four km resurfaced	Achieved
New Vai Town, Caldwell (World Bank) and 35 minor river crossings built or improved by June 2011.	Vai Town Bridge completed. Caldwell consultancy in award process	Good progress
Six hundred kms of roads under maintenance.	Maintenance ongoing	Achieved
Four hundred kms (World Bank) of rural feeder roads rehabilitated by 2011.	Rehabilitation of 200 km of feeder roads started in 2011 under World Bank/International Labour Organization (ILO)	Good progress
One hundred twenty-five kms of primary roads rehabilitated by end 2010 using labor-based methods.	Rehabilitation of Fish Town – Harper Road and 125 km primary roads ongoing	Good progress
Two hundred twenty-nine drainage points constructed by 2010.	229 drainage points constructed at Fishtown-Harper Road	Achieved
Ports. Seventy percent of the general cargo operations by professional terminal operator by 2010	Private concession effective in 2010 and handles near 100 percent of general cargo	Achieved
Landlord Port Authority established by 2010.	Concession agreement became effective in October 2010	Achieved
Water and Sanitation. Household water connections in Monrovia to 50,000 by 2010.	Not available	Not available
Seventy-five km of transmission mains and over 200 km of distribution lines rehabilitated by 2010.	Not available	Not available
Treated water in Monrovia increased from 2 million gallons per day (mgd) to 6 mgd by 2010.	4.2 mgd in Oct 2010	Good progress
One sewage stabilization pond, and 31 public toilets, rehabilitated/constructed by 2010.	Not available	Not available
Forty percent of solid waste disposed of in a sanitary manner annually (compared to 25 percent).	Forty percent of solid waste collected and disposed	Achieved
Energy. Selection of a Management Contractor for Monrovia Electricity Concession by 2009.	Management Contractor selected	Achieved
Special Purpose Company for regional transmission operation formed by 2010.	Special Service Company not yet created	No progress
Feasibility Study for the interconnections to Côte D'Ivoire, Guinea and Sierra Leone by June 2010.	Feasibility study completed	Achieved
Pillar III: Facilitating Pro-Poor Growth		
4. Improved agriculture and natural resources management to generate pro-poor growth		
Agriculture. Number of markets where seed rice is available has increased from three in 2007 to seven in 2009.	-	No progress

Objective / Result Indicator	Actual Results (as of 12/20/11)	Progress Made
Local seed multiplication facility established and produces 1000 million tons of certified seed.	-	No progress
Two new sector policies completed by 2010.	-	No progress
At least three markets constructed/rehabilitated by 2010.	-	No progress
Reduced tariffs on rice and agricultural inputs.	Not available	Not available
Forest. Two community forestry concessions by 2010.	Sites established but not operational	Some progress
Community Rights Law approved by 2009.	Approved 2 years later than required by 2006 Forest Law	Achieved
Declaration of three new Protected Areas by 2010.	One Protected Area declared	Some progress
Determine carbon storage by 2009.	Done in 2009	Achieved
Mining. Large-scale exploration and mining licenses issued through/ recorded in mining cadastre system.	All new licenses are issued by the Mining Cadastre Information Management System	Achieved
Transparent and internationally-competitive mineral asset tendering procedures are consistently applied.	New mining contracts completed	Achieved
Two reports of payments minerals published.	Two reports published	Achieved
Adopt new environmental and social framework for minerals.	Update is delayed	No progress
Land. Policy framework for land tenure reform adopted.	Not yet adopted	No progress
5. Improved business and investment climate		
Creation of Liberian Better Business Forum (LBBF).	LBBF set up in 2007	Achieved
Creation of at least one commercial microfinance bank.	Access Bank (2009)	Achieved
Identification of barriers to business formalization.	New registry in place	Achieved
Redrafting Investment Code.	New code in 2010	Achieved
Modern business registry operational.	Working by 2011	Achieved
Two business-related reforms enacted.	Eight reforms implemented	Achieved
Access Bank Liberia manages 20,000 accounts by 2011.	28,000 by 2010	Achieved
Functioning one-stop shop service for customs facility.	One-Stop shop since 2010	Achieved
6. Increased access to social protection and social services in the face of shocks		
Cash-for-work program reaches 17,000 households by 2010.	17,000 reached	Achieved
One thousand girls have received training for business.	1,250 girls have received training	Achieved
Fifty percent of road contracts use labor-based methods.	Thirty percent use labor-based methods	Good progress
Food security. School-feeding in five counties in 2008/09.	Results achieved	Achieved
Social Services. Twenty-five clinics meet standards.	Standards met	Achieved
Twenty schools and 20 health facilities rehabilitated by 2010.	Ten schools and 5 health facilities rehabilitated	Good progress
Ninety percent of Community Empowerment Project (CEP) II sub-projects reflect beneficiary priorities.	Sixty-nine percent completed	Good progress

Appendix C
Statistical Supplement

Objective / Result Indicator	Actual Results (as of 12/20/11)	Progress Made
Pillar I: Rebuilding Core State Functions		
1. Improved efficiency of budget preparation and execution and enhanced revenue administration		
Budgeting. Eighty percent of vouchers can be approved and paid by the Ministry of Finance by 2009 (compared to 60 percent in 2006).	One hundred percent in 2010	Achieved
Quarterly expenditure reports posted within 6 weeks by 2009 (compared to 3 months after in 2007).	The Quarterly report is published in 45 days	Achieved
Three modules of the Integrated Financial Management Information System (IFMIS) system operational by 2011.	First module expected in 2012	Some progress
Less than 20 percent of procurement on less competitive methods without justification by 2010 (80 percent in 2008).	68.3 percent in 2010	Some progress
General Auditing Commission audits five ministries for Parliament by 2009.	Twenty-two audits in 2009	Achieved
Internal audits produced for 3 key ministries by 2009.	Decision taken to set up internal audits	Some progress
Budget linked to medium-term framework by 2010.	Medium-Term Expenditure Framework established, but lined to budget.	Some progress
Tax Administration. New Integrated Tax Administration System (ITAS) operational by 2010.	ITAS started in Oct 2010	Achieved
Tax administration. Risk management systems implemented and post audit systems enhanced by 2010.	-	No progress
2. Increased professionalization and human resource management of the civil service		
Professionalization. Senior Executive Service (SES) Scheme has recruited 70 percent staff by 2009.	Ninety-seven percent of staff at post	Achieved
Three ministries implement restructuring plans based on new mandates, organizational structures and staffing plans.	One agency implemented	Some progress
Civil Service Reform (CSR) Strategy in place by 2009.	CSR Strategy approved	Achieved
Development of a plan for Liberia Institute of Public Administration (LIPA) training delivery by early 2009, and 25 staff trained by 2010.	No training plan and no training	No progress
Performance evaluation based on merit is designed and linked to compensation and promotion systems by 2011.	System is being designed	Some progress
Human Resource Management of Civil Service. Personnel records maintained with matching payroll records.	Records created with matching on-going	Good progress
Personnel file includes biometric information for 100 percent of employees.	Biometric ID for 45 percent of personnel	Good progress
Rationalization of civil service grades and development of a well-defined salary structure.	Re-grading done; new pay approved	Achieved
Retirement age and rules are fully enforced.	Fully implemented	Achieved

Objective / Result Indicator	Actual Results (as of 12/20/11)	Progress Made
Pillar II: Rehabilitating Infrastructure		
3. Improved access to key infrastructure services		
Transport. Cotton Tree – Buchanan road corridor by 2010; Monrovia - Ganta corridor under Output and Performance-Based Road Contract (OPRC) by end 2011.	Cotton Tree - Bokay Town complete. Bokay - Town to Buchanan procured. Monrovia - Ganta bids invited 12/2010;	Good progress
Draft legislation on Road Authority and Road Maintenance Fund by 2011.	In preparation	Some progress
Twenty-four kms of Monrovia roads resurfaced.	Twenty-four km resurfaced	Achieved
New Vai Town, Caldwell (World Bank) and 35 minor river crossings built or improved by June 2011.	Vai Town Bridge completed. Caldwell consultancy in award process	Good progress
Six hundred kms of roads under maintenance.	Maintenance ongoing	Achieved
Four hundred kms (World Bank) of rural feeder roads rehabilitated by 2011.	Rehabilitation of 200 km of feeder roads started in 2011 under World Bank/International Labour Organization (ILO)	Good progress
One hundred twenty-five kms of primary roads rehabilitated by end 2010 using labor-based methods.	Rehabilitation of Fish Town – Harper Road and 125 km primary roads ongoing	Good progress
Two hundred twenty-nine drainage points constructed by 2010.	229 drainage points constructed at Fishtown-Harper Road	Achieved
Ports. Seventy percent of the general cargo operations by professional terminal operator by 2010	Private concession effective in 2010 and handles near 100 percent of general cargo	Achieved
Landlord Port Authority established by 2010.	Concession agreement became effective in October 2010	Achieved
Water and Sanitation. Household water connections in Monrovia to 50,000 by 2010.	Not available	Not available
Seventy-five km of transmission mains and over 200 km of distribution lines rehabilitated by 2010.	Not available	Not available
Treated water in Monrovia increased from 2 million gallons per day (mgd) to 6 mgd by 2010.	4.2 mgd in Oct 2010	Good progress
One sewage stabilization pond, and 31 public toilets, rehabilitated/constructed by 2010.	Not available	Not available
Forty percent of solid waste disposed of in a sanitary manner annually (compared to 25 percent).	Forty percent of solid waste collected and disposed	Achieved
Energy. Selection of a Management Contractor for Monrovia Electricity Concession by 2009.	Management Contractor selected	Achieved
Special Purpose Company for regional transmission operation formed by 2010.	Special Service Company not yet created	No progress
Feasibility Study for the interconnections to Côte D'Ivoire, Guinea and Sierra Leone by June 2010.	Feasibility study completed	Achieved

Objective / Result Indicator	Actual Results (as of 12/20/11)	Progress Made
Pillar III: Facilitating Pro-Poor Growth		
4. Improved agriculture and natural resources management to generate pro-poor growth		
Agriculture. Number of markets where seed rice is available has increased from three in 2007 to seven in 2009.	-	No progress
Local seed multiplication facility established and produces 1000 million tons of certified seed.	-	No progress
Two new sector policies completed by 2010.	-	No progress
At least three markets constructed/rehabilitated by 2010.	-	No progress
Reduced tariffs on rice and agricultural inputs.	Not available	Not available
Forest. Two community forestry concessions by 2010.	Sites established but not operational	Some progress
Community Rights Law approved by 2009.	Approved 2 years later than required by 2006 Forest Law	Achieved
Declaration of three new Protected Areas by 2010.	One Protected Area declared	Some progress
Determine carbon storage by 2009.	Done in 2009	Achieved
Mining. Large-scale exploration and mining licenses issued through/ recorded in mining cadastre system.	All new licenses are issued by the Mining Cadastre Information Management System	Achieved
Transparent and internationally-competitive mineral asset tendering procedures are consistently applied.	New mining contracts completed	Achieved
Two reports of payments minerals published.	Two reports published	Achieved
Adopt new environmental and social framework for minerals.	Update is delayed	No progress
Land. Policy framework for land tenure reform adopted.	Not yet adopted	No progress
5. Improved business and investment climate		
Creation of Liberian Better Business Forum (LBBF).	LBBF set up in 2007	Achieved
Creation of at least one commercial microfinance bank.	Access Bank (2009)	Achieved
Identification of barriers to business formalization.	New registry in place	Achieved
Redrafting Investment Code.	New code in 2010	Achieved
Modern business registry operational.	Working by 2011	Achieved
Two business-related reforms enacted.	Eight reforms implemented	Achieved
Access Bank Liberia manages 20,000 accounts by 2011.	28,000 by 2010	Achieved
Functioning one-stop shop service for customs facility.	One-Stop shop since 2010	Achieved
6. Increased access to social protection and social services in the face of shocks		
Cash-for-work program reaches 17,000 households by 2010.	17,000 reached	Achieved
One thousand girls have received training for business.	1,250 girls have received training	Achieved
Fifty percent of road contracts use labor-based methods.	Thirty percent use labor-based methods	Good progress
Food security. School-feeding in five counties in 2008/09.	Results achieved	Achieved
Social Services. Twenty-five clinics meet standards.	Standards met	Achieved
Twenty schools and 20 health facilities rehabilitated by 2010.	Ten schools and 5 health facilities rehabilitated	Good progress
Ninety percent of Community Empowerment Project (CEP) II sub-projects reflect beneficiary priorities.	Sixty-nine percent completed	Good progress

Appendix C. Statistical Supplement

Figure C.1 Liberia at a Glance

Key Development Indicators (2009)	Liberia	Sub-Saharan Africa	Low Income
Population, mid-year (millions)	4.0	819	828
Surface area (thousand sq. km)	*111*	24,242	17,838
Population growth	4.3	2.5	2.2
Urban population (% of total pop.)	61	36	28
GNI (Atlas method, US$ billions)	0.7	897	389
GNI per capita (Atlas method, US$)	160	1,095	470
GNI per capita (PPP, international $)	290	1,981	1,131
GDP growth (%)	4.6	5.2	6.2
GDP per capita growth (%)	0.3	2.7	3.9
(most recent estimate, 2003–08)			
Poverty headcount ratio at $1.25/day (PPP, %)	84	51	..
Poverty headcount ratio at $2.00/day (PPP, %)	95	73	..
Life expectancy at birth (years)	58	52	57
Infant mortality (per 1,000 live births)	80	83	77
Child malnutrition (% of children under 5)	20	25	28
Adult literacy, male (% of ages 15 and older)	63	72	73
Adult literacy, female (% of ages 15 and older)	53	54	59
Gross primary enrollment, male (% of age group)	96	105	107
Gross primary enrollment, female (% of age group)	86	95	100
Access to an improved water source (% of population)	68	60	64
Access to improved sanitation facilities (% of population)	17	31	35

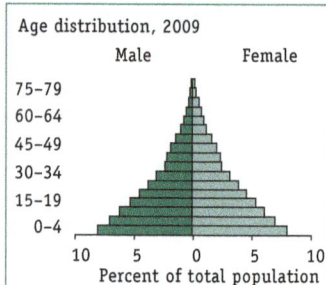

Age distribution, 2009

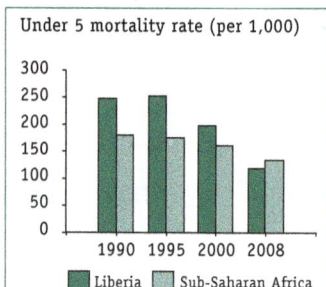

Under 5 mortality rate (per 1,000)

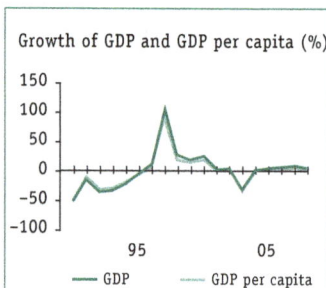

Growth of GDP and GDP per capita (%)

Net Aid Flows (US$ millions)	1980	1990	2000	2009
Net ODA and offical aid	97	117	67	1,250
Top 3 donors (in 2007):				
Germany	11	7	–1	317
United States	32	19	16	276
European Commission	4	8	13	50
Aid (% of GNI)	10.4	*102*	17.4	185.8
Aid per capita (US$)	51	52	24	330

Long-Term Economic Trends

	1980	1990	2000	2009
Consumer prices (annual % change)	14.7	*9.1*	*12.1*	*11.7*
GDP implicit deflator (annual % change)	9.1	–0.2	–1.3	7.4
Exchange rate (annual average, local per US$)	1.0	1.0	41.0	68.3
Terms of trade index (2000 = 100)	..	..	..	..

	1980	1990	2000	2009	1980–90	1990–2000	2000–09
					(average annual growth %)		
Population, mid-year (millions)	1.9	2.2	2.8	4.0	1.3	2.7	3.7
GRP (US$ millions)	954	384	561	876	–7.0	4.1	0.0
	(% of GDP)						
Agriculture	35.9	54.4	72.0	*61.3*	..	..	..
Industry	28.1	16.8	11.6	*16.8*	..	..	..
Manufacturing	7.7	..	9.5	*12.7*	..	..	..
Services	36.0	28.8	16.4	*21.9*	..	..	..
Household final consumption expenditure	66.1	..	89.1	202.3	..	..	..
General gov't final consumption expenditure	19.1	..	14.4	19.3	..	..	..
Gross capital formation	..	..	4.9	20.0	..	..	..
Export of goods and services	64.3	..	21.5	31.1	..	..	..
Imports of goods and services	64.4	..	26.0	172.6	..	..	..
Gross savings	..	..	..	*–126.8*			

Balance of payments and Trade (US$ millions)	2000	2009
Total merchandise exports (fob)	120	*260*
Total merchandise imports (cif)	182	*667*
Net trade in goods and services	−25	*−1,183*
Current account balance as a % of GRP	−23.3	*−26.1*
Workers' remittances and compensation of employees (receipts)	..	54
Reserves, including gold	*2*	*85*
Central Government Finance (% of GDP)		
Current revenue (including grants)	12.8	27.5
Tax revenue	..	20.8
Current expenditure	7.5	30.2
Overall surplus/deficit	−0.7	−6.4
Highest marginal tax rate (%)		
Individual	..	..
Corporate	..	..
External Debt and Resource Flows (US$ millions)		
Total debts outstanding and disbursed	2,809	1,660
Total debt service	1	64
Debt relief (HIPC, MDRI)	2,998	..
Total debt (% of GDP)	500.8	189.4
Total debt service (% of exports)	0.5	*5,370.2*
Foreign direct investment (net inflows)	21	378
Portfolio equity (net inflows)	0	0

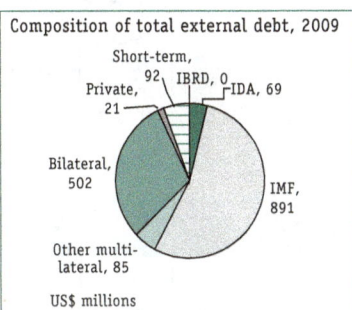

Governance indicators, 2000 and 2009

- Voice and accountability
- Political stability
- Regulatory quality
- Rule of law
- Control of corruption

Country's percentile rank (0–100)
higher values imply better ratings

Composition of total external debt, 2009

Short-term, 92
Private, 21
IBRD, 0
IDA, 69
Bilateral, 502
Other multi-lateral, 85
IMF, 891

US$ millions

Private Sector Development	2000	2009
Time required to start a business (days)	..	20
Cost to start a business (% of GNI per capita)	..	52.9
Time required to register property (days)	..	50
Ranked as a major constraint to business (% of managrs surveyed who agreed)		
n.a.	..	..
n.a.	..	..
Stock market capitalization (% of GDP)	..	..
Bank capital to asset ratio (%)	..	..

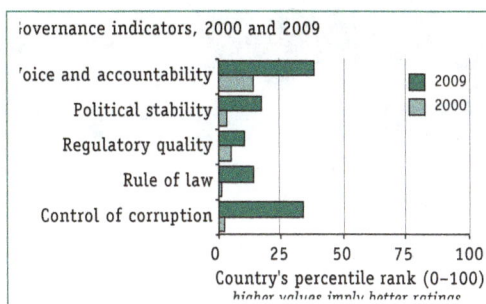

Technology and Infrastructure	2000	2008
Paved roads (% of total)	6.2	..
Fixed line and mobile phone subscribers (per 100 people)	0	29
High technology exports (% of manufactured exports)	..	..
Environment		
Agricultural land (% of land area(	27	*27*
Forest area (% of land area)	35.9	*315*
Terrestrial protected areas (% of surface area)	..	15.0
Freshwater resources per capita (cu. meters)	*65,427*	*52,723*
Freshwater withdrawal (billion cubic meters)	0.1	..
CO2 emissions per capita (mt)	0.15	*0.19*
GDP per unit of energy use (2005 PPP $ per kg of oil equivalent)	..	..
Energy use per capita (kg of oil equivalent)	..	..

World Bank Group portfolio (US$ millions)	2000	2009
IBRD		
Total debt outstanding and disbursed	130	0
Disbursements	0	0
Principal repayments	0	0
Interest payments	0	0
IDA		
Total debt outstanding and disbursed	100	69
Disbursements	0	0
Total debt service	0	4
IFC *(fiscal year)*		
Total disbursed and outstanding portfolio	4	4
of which IFC own account	4	4
Disbursements for IFC own account	4	4
Portfolio sales, prepayments and repayments for IFC own account	0	0
MIGA		
Gross exposure	—	—
New guarantees	—	—

Source: Development Economics, Development Data Group (DECDG).
Note: Figures in italics are for years other than those specified. 2009 data are preliminary. .. indicates data are not available; — indicates observation is not applicable.
GDP= gross domestic product; GNI= gross national income; HIPC= Highly-Indebted Poor Country Initiative; IBRD= International Bank for Reconstruction and Development; IDA= International Development Association; IFC= International Finance Corporation; IMF= International Monetary Fund; MDRI= Multilateral Debt Relief Initiative; MIGA= Multilateral Investment Guarantee Association; ODA= official development assistance; PPP= purchasing power parity.

Table C.1 — Liberia: Economic and Social Indicators, 1990–2010

Indicators	1997	1998	1999	2000	2001	2002	2003
Growth and Inflation							
GDP growth (annual %)	106.3	29.7	22.9	25.7	2.9	3.7	−31.3
GDP per capita growth (annual %)	92.6	20.5	15.2	19.7	−0.3	1.7	−32.2
GNI per capita, Atlas method (current US$)	120	130	120	140	140	150	110
GNI per capita, PPP (current int'l US$)	220	260	260	290	320	360	260
Inflation, consumer prices (annual %)	..	..	..	..	..	14.2	10.3
Composition of GDP (%)							
Agriculture, value added (% of GDP)	77.0	78.6	76.2	72.0	73.3	75.5	71.6
Industry, value added (% of GDP)	10.2	7.1	7.2	11.6	9.6	8.0	10.6
Services, etc., value added (% of GDP)	12.8	14.3	16.6	16.4	17.1	16.4	17.7
Gross fixed capital formation (% of GDP)	..	..	..	..	4.9	4.7	9.4
Gross domestic savings (% of GDP)	..	..	..	..	−3.4	−3.3	−3.2
External Accounts							
Exports of goods and services (% of GDP)	8.8	10.8	14.6	21.5	23.2	19.9	32.4
Imports of goods and services (% of GDP)	72.0	39.3	41.7	26.0	31.6	27.9	44.9
Current account balance (% of GDP)	..	..	..	..	..	..	..
External debt stocks (% of GNI)	911.7	794.2	761.2	718.7	743.0	717.1	1022.7
Total debt service (% of GNI)	0.1	0.3	0.8	0.2	0.2	0.2	0.1
Total reserves in months of imports	..	..	..	..	..	..	..
Social Indicators							
Health							
Immunization, DPT (% of children ages 12-23 months)	..	..	50.0	46.0	42.0	39.0	35.0
Life expectancy at birth, total (years)	43.2	44.0	44.9	46.0	47.1	48.4	49.6
Mortality rate, infant (per 1,000 live births)	130.7	125.4	119.8	115.1	110.2	105.9	101.0
Out-of-pocket health expenditure (% of private expenditure on health)	..	52.2	52.2	52.2	52.2	52.2	52.2
Health expenditure, public (% of GDP)	..	1.4	1.5	1.3	1.5	1.0	1.2
Population							
Population growth (annual %)	6.9	7.4	6.5	4.9	3.2	1.9	1.4
Population, total (in millions)	2.4	2.5	2.7	2.8	2.9	3.0	3.0
Education							
School enrollment, primary (% gross)	..	..	93.9	111.7	..	..	..
School enrollment, secondary (% gross)	..	..	31.1	34.8	..	..	..
School enrollment, tertiary (% gross)	..	..	8.1	16.1	..	..	..

Source: World Bank World Development Indicators (December 2011 Update).
Note: DPT = diphtheria, pertussis, and tetanus; GDP = gross domestic product; GNI = gross national income; PPP = purchasing power parity. Sub-Saharan Africa includes developing countries only.

	2004	2005	2006	2007	2008	2009	2010	1997–2003	2004–10
	2.6	5.3	7.8	9.4	7.1	4.6	5.5	22.8	6.0
	0.8	2.3	3.5	4.3	1.8	-0.3	1.3	16.7	2.0
	120	130	130	150	180	190	200	130	157
	260	270	260	300	320	340	340	281	299
	7.8	10.8	7.3	11.4	17.5	7.4	..	12.2	10.4
	68.2	65.8	56.9	55.0	61.3	..	..	74.9	61.4
	13.4	15.7	17.1	18.9	16.8	..	..	9.2	16.4
	18.4	18.4	26.0	26.1	21.9	..	..	15.9	22.2
	13.2	16.4	..	..	..	..	..	6.4	14.8
	−0.7	2.4	−34.6	−142.5	−121.5	..	..	−3.3	−59.4
	37.3	37.9	28.6	28.3	31.1	..	..	18.7	32.6
	51.2	51.9	83.2	190.9	172.6	..	..	40.5	110.0
	−34.7	−34.6	−28.2	−30.4	−42.1	−31.5	−42.2	..	−34.8
	1021.0	934.2	926.8	664.7	464.9	225.4	28.3	809.8	609.4
	0.2	0.2	0.2	114.7	138.9	8.7	0.7	0.3	37.6
	0.2	0.2	0.5	0.7	0.8	2.4	..	..	0.8
	31.0	60.0	60.0	60.0	64.0	64.0	64.0	42.4	57.6
	50.8	51.9	53.0	53.9	54.7	55.5	..	46.2	53.3
	96.4	92.1	88.3	84.3	80.6	77.6	73.6	115.4	84.7
	52.2	52.2	52.2	52.2	52.2	52.2	..	52.2	52.2
	1.3	1.6	1.9	2.8	3.9	5.3	..	1.3	2.8
	1.8	2.9	4.0	4.8	5.1	4.7	4.0	4.6	3.9
	3.1	3.2	3.3	3.5	3.7	3.8	4.0	2.8	3.5
	..	..	..	101.0	96.0	..	..	102.8	98.5
	..	..	..	..	..	..	..	33.0	..
	..	..	..	..	..	..	..	12.1	..

Table C.2 — Liberia and Comparators: Key Economic and Social Indicators, Average 2004–10

Indicators	Liberia	DRC	Burundi	Niger	Mozambique	
Growth and Inflation						
GDP growth (annual %)	6.0	5.8	3.8	4.3	7.5	
GDP per capita growth (annual %)	2.0	2.8	0.8	0.7	4.9	
GNI per capita, Atlas method (current US$)	157	146	126	299	351	
GNI per capita, PPP (current international $)	299	284	370	657	744	
Inflation, consumer prices (annual %)	10.4	14.5	10.6	3.5	9.6	
Composition of GDP (%)						
Agriculture, value added (% of GDP)	61.4	44.0	37.5	...	29.1	
Industry, value added (% of GDP)	16.4	26.6	19.5	...	25.1	
Services, etc., value added (% of GDP)	22.2	29.4	43.1	...	45.8	
Gross fixed capital formation (% of GDP)	14.8	18.7	13.3	17.1	18.7	
Gross domestic savings (% of GDP)	−59.4	7.3	−18.0	8.7	5.5	
External Accounts						
Exports of goods and services (% of GDP)	32.6	24.4	10.6	15.6	31.2	
Imports of goods and services (% of GDP)	110.0	36.9	42.1	25.1	44.4	
Current account balance (% of GDP)	−34.8	...	−12.0	−11.8	−11.3	
External debt stocks (% of GNI)	609.4	126.9	126.5	33.7	50.2	
Total debt service (% of GNI)	37.6	4.0	3.7	1.4	0.8	
Total reserves in months of imports	0.8	...	4.8	3.8	4.4	
Social Indicators						
Health						
Immunization, DPT (% of children ages 12-23 months)	57.6	65.1	91.9	57.7	77.1	
Life expectancy at birth, total (years)	53.3	47.3	48.4	52.5	48.5	
Mortality rate, infant (per 1,000 live births)	84.7	114.9	91.3	79.1	100.4	
Out-of-pocket health expenditure (% of private expenditure on health)	52.2	84.2	65.2	94.9	41.6	
Health expenditure, public (% of GDP)	2.8	2.9	4.7	3.0	3.7	
Population						
Population growth (annual %)	3.9	2.8	2.9	3.5	2.4	
Population, total (in millions)	3.5	60.8	7.7	14.0	21.8	
Education						
School enrollment, primary (% gross)	98.5	90.6	121.3	55.1	107.5	
School enrollment, secondary (% gross)	...	35.7	17.4	11.0	18.2	
School enrollment, tertiary (% gross)	...	5.2	2.6	1.2	1.3	

Source: World Bank, World Development Indicators (December 2011 Update).
Note: DPT = diphtheria, pertussis, and tetanus; GDP = gross domestic product; GNI = gross national income; HIPC= Highly-Indebted Poor Country Initiative; IDA= International Development Association; PPP = purchasing power parity. Sub-Saharan Africa includes developing countries only.

	Sierra Leone	Cote d'Ivoire	Ghana	IDA only	HIPC	Low income	Sub-Saharan Africa
	6.0	2.1	6.3	6.2	5.4	5.9	5.2
	2.8	0.3	3.8	3.8	2.7	3.7	2.6
	283	983	833	628	503	409	955
	709	1,679	1,379	1,391	1,140	1,090	1,893
	13.1	2.7	13.7	...	...	...	...
	49.8	23.6	33.5	26.4	26.8	28.0	15.2
	23.1	25.6	22.0	27.8	26.9	24.3	31.3
	27.0	50.8	44.5	45.7	46.3	47.7	53.6
	14.5	10.4	23.2	21.6	21.2	21.1	20.3
	3.5	18.2	5.9	12.6	10.8	10.1	16.4
	20.2	47.1	29.5	28.1	29.1	20.6	32.3
	31.2	39.5	46.8	34.7	40.0	32.2	34.7
	−10.4	2.2	−8.3	...	...	...	...
	79.5	68.2	36.1	...	...	39.7	27.4
	1.0	2.8	1.4	2.3	2.0	1.5	2.2
	4.6	2.8	3.4	6.3	5.2	4.5	6.6
	73.0	76.6	89.0	73.3	74.5	77.1	69.5
	45.3	52.5	61.9	56.4	54.0	57.4	52.5
	121.8	90.0	53.9	77.5	80.9	74.5	81.7
	88.8	95.9	78.6	89.0	84.6	83.0	59.5
	1.3	0.9	3.2	2.1	2.5	2.0	2.7
	3.1	1.8	2.4	2.3	2.6	2.1	2.5
	5.4	18.7	22.7	1063.7	589.4	749.0	793.7
	...	76.8	97.4	96.8	...	99.3	95.8
	...	...	51.6	38.6	...	35.7	32.9
	...	8.7	6.5	7.2	...	5.8	5.8

Donor	1997	1998	1999	2000	2001	2002	2003
Bilateral donors							
Australia	..	..	..	..	0.13	..	..
Austria	0.27	0.02	0.02	0.04	0.01	0.08	0.43
Belgium	0.61	0.49	0.05	..	..	..	0.23
Canada	..	0.34	0.10	0.19	0.30	0.34	1.77
Denmark	0.14	0.41	0.29	0.09	0.03	0.06	0.25
Finland	0.27	0.57	0.81	0.55	0.90	0.46	1.47
France	0.88	1.34	0.03	0.80	1.49	1.74	1.29
Germany	−5.73	−2.47	−6.85	−1.28	−6.46	−2.14	−3.21
Greece	..	..	..	..	..	..	0.16
Ireland	0.33	0.31	0.25	0.19	0.68	0.62	3.04
Italy	..	..	..	..	..	..	..
Japan	0.45	..	1.47	0.02	0.05	0.02	..
Korea	..	0.01	..	..	..	..	..
Luxembourg	..	..	..	..	..	0.28	0.45
Netherlands	8.26	6.42	3.16	2.00	2.25	2.88	8.98
New Zealand	..	..	0.05	..	..	..	0.18
Norway	2.18	4.47	1.51	0.29	0.65	1.94	8.98
Portugal	..	..	..	..	..	..	..
Spain	0.15	0.33	0.71	..	0.11	..	0.46
Sweden	5.77	7.57	3.59	1.44	1.14	1.07	5.14
Switzerland	1.12	2.03	1.96	0.36	0.57	1.67	2.82
United Kingdom	4.26	0.78	1.08	3.28	1.17	2.85	7.63
United States	12.00	8.67	36.40	15.87	12.61	15.08	30.21
DAC Countries, Total	30.96	31.29	44.63	23.84	15.63	26.95	70.28
Chinese Taipei	1.00	..	..	..	..	..	..
Czech Republic	..	..	..	..	..	..	0.04
Iceland	..	..	..	..	..	..	..
Israel	0.02	0.01	0.01	..	0.01	0.01	..
Kuwait	..	..	..	..	..	..	..
Poland	..	..	0.01	..	..	0.00	0.00
Slovak Republic	..	..	..	..	..	..	..
Slovenia	..	..	..	..	..	..	..
Turkey	..	..	..	..	..	..	..
United Arab Emirates	..	..	..	..	..	..	0.01
Other donors	..	..	..	..	..	..	..
Non−DAC Countries, Total	1.02	0.01	0.02	..	0.01	0.01	0.05

2004	2005	2006	2007	2008	2009	2010	Total 1997–2003	Total 2004–10
..	..	..	..	..	0.01	0.26	0.13	0.27
0.73	0.33	..	..	..	..	7.85	0.87	8.91
..	0.51	1.23	0.29	..	0.01	0.13	1.38	2.17
1.04	2.93	1.59	2.91	1.95	2.20	1.10	3.04	13.72
0.09	3.81	5.67	6.45	12.30	8.81	9.87	1.27	47.00
2.76	1.71	1.34	2.05	3.08	2.12	0.67	5.03	13.73
0.82	0.55	2.05	1.13	26.84	0.30	232.04	7.57	263.73
−3.08	1.32	8.96	10.03	316.60	28.07	50.14	−28.14	412.04
0.16	0.03	0.07	..	0.09	0.03	0.01	0.16	0.39
2.74	4.34	7.27	13.24	12.94	9.81	10.60	5.42	60.94
1.95	0.02	..	0.01	0.81	75.41	1.94	0.00	80.14
..	..	17.40	12.46	13.98	14.71	134.31	2.01	192.86
..	..	0.01	0.20	10.33	0.01	0.04	0.01	10.59
0.65	..	0.11	..	0.08	0.08	0.41	0.73	1.33
8.62	7.20	6.53	2.85	19.99	..	40.01	33.95	85.20
0.05	0.09	..	..	..	..	..	0.23	0.14
11.64	7.14	8.94	28.17	33.84	15.37	22.84	20.02	127.94
0.08	0.58	0.18	0.24	0.21	..	..	0.00	1.29
..	1.53	1.26	3.55	24.29	5.75	1.83	1.76	38.21
12.53	14.79	15.18	19.78	26.27	41.98	26.79	25.72	157.32
3.20	3.17	5.98	10.63	7.23	5.80	4.71	10.53	40.72
16.46	7.54	15.27	12.36	32.40	33.40	25.58	21.05	143.01
102.51	86.35	88.39	102.73	275.99	96.93	131.37	130.84	884.27
162.95	143.94	187.43	229.08	819.22	340.80	702.50	243.58	2,585.92
..	..	..	..	..	..	..	1.00	0.00
0.13	0.11	0.28	0.41	0.38	0.56	0.33	0.04	2.20
..	..	..	0.10	0.53	0.21	0.35	0.00	1.19
0.01	..	..	0.01	0.04	0.05	0.04	0.06	0.15
..	..	..	..	..	..	..	0.00	0.00
..	..	0.01	..	0.01	..	..	0.01	0.02
..	..	..	..	25.07	..	..	0.00	25.07
..	..	..	..	0.01	0.01	..	0.00	0.02
..	..	0.15	0.12	0.60	0.08	0.03	0.00	0.98
0.01	0.05	0.05	0.60	0.03	0.04	1.45	0.01	2.23
..	..	..	..	0.35	..	..	0.00	0.35
0.15	0.16	0.49	1.24	27.02	0.95	2.20	1.12	32.21

(Table continues on the following page.)

Appendix C: Statistical Supplement ■ 137

Table C.3	Total Net Disbursements of Official Development Assistance and Official Aid, 1990–2010 (in current US$ million) (cont.)						
Donor	**1997**	**1998**	**1999**	**2000**	**2001**	**2002**	**2003**
Multilaterals							
AfDF	..	..	..	..	..	..	..
BADEA	..	..	..	..	..	..	..
EU Institutions	16.43	23.44	9.76	12.71	8.82	9.24	14.92
GAVI	..	..	..	..	..	..	..
GEF	..	..	..	..	..	0.26	0.37
Global Fund	..	..	..	..	..	..	..
IDA	..	..	..	..	..	..	..
IFAD	..	..	..	..	..	..	..
IMF (Concessional Trust Funds)	..	−0.60	−0.60	−0.37	−0.24	..	..
Islamic Dev. Bank	..	..	..	..	..	..	..
UNAIDS	..	..	..	..	..	..	..
UNDP	7.91	7.26	2.60	2.01	2.13	0.77	1.04
UNFPA	0.06	0.68	0.92	0.74	0.82	0.53	0.56
UNHCR	2.28	2.50	6.08	11.72	5.80	8.33	5.89
UNICEF	1.95	2.09	2.21	1.70	1.77	1.48	5.39
UNPBF	..	..	..	..	..	..	..
UNTA	2.08	0.98	1.72	2.39	1.34	2.60	1.95
WFP	13.05	4.34	26.61	12.68	2.40	4.99	6.49
Multilateral Agencies, Total	43.76	40.69	49.30	43.58	22.84	28.20	36.61
All Donors, Total	75.74	71.99	93.95	67.42	38.48	55.16	106.94

Source: DAC.

Note: AfDF= African Development Fund of African Development Bank; African Bank for Economic Development in Africa; DAC= Development Assistance Committee of Organisation for Economic Co−operation and Development; EU= European Union; GAVI=Global Alliance for Vaccines and Immunizations; GEF= Global Environmental Fund; IDA= International Development Association; IFAD= International Fund for Agricultural Development; IMF= International Monetary Fund; UNAIDS= United Nations Programme on HIV and AIDS; UNDP= United Nations Development Programme; UNFPA= United Nations Population Fund; UNHCR= United Nations High Commissioner for Refugees; UNICEF= United Nations Children's Fund; UNPBF= United Nations Peace building Fund; UNTA= United Nations Regular Programme of Technical Assistance; WFP= World Food Program.

2004	2005	2006	2007	2008	2009	2010	Total 1997–2003	Total 2004–10
..	..	..	−6.11	−26.21	4.02	4.57	0.00	−23.73
..	..	0.14	0.03	..	..	..	0.00	0.17
30.36	52.99	44.24	39.46	48.59	59.54	90.92	95.32	366.10
..	..	..	2.74	3.04	2.41	1.88	0.00	10.07
0.22	1.00	..	..	0.83	2.64	..	0.63	4.69
5.06	9.16	10.11	4.44	15.66	..	20.67	0.00	65.10
..	..	1.13	407.05	4.60	42.45	40.14	0.00	495.37
..	..	..	..	..	..	−10.25	0.00	−10.25
..	..	..	..	319.99	27.82	539.66	−1.81	887.47
..	..	..	..	..	..	0.30	0.00	0.30
..	..	0.01	0.18	..	0.04	0.33	0.00	0.56
5.34	4.13	4.17	5.37	7.19	7.59	8.74	23.72	42.53
0.86	0.78	2.25	3.66	3.69	2.59	5.89	4.31	19.72
0.19	4.16	1.78	3.78	6.33	2.19	1.09	42.60	19.52
3.17	3.78	4.05	6.11	5.57	5.73	5.35	16.59	33.76
..	..	..	..	1.50	7.98	6.41	0.00	15.89
1.88	2.39	1.59	2.06	0.44	..	..	13.06	8.36
3.07	..	3.06	2.30	13.53	5.82	2.25	70.56	30.03
50.15	78.39	72.53	471.07	404.75	170.82	717.95	264.98	1,965.66
213.25	222.49	260.45	701.39	1,250.99	512.57	1,422.65	509.68	4,583.79

Table C.4	Liberia: World Bank Projects by Sector Board, FY1997–2011 (Commitment amounts in US$ million)								
Sector Board	1997–2004	2005	2006	2007	2008	2009	2010	2011	Total
Agriculture and Rural Development				0.1	6.9		12.0	16.0	35.0
Economic Policy					430.0	44.3		11.0	485.3
Education								40.0	40.0
Energy and Mining					0.4		1.2	10.0	11.6
Environment			1.0	2.8	0.8		3.0	1.0	8.5
Financial Management				1.9		3.7		0.5	6.1
Gender and Development						6.6			6.6
Global Information/ Communications Technology								25.6	25.6
Health, Nutrition and Population				8.5					8.5
Poverty Reduction					0.7				0.7
Public Sector Governance			0.6		14.5			7.0	22.1
Social Protection		6.0		16.3	3.4		16.0		41.7
Transport			30.0	25.0	50.8	77.4	47.0	176.6	406.8
Urban Development							18.4	4.0	22.4
Total	0.0	6.0	31.6	54.6	507.5	132.0	97.5	291.7	1,120.9

Source: World Bank database.

Note: Includes International Development Association (IDA) financing and Trust Funds.

Table C.5 Liberia: World Bank Projects by Sector , FY1997–2011 (Number of projects)

Sector Board	1997–2004	2005	2006	2007	2008	2009	2010	2011	Total
Agriculture and Rural Development				1	2		1	2	6
Economic Policy					1	2		1	4
Education								1	1
Energy and Mining					1		2	1	4
Environment			1	1	1		1	1	5
Financial Management				1		1		1	3
Gender and Development						1			1
Global Information/ Communications Technology								1	1
Health, Nutrition and Population				1					1
Poverty Reduction					1				1
Public Sector Governance			1		3			1	5
Social Protection		1		1	2		1		5
Transport			1	2	1	3	1	1	9
Urban Development							1	1	2
Total		1	3	7	12	7	7	11	48

Source: World Bank database.

Note: Includes projects financed by the International Development Association (IDA) and Trust Funds.

Approval Fiscal Year	Project ID	Project Name	Product Line	Sector Board	Instrument Type	WB Commit-ments	IDA Commit-ments	
Closed Projects								
2005	P098266	Community Empowerment Emergency Recovery Loan	SF	Social Protection	IL	6	0	
2006	P076740	Sapo National Park	GEF	Environment	IL	1	0	
2007	P101456	Liberia Infrastructure Rehabilitation Project	SF	Transport	IL	8	0	
2007	P104287	Development Forestry Sector Management Project	SF	Environment	IL	3	0	
2007	P104426	Liberia- Avian Flu Rapid Assessment	RE	Agriculture and Rural Development	IL	0	0	
2007	P104727	Liberia Public Financial Management Capacity Building	RE	Financial Management	IL	2	0	
2007	P105282	Health Systems Reconstruction	IDA	Health, Nutrition and Population	IL	9	9	
2008	P102904	Liberia Judicial System Reform	RE	Public Sector Governance	IL	1	0	
2008	P102915	Re-engagement and Reform Support Program	IDA	Economic Policy	DPO	430	430	
2008	P106048	Liberia: Extractive Industries Transparency	RE	Energy and Mining	IL	0	0	
2008	P109195	Emergency Senior Executive Service Project	SF	Public Sector Governance	IL	2	0	
2008	P109827	Pilot Project to Strengthen the Sexual and Reproductive Health and Rights for the War-Affected Vulnerable Youth in Liberia	RE	Social Protection	IL	0	0	

Trust Fund Commit-ments	Latest DO	Latest IP	Latest risk rating	Project Status	Closing Date	IEG Outcome	IEG Risk to DO Outcome
6	S	S		Closed	12/31/08		
1				Closed	9/30/10		
8	S	MS		Closed	9/30/10		
3	MS	MS		Closed	12/31/11		
0				Closed	6/30/08		
2				Closed	12/31/09		
0	MS	MS		Closed	10/1/11		
1				Closed	7/31/11		
0	S	S		Closed	9/30/08	S	Significant
0				Closed	12/31/10		
2	S	S		Closed	6/30/11		
0				Closed	10/31/10		

(Table continues on the following page.)

Table C.6		Liberia: List of World Bank Approved Projects, 2004–11						(cont.)
Approval Fiscal Year	Project ID	Project Name	Product Line	Sector Board	Instrument Type	WB Commitments	IDA Commitments	
2008	P110165	Support to Poverty Reduction Strategy Preparation	RE	Poverty Reduction	IL	1	0	
2008	P112107	Liberia Emergency Food Support for Vulnerable Women and Children	SF	Agriculture and Rural Development	IL	4	0	
2009	P113450	Reengagement and Reform Support Program 2	IDA	Economic Policy	DPO	4	4	
2009	P114846	Liberia Debt Reduction Grant	DR	Economic Policy	DR	40	0	
2010	P117582	Liberia Phase II - Extractive Industries Transparency Initiative	RE	Energy and Mining	IL	0	0	
2010	P118075	Liberia - Support from Extractive Industries -Technical Advisory Facility	RE	Energy and Mining	IL	1	0	
2011	P117279	Third Reengagement and Reform Support Program	IDA	Economic Policy	DPO	11	11	
Active Projects								
2006	P100160	Emergency Infrastructure Project (EIP)	IDA	Transport	IL	30	30	
2007	P103276	EIP Supplemental Component	IDA	Transport	IL	17	17	
2007	P105683	Community Empowerment II	IDA	Social Protection	IL	16	5	
2008	P104716	Agriculture and Infrastructure Development Project	IDA	Transport	IL	51	37	
2008	P105830	Establishment of Protected Areas Network	GEF	Environment	IL	1	0	

Trust Fund Commit-ments	Latest DO	Latest IP	Latest risk rating	Project Status	Closing Date	IEG Outcome	IEG Risk to DO Outcome
1				Closed	3/31/11		
4	S	S		Closed	12/31/10		
0	S	S		Closed	6/30/10	S	Significant
40				Closed	1/31/11		
0				Closed	12/31/10		
1				Closed	10/31/11		
0				Closed	6/30/11		
0	S	MS		Active	3/31/12		
0				Active			
11	S	S		Active	7/31/12		
14	S	MS		Active	10/31/13		
1				Active	11/30/12		

(Table continues on the following page.)

Approval Fiscal Year	Project ID	Project Name	Product Line	Sector Board	Instrument Type	WB Commit-ments	IDA Commit-ments	
2008	P107248	Economic Governance and Institutional Reform	IDA	Public Sector Governance	IL	11	11	
2008	P112083	Agricultural Infrastructure and Develop-ment Project –	SF	Agriculture and Rural Development	IL	3	0	
2008	P112084	Additional Financing to CEP - Public Works Program	SF	Social Protection	IL	3	0	
2009	P109775	Public Financial Management – IFMIS	RE	Financial Management	IL	4	0	
2009	P110571	Economic Empowerment of Adolescent Girls and Young Women in Liberia	RE	Gender and Development	IL	7	0	
2009	P113099	Urban and Rural Infrastructure Rehabilitation Project	IDA	Transport	IL	53	44	
2009	P117005	Emergency Infrastructure Rehabilitation Project	IDA	Transport	IL	8	8	
2009	P117019	Agriculture and Infrastructure Development Project	IDA	Transport	IL	16	16	
2010	P106063	West Africa Fisheries - Phase 1 *	IDA	Agriculture and Rural Development	IL	12	9	
2010	P115664	Emergency Monrovia Urban Sanitation Project	RE	Urban Development	IL	18	0	
2010	P117010	Land Sector Reforms: Rehabilitation and Reform of Land Rights	RE	Environment	IL	3	0	
2010	P121686	Youth, Employment, Skills Project	IDA	Social Protection	IL	16	6	
2010	P121770	Liberia - Urban and Rural Infrastructure Rehabilitation Project	IDA	Transport	IL	47	20	

Trust Fund Commit-ments	Latest DO	Latest IP	Latest risk rating	Project Status	Closing Date	IEG Outcome	IEG Risk to DO Outcome
0	MS	MS		Active	12/31/13		
3				Active			
3				Active			
4	S	S		Active	3/31/12		
7				Active	12/31/12		
9	S	MS		Active	6/30/14		
0				Active			
0				Active			
3	MS	MS		Active	12/31/17		
18	S	S		Active	12/31/13		
3				Active	4/30/13		
10	S	MS		Active	6/30/13		
27				Active			

(Table continues on the following page.)

| Table C.6 | | | | Liberia: List of World Bank Approved Projects, 2004–11 | | | | | (cont.) |

Approval Fiscal Year	Project ID	Project Name	Product Line	Sector Board	Instrument Type	WB Commit- ments	IDA Commit- ments	
2011	P114580	Liberia: Expansion of Protected Areas Network – II	GEF	Environment	IL	1	0	
2011	P116273	West Africa Reg. Comm. Infrastructure Program *	IDA	Global Information/ Communications Technology	IL	26	26	
2011	P117662	Fast Track Initiative Grant for Basic Education	RE	Education	IL	40	0	
2011	P120660	Liberia Electricity System Enhancement Project	IDA	Energy and Mining	IL	10	10	
2011	P122065	West Africa Agric Prod Program (WAAPP-1C) *	IDA	Agriculture and Rural Development	IL	14	6	
2011	P123361	PFM Strengthening and Reform Coordination	IDF	Financial Management	IL	0	0	
2011	P124643	Economic Governance and Institutional Reform	IDA	Public Sector Governance	IL	7	7	
2011	P124664	Emergency Monrovia Urban Sanitation Project (EMUS)	IDA	Urban Development	IL	4	4	
2011	P124844	West Africa Regional Fisheries Program APL A1 Additional Financing *	IDA	Agriculture and Rural Development	IL	2	2	
2011	P125574	Liberia Road Asset Management Project	IDA	Transport	IL	177	68	

Source: World Bank database.

* Regional projects. Amounts showing correspond to Liberia only.

Note: CEP= Community Empowerment Project; DPO=Development Policy Operation; DR=Debt Reduction Facility; DO=Development Outcome; EIP= Emergency Infrastructure Project; ERL= Economic Recovery Loan; IDA=International Development Association; GEF=Global Environmental Facility; IDF=Institutional Development Fund; IFMIS= Integrated Financial Management Information System; IL=Investment Lending; IEG= Independent Evaluation Group; PFM= public financial management; RE=Recipient Executed Activities; SF=Special Financing.

Trust Fund Commit-ments	Latest DO	Latest IP	Latest risk rating	Project Status	Closing Date	IEG Outcome	IEG Risk to DO Outcome
1				Active	7/31/13		
0	S	S	Moderate	Active	9/30/15		
40	S	MS	Substantial	Active	6/30/13		
0	S	S		Active	12/31/14		
8	S	S		Active	6/30/16		
0				Active	6/30/14		
0				Active			
0				Active			
0				Active			
109	S	S		Active	6/30/22		

Rating Scale for Latest DO and IEG Outcome Ratings: HS=Highly Satisfactory; S=Satisfactory; MS=Moderately Satisfactory; MU=Moderately Unsatisfactory; U=Unsatisfactory; HU=Highly Unsatisfactory. Rating Scale for IEG Risk to Development Outcome Ratings: High; Significant; Moderate; Negligible to Low; Non-Evaluable.

Table C.7		Liberia: World Bank Delivered Analytical and Advisory Work, 2004–11			
Delivery Fiscal year	Project ID	Project Name	Output Type	Report Type	Sector Board
Economic and Sector Work					
2008	P101546	Liberia Agricultural Sector Review	Report	Rural Development Assessment	Agriculture and Rural Development
2008	P103699	Sustainable Livelihoods Approach to Define Land Tenure Priorities in Post-Conflict Liberia	Report	Other Environmental Study	Environment
2008	P107324	Diagnostic Trade Integration Study	Report	Foreign Trade, Foreign Direct Investment, and Capital Flows Study	Economic Policy
2009	P107304	Rapid Public Expenditure Management and Fiduciary Accountability Review (PEMFAR)	Report	Public Expenditure Review (PER)	Public Sector Governance
2010	P113275	Policy Note on Pro-poor Growth	Policy Note	Not assigned	Economic Policy
2010	P118478	Liberia Energy Policy	Report	Energy Study	Energy and Mining
2010	P118706	Investment Climate Policy Note	Policy Note	Not assigned	Financial and Private Sector Development
2011	P115820	Debt Management Performance Assessment (DeMPA) Assessment	Report	General Economy, Macroeconomics, and Growth Study	Economic Policy
2011	P122596	Reports on the Observance of Standards and Codes (ROSC) Accounting and Auditing	Report	Accounting and Auditing Assessment (ROSC)	Financial Management
2011	P124620	Liberia Infrastructure and Resource Concessions	Policy Note	Not assigned	Energy and Mining
Non-lending technical assistance					
2007	P090894	Petroleum Procurement Under Bank International Competitive Bidding (ICB) rules	Institutional Development Plan		Energy and Mining
2007	P101802	Telecommunications Sector Reform	"How-To" Guidance		Global Information/ Communications Technology
2007	P105055	Liberia Community Broadcasting	"How-To" Guidance		Social Development

Delivery Fiscal year	Project ID	Project Name	Output Type	Report Type	Sector Board
2008	P089266	Support for Economic Management	Institutional Development Plan		Financial Management
2008	P091984	Forestry Management	Institutional Development Plan		Agriculture and Rural Development
2008	P100440	Liberia Rapid Results Initiative	Knowledge-Sharing Forum		Public Sector Governance
2008	P107169	Telecom Sector Reform	"How-To" Guidance		Global Information/ Communications Technology
2008	P107212	Liberia Mining Technical Assistance	Institutional Development Plan		Energy and Mining
2009	P103243	Health Sector Dialogue	Client Document Review		Health, Nutrition and Population
2009	P112448	Transition Support Fund	Institutional Development Plan		Urban Development
2009	P115019	Financial Sector Revitalization Strategy	"How-To" Guidance		Financial and Private Sector Development
2010	P088679	Multi-sector Grant Infrastructure Project	Institutional Development Plan		Urban Development
2010	P100995	Public Procurement Reform	Institutional Development Plan		Procurement
2010	P103759	Public Sector Reform	Client Document Review		Public Sector Governance
2010	P112372	Preparation of Monrovia Slum Upgrading Program	Institutional Development Plan		Urban Development
2010	P121400	Liberia Fisheries Citizens Report Card Survey	Model/Survey		Social Development
2011	P103454	Education Sector Strategy and Education-For-All (EFA) Plan	Institutional Development Plan		Education
2011	P117636	Health Systems for Outcomes	"How-To" Guidance		Health, Nutrition and Population

(Table continues on the following page.)

Table C.7	Liberia: World Bank Delivered Analytical and Advisory Work, 2004–11 (cont.)				
Delivery Fiscal year	Project ID	Project Name	Output Type	Report Type	Sector Board
Main publications*					
2005	31443	Community Cohesion in Liberia. A post-war rapid social assessment	Brief		
2006	38024	Mini-diagnostic analysis of the investment climate	Working Paper		
2009	WPS4742	Rice prices and poverty in Liberia	Policy Research Working Paper		
2011	58020	Policy options to attract nurses to rural Liberia : evidence from a discrete choice experiment	Working Paper		
2011	58021	Health worker attitudes toward rural service in Liberia : results from qualitative research	Working Paper		
2011	63635	Liberia education country status report : out of the ashes - learning lessons from the past to guide education recovery in Liberia	Working Paper		
2011	WPS5597	Liberia's infrastructure: a continental perspective	Policy Research Working Paper		

Source: World Bank database.

* List includes Liberia-specific major reports. Report numbers are shown

Table C.8a	Project Ratings for Liberia and Comparators, FY2004–11									
	Total Evaluated ($US Millions)		Outcome % Satisfactory		Risk to Development Objective % Moderate or Lower Satisfactory		Sustainability % Likely		Institutional Development Impact % Substantial	
Country/Region	$M	No	$	No	$	No	$	No	$	No
Liberia	405.2	2	100.0	100.0	0.0	0.0				
Democratic Republic of Congo	342.5	3	16.1	33.3	0.0	0.0	21.7	50.0	21.7	50.0
Burundi	317.0	9	91.9	88.9	45.3	37.5	100.0	100.0	0.0	0.0
Niger	435.2	13	72.5	53.8	56.3	54.5	65.0	50.0	0.0	0.0
Mozambique	1,202.1	21	95.5	85.7	94.1	83.3	100.0	66.7	100.0	66.7
Sierra Leone	175.0	9	69.6	77.8	61.8	66.7	8.1	50.0	4.5	33.3
Côte d'Ivoire	556.2	10	66.8	40.0	0.5	25.0	0.0	0.0	0.0	0.0
Ghana	1,384.4	24	64.0	58.3	42.8	33.3	19.5	33.3	54.6	33.3
Sub-Saharan Africa	18,426.1	426	71.7	66.2	49.6	46.4	65.3	63.9	51.0	46.1
World Bank	108,072.5	1,800	84.4	77.0	71.6	61.2	87.6	80.1	64.9	54.6

Source: World Bank database, January 2012.

Table C.8b	Portfolio Status Indicators, Liberia and Comparators FY2011					
Country	# Projects	# Projects At Risk	% At Risk	Net Commitment Amt (US$ million)	Commitment At Risk (US$)	% Commitment at Risk
Liberia	8	0	0.0	282	0	0.0
Democratic Republic of Congo	16	11	68.8	2,023	1,718	84.9
Burundi	11	0	0.0	372	0	0.0
Niger	10	4	40.0	382	110	28.8
Mozambique	19	4	21.1	976	243	24.9
Sierra Leone	8	1	12.5	183	22	12.0
Côte d'Ivoire	8	2	25.0	644	135	21.0
Ghana	19	2	10.5	1,423	77	5.4
Sub-Saharan Africa	434	105	24.2	37,010	7,801	21.1
World Bank	1,454	302	20.8	165,792	22,573	13.6

Source: World Bank databases, January 2012.

Table C.9	Liberia: Portfolio Status Indicators, FY2004–11					
Fiscal year	# Projects	# Projects At Risk	% At Risk	Net Commitment Amt	Commitment At Risk	% Commitment at Risk
2004						
2005						
2006	1	0	0.0	30	0	0.0
2007	3	1	33.3	60	47	77.5
2008	5	1	20.0	108	47	43.1
2009	7	2	28.6	180	14	7.5
2010	7	1	14.3	202	5	2.5
2011	8	0	0.0	282	0	0.0

Source: World Bank databases, January 2012.

Country/Region	FY04	FY05	FY06	FY07	FY08	FY09	FY10	FY11	Average	Total 2004–11	Budget Distribution %
Table C.10 Comparative Bank Budget (Direct Costs by Service), 2004–11 (in millions USD)											
LIBERIA											
Project Supervision	-	-	0.0	0.7	1.4	1.3	2.0	2.2	0.9	7.5	34
Lending	0.1	0.2	0.2	0.7	0.5	0.8	1.3	1.3	0.6	5.1	23
Economic and Sector Work	0.2	1.0	1.3	1.4	0.8	0.4	0.6	0.6	0.8	6.2	28
Other	0.5	0.1	0.2	0.4	0.6	0.4	0.5	0.4	0.4	3.1	14
Total	0.8	1.3	1.7	3.2	3.2	2.8	4.3	4.5	2.7	21.8	100%
DEPARTMENT (LIBERIA, GHANA, SIERRA LEONE)											
Project Supervision	2.8	3.4	3.6	4.5	6.1	5.4	6.4	6.5	4.8	38.7	41
Lending	2.6	2.4	2.1	2.9	2.3	3.1	5.5	5.3	3.3	26.3	28
Economic and Sector Work	1.8	2.1	3.3	3.3	1.8	1.4	1.6	2.0	2.1	17.2	18
Other	1.8	1.4	1.2	1.7	1.6	1.7	1.5	1.0	1.5	12.1	13
Total	9.0	9.3	10.2	12.4	11.8	11.5	15.2	14.9	11.8	94.2	100%
AFRICA											
Project Supervision	42.2	49.8	52.4	53.2	60.9	60.5	69.7	71.9	57.6	460.8	33
Lending	46.4	40.6	39.7	39.1	37.8	45.0	46.9	44.4	42.5	339.8	25
Economic and Sector Work	35.6	35.9	39.2	37.7	42.5	43.9	46.1	43.9	40.6	324.7	24
Other	30.0	34.2	30.1	32.2	30.6	29.9	30.9	33.6	31.4	251.4	18
Total	154.1	160.5	161.4	162.2	171.8	179.3	193.6	193.7	172.1	1,376.7	100%
WORLD BANK											
Project Supervision	167.0	178.5	190.5	199.3	217.9	231.5	252.2	256.6	211.7	1,693.4	33
Lending	157.2	151.8	156.0	149.6	147.6	151.2	157.1	147.0	152.2	1,217.4	23
Economic and Sector Work	154.8	158.5	169.0	162.4	187.1	197.8	206.2	202.9	179.8	1,438.7	28
Other	105.2	99.5	103.6	105.2	104.7	104.2	109.3	117.3	106.1	849.1	16
Total	584.2	588.2	619.1	616.5	657.4	684.7	724.8	723.8	649.8	5,198.6	100%

Source: Internal World Bank database as of January 2012.

Note: "Other" includes country program support, client training and impact evaluation services. "Total" includes all Country Services.

| Table C.11 | Liberia: Direct Costs by Service and Source of Finance, 2004–11 (in million USD) |

	FY04	FY05	FY06	FY07	FY08	FY09	FY10	FY11	Average	Total 2004–11	Budget Distribution %
LIBERIA											
BANK INTERNAL FUND											
Project Supervision	-	-	0.0	0.7	1.4	1.3	2.0	2.2	0.9	7.5	34
Lending	0.1	0.2	0.2	0.7	0.5	0.8	1.3	1.3	0.6	5.1	23
Economic and Sector Work	0.2	1.0	1.3	1.4	0.8	0.4	0.6	0.6	0.8	6.2	28
Other	0.5	0.1	0.2	0.4	0.6	0.4	0.5	0.4	0.4	3.1	14
Bank Budget Total	0.8	1.3	1.7	3.2	3.2	2.8	4.3	4.5	2.7	21.8	100%
TRUST FUNDS											
Project Supervision	-	-	0.3	-	0.3	0.6	0.6	1.1	0.4	2.9	11
Lending	-	-	-	2.5	4.8	2.5	1.0	0.3	1.4	11.0	42
Economic and Sector Work	-	1.1	3.0	1.2	1.7	1.6	1.9	1.1	1.4	11.6	44
Other	-	0.0	0.1	0.0	0.2	0.1	0.6	0.7	0.2	1.7	7
Trust Funds Total	-	1.1	3.3	3.7	6.8	4.7	3.6	2.9	3.3	26.0	100%
TOTAL	0.8	2.4	5.0	6.8	10.0	7.5	7.9	7.4	6.0	47.9	
AFRICA											
BANK INTERNAL FUND											
Project Supervision	42.2	49.8	52.4	53.2	60.9	60.5	69.7	71.9	57.6	460.8	33
Lending	46.4	40.6	39.7	39.1	37.8	45.0	46.9	44.4	42.5	339.9	25
Economic and Sector Work	35.6	35.9	39.2	37.7	42.5	43.9	46.1	43.9	40.6	324.7	24
Other	30.0	34.2	30.1	32.2	30.6	29.9	30.9	33.6	31.4	251.4	18
Bank Budget Total	154.1	160.5	161.4	162.2	171.9	179.3	193.6	193.7	172.1	1,376.7	100%
TRUST FUNDS											
Project Supervision	6.5	3.8	4.1	12.2	14.3	19.4	22.2	27.0	13.7	109.6	20
Lending	19.2	11.8	8.1	12.0	12.4	8.3	7.4	6.9	10.8	86.0	16
Economic and Sector Work	39.2	31.0	29.0	30.6	33.5	37.8	44.8	44.3	36.3	290.3	54
Other	6.6	6.1	5.0	5.5	5.0	6.8	4.8	9.0	6.1	48.8	9
Trust Funds Total	71.5	52.8	46.2	60.2	65.3	72.3	79.2	87.2	66.8	534.7	100%
TOTAL	225.6	213.3	207.6	222.4	237.1	251.6	272.8	280.9	238.9	1,911.4	

Source: Internal World Bank database as of January 2012.

Note: "Other" includes country program support, client training and impact evaluation services. "Total" includes all Country Services.

Table C.12	Liberia: Millennium Development Goals				
		1990	1995	2000	2009
Goal 1: Eradicate extreme poverty and hunger					
Employment to population ratio, 15+, total (%)		66	65	65	66
Employment to population ratio, ages 15-24, total (%)		57	56	56	57
Income share held by lowest 20%		..	..	..	6.4
Malnutrition prevalence, weight for age (% of children under 5)		..	..	22.8	20.4
Poverty gap at $1.25 a day (PPP) (%)		..	..	..	41
Poverty headcount ratio at $1.25 a day (PPP) (% of population)		..	..	..	84
Prevalence of undernourishment (% of population)		30	32	36	33
Vulnerable employment, total (% of total employment)		..	..	..	..
Goal 2: Achieve universal primary education					
Literacy rate, youth female (% of females ages 15-24)		..	..	..	80
Literacy rate, youth male (% of males ages 15-24)		..	..	..	70
Persistence to last grade of primary, total (% of cohort)		..	..	..	..
Primary completion rate, total (% of relevant age group)		..	..	..	58
Total enrollment, primary (% net)		..	..	75	..
Goal 3: Promote gender equality and empower women					
Proportion of seats held by women in national parliaments (%)		..	6	8	13
Ratio of female to male primary enrollment (%)		..	..	72	90
Ratio of female to male secondary enrollment (%)		..	..	71	75
Ratio of female to male tertiary enrollment (%)		..	..	74	..
Share of women employed in the nonagricultural sector (% of total nonagricultural employment)		..	..	11.4	..
Goal 4: Reduce child mortality					
Immunization, measles (% of children ages 12-23 months)		..	..	63	64
Mortality rate, infant (per 1,000 live births)		165	169	134	80
Mortality rate, under-5 (per 1,000)		247	253	198	112
Goal 5: Improve maternal health					
Adolescent fertility rate (births per 1,000 women ages 15-19)		..	..	148	140
Births attended by skilled health staff (% of total)		..	..	51	46
Contraceptive prevalence (% of women ages 15-49)		..	..	10	11
Maternal mortality ratio (modeled estimate, per 100,000 live births)		1100	1400	1100	990
Pregnant women receiving prenatal care (%)		..	..	85	79
Unmet need for contraception (% of married women ages 15-49)		..	..	..	36
Goal 6: Combat HIV/AIDS, malaria, and other diseases					
Children with fever receiving antimalarial drugs (% of children under age 5 with fever)		..	..	..	67
Condom use, population ages 15-24, female (% of females ages 15-24)		..	..	..	9
Condom use, population ages 15-24, male (% of males ages 15-24)		..	..	..	19
Incidence of tuberculosis (per 100,000 people)		200	220	240	280

(Table continues on the following page.)

Table C.12	Liberia: Millennium Development Goals (cont.)				
		1990	1995	2000	2009
Prevalence of HIV, female (% ages 15-24)		..	..	..	1.3
Prevalence of HIV, male (% ages 15-24)		..	..	..	0
Prevalence of HIV, total (% of population ages 15-49)		0.4	1.2	1.4	1.7
Tuberculosis case detection rate (all forms)		47	33	22	46
Goal 7: Ensure environmental sustainability					
CO2 emissions (kg per PPP $ of GDP)		0.6	1.4	0.4	0.5
CO2 emissions (metric tons per capita)		0.2	0.2	0.2	0.2
Forest area (% of land area)		42	39	36	31
Improved sanitation facilities (% of population with access)		11	13	14	17
Improved water source (% of population with access)		58	61	65	68
Marine protected areas (% of total surface area)		..	..	..	0
Terrestrial protected areas (% of total surface area)		..	..	..	15
Goal 8: Develop a global partnership for development					
Debt service (PPG and IMF only, % of exports, excluding workers' remittances)		..	..	0	0
Internet users (per 100 people)		0	0	0	0.5
Mobile cellular subscriptions (per 100 people)		0	0	0	19
Net ODA received per capita (current US$)		52	63	24	330
Telephone lines (per 100 people)		0	0	0	0
Other					
Fertility rate, total (births per woman)		6.5	6.2	6.1	5.9
GNI per capita, Atlas method (current US$)		250	130	140	160
GNI, Atlas method (current US$) (billions)		0.6	0.3	0.4	0.7
Gross capital formation (% of GDP)		..	..	4.9	20
Life expectancy at birth, total (years)		49	51	54	58
Literacy rate, adult total (% of people ages 15 and above)		..	43	..	58
Population, total (millions)		2.2	1.9	2.8	4
Trade (% of GDP)		..	80.8	47.5	203.7

Source: World Development Indicators as of January 2012.

Note: CO2= carbon dioxide; GDP= gross domestic product; GNI= gross national income; HIV= human immunodeficiency virus; IMF= International Monetary Fund; ODA= official development assistance; PPG= public and publicly-guaranteed debt; PPP= purchasing power parity;

Appendix D

Guide to IEG's Country Program
Evaluation Methodology

This methodological note describes the key elements of IEG's Country Program evaluation (CPE) methodology.[1]

CPEs rate the outcomes of World Bank Group assistance programs, not the clients' overall development progress

A World Bank Group assistance program needs to be assessed on how well it met its particular objectives, which are typically a subset of the client's development objectives. If a World Bank Group assistance program is large in relation to the client's total development effort, the program outcome will be similar to the client's overall development progress. However, most World Bank Group assistance programs provide only a fraction of the total resources devoted to a client's development by development partners, stakeholders, and the government itself. In CPEs, IEG rates only the outcome of the World Bank Group's program, not the client's overall development outcome, although the latter is clearly relevant for judging the program's outcome.

The experience gained in CPEs confirms that World Bank Group program outcomes sometimes diverge significantly from the client's overall development progress. CPEs have identified World Bank Group assistance programs which had:

- Satisfactory outcomes matched by good client development;
- Unsatisfactory outcomes in client countries which achieved good overall development results, notwithstanding the weak World Bank Group program; and,
- Satisfactory outcomes in client countries which did not achieve satisfactory overall results during the period of program implementation.

Assessments of assistance program outcome and World Bank Group performances are not the same

By the same token, an unsatisfactory World Bank Group assistance program outcome does not always mean that World Bank Group performance was also unsatisfactory, and *vice-versa*. This becomes clearer once we consider that the World Bank Group's contribution to the outcome of its assistance program is only part of the story. The assistance program's outcome is determined by the joint impact of four agents: (a) the client; (b) the World Bank Group; (c) partners and other stakeholders; and (d) exogenous forces (for example, events of nature, international economic shocks, and so on). Under the right circumstances, a negative contribution from any one agent might overwhelm the positive contribution from the other three, and lead to an unsatisfactory outcome.

IEG measures World Bank Group performance primarily on the basis of contributory actions the World Bank Group directly controlled. Judgments regarding World Bank Group performance typically consider the relevance and implementation of the strategy, the design and supervision of the World Bank Group's lending and financial support interventions, the scope, quality and follow-up of diagnostic work and other analytic and advisory activities

(AAA), the consistency of the World Bank Group's lending and financial support with its non-lending work and with its safeguard policies, and the World Bank Group's partnership activities.

Rating Assistance Program Outcome

In rating the outcome (expected development impact) of an assistance program, IEG gauges the extent to which major strategic objectives were relevant and achieved, without any shortcomings. In other words, did the World Bank Group do the right thing, and did it do it right. Programs typically express their goals in terms of higher-order objectives, such as poverty reduction. The country assistance strategy (CAS) may also establish intermediate goals, such as improved targeting of social services or promotion of integrated rural development, and specify how they are expected to contribute toward achieving the higher-order objective. IEG's task is then to validate whether the intermediate objectives were the right ones and whether they produced satisfactory net benefits, and whether the results chain specified in the CAS was valid. Where causal linkages were not fully specified in the CAS, it is the evaluator's task to reconstruct this causal chain from the available evidence, and assess relevance, efficacy, and outcome with reference to the intermediate and higher-order objectives.

For each of the main objectives, the CPE evaluates the relevance of the objective, the relevance of the World Bank Group's strategy toward meeting the objective, including the balance between lending and non-lending instruments, the efficacy with which the strategy was implemented and the results achieved. This is done in two steps. The first is a top-down review of whether the World Bank Group's program achieved a particular World Bank Group objective or planned outcome and had a substantive impact on the country's development. The second step is a bottom-up review of the World Bank Group's products and services (lending, analytical and advisory services, and aid coordination) used to achieve the objective. Together these two steps test the consistency of findings from the products and services and the development impact dimensions. Subsequently, an assessment is made of the relative contribution to the results achieved by the World Bank Group, other development partners, the government and exogenous factors.

Evaluators also assess the degree of client ownership of international development priorities, such as the Millennium Development Goals, and World Bank Group corporate advocacy priorities, such as safeguards. Ideally, any differences on dealing with these issues would be identified and resolved by the CAS, enabling the evaluator to focus on whether the trade-offs adopted were appropriate. However, in other instances, the strategy may be found to have glossed over certain conflicts, or avoided addressing key client development constraints. In either case, the consequences could include a diminution of program relevance, a loss of client ownership, and/or unwelcome side-effects, such as safeguard violations, all of which must be taken into account in judging program outcome.

IEG utilizes six rating categories for **outcome**, ranging from highly satisfactory to highly unsatisfactory:

Highly Satisfactory:	The assistance program achieved at least acceptable progress toward all major relevant objectives, and had best practice development impact on one or more of them. No major shortcomings were identified.
Satisfactory:	The assistance program achieved acceptable progress toward all major relevant objectives. No best practice achievements or major shortcomings were identified.
Moderately Satisfactory:	The assistance program achieved acceptable progress toward most of its major relevant objectives. No major shortcomings were identified.
Moderately Unsatisfactory:	The assistance program did not make acceptable progress toward most of its major relevant objectives, or made acceptable progress on all of them, but either (a) did not take into adequate account a key development constraint or (b) produced a major shortcoming, such as a safeguard violation.
Unsatisfactory:	The assistance program did not make acceptable progress toward most of its major relevant objectives, and either (a) did not take into adequate account a key development constraint or (b) produced a major shortcoming, such as a safeguard violation.
Highly Unsatisfactory:	The assistance program did not make acceptable progress toward any of its major relevant objectives and did not take into adequate account a key development constraint, while also producing at least one major shortcoming, such as a safeguard violation.

The **institutional development impact (IDI)** can be rated at the project level as: *high, substantial, modest,* or *negligible.* IDI measures the extent to which the program bolstered the Client's ability to make more efficient, equitable and sustainable use of its human, financial, and natural resources. Examples of areas included in judging the institutional development impact of the program are:

- the soundness of economic management;
- the structure of the public sector, and, in particular, the civil service;
- the institutional soundness of the financial sector;
- the soundness of legal, regulatory, and judicial systems;
- the extent of monitoring and evaluation systems;
- the effectiveness of aid coordination;
- the degree of financial accountability;
- the extent of building capacity in nongovernmental organizations; and,
- The level of social and environmental capital.

IEG is, however, increasingly factoring IDI impact ratings into program outcome ratings, rather than rating them separately.

Sustainability can be rated at the project level as *highly likely, likely, unlikely, highly unlikely,* or, if available information is insufficient, *non-evaluable.* Sustainability measures the resilience to risk of the development benefits of the country program over time, taking into account eight factors:

- technical resilience;

- financial resilience (including policies on cost recovery);

- economic resilience;

- social support (including conditions subject to safeguard policies);

- environmental resilience;

- ownership by governments and other key stakeholders;

- Institutional support (including a supportive legal/regulatory framework, and organizational and management effectiveness); and, resilience to exogenous effects, such as international economic shocks or changes in the political and security environments.

At the program level, IEG is increasingly factoring sustainability into program outcome ratings, rather than rating them separately.

Risk to Development Outcome. According to the 2006 harmonized guidelines, sustainability has been replaced with a "risk to development outcome," defined as the risk, at the time of evaluation, that development outcomes (or expected outcomes) of a project or program will not be maintained (or realized). The risk to development outcome can be rated at the project level as *high, significant, moderate, negligible to low, non-evaluable.*

Note

1. In this note, *assistance program* refers to products and services generated in support of the economic development of a Client country over a specified period of time, and *client* refers to the country that receives the benefits of that program.

Appendix E
List of People Met

Aagon Tingba	Director, Training Unit	Ministry of Finance
Akindele Beckley	Program Director, Infrastructure Implementation Unit	Ministry of Public Works
Amara Konneh	Minister	Ministry of Planning and Economic Affairs
Andrew Tehmeh		Ministry of Gender
Annete Kiawu		Ministry of Gender
Arabella Greaves	Technical Advisor - Project Coordinator	Ministry of Health and Social Welfare
Arebela Greaves,	Project Coordinator	Ministry of Health
Augustine Blamah	Director of Budget	Ministry of Finance
Beauford O. Weeks, I. Msc.	Assistant Minister for Energy	Ministry for Energy
Carlton Miller	Director of Mines	Ministry of Land Mines and Energy
Chris Sokpor	Head - Ministry of Finance/Public Financial Management Unit	Ministry of Finance
D. Emmanuel Williams	Acting Assistant Minister	Ministry of Planning and Economic Affairs
D. Wisseh Kay		Bureau of National Fisheries (BNF)
Decontee Sackie	Director Custom	Ministry of Finance
Dr. Brandy	Land Commission, Head	World Bank Project Coordinator
Dr. Edward Liberty	Director Liberia Institute of Statistics and Geo-Information Services (LISGIS)	LISGIS
Dr. Roosevelt Gasolin Jayjay	Minister,	Ministry of Mines, Land, and Energy
Drayton Hinneh,	Director	Ministry of Finance
Edward Liberty	Director	Liberia Institute of Statistics and Geo-Information Services (LISGIS)
Elfrieda Stewart Tamba	Deputy Minister for Revenue	Ministry of Finance
Emmanuel Sherman	Director, Geological Survey	Ministry of Land Mines and Energy
Emmet Crayton		Ministry of Gender
Eva Lotter	Economic Empowerment of Adolescent Girls (EPAG) Coordinator	Gender Ministry
Frances Johnson Morris	Chair	Liberia Anti Corruption Commission (LACC)
Gabriel Fernandez	National Social Protection Coordinator	Ministry of Planning and Economic Affairs
George Dayrall	Liberia Agency for Community Empowerment (LACE)	LACE Office
Glasgow B. Togba		Bureau of National Fisheries (BNF)
Harold J. Monger	Director General	Liberia Institute of Public Administration
Harold Monger	Head of Liberian Institute of Public Administration (LIPA)	Liberian Institute of Certified Public Accountants (LICPA)

Harris F. Tarnue, Sr.	Deputy Director General	Liberia Institute of Public Administration
Hon. Francis Karpeh	Deputy Minister	Ministry of Finance
Hon. Varbah Gayflor	Minister	Ministry of Gender
Honorable T. Felix Morlu	Geologist/Assistant Minister	Ministry of. Lands, Mines and Energy
J. Ebenezer Kolliegbo	Deputy Minister	Ministry of Transport
James B. Dennis	Land Commission	World Bank Project Coordinator
James Dorbor Jallah		Liberian Institute of Certified Public Accountants (LICPA)
James F. Kollie, Jr	Deputy National Coordinator	Liberia Reconstruction and Development Committee
James Jallah	Deputy Minister for Sectoral and Regional Planning	Ministry of Planning and Economic Affairs
Johansen Voker		Environmental Protection Agency of Liberia
Kederick F. Johnson	Assistant Director	Forest Development Authority,
L. Issah Braimah		Bureau of National Fisheries (BNF)
Anyaa Vohiri		Environmental Protection Agency of Liberia
Mohammed Swaray	Resource Management Unit,	Ministry of Finance
Moses D. Wogbeh, Sr.	Director	Forest Development Authority,
Moses Zinnah	Project Management Unit Director	Ministry of Agriculture
Mr. A. Ndebehwolie Borley		Gender Ministry
Nathaniel T. Blama		Environmental Protection Agency of Liberia
Natty Davis	Chairman	National Investment Commission
Negballe Warner	Former Executive Secretary	Liberia Extractive Industries Transparency Initiative (LEITI)
Nortu Jappah	Managing Director -	Liberia Water and Sewer Corporation (LWSC)
Nuran Ercan	Procurement Advisor, Agriculture Sector Rehabilitation Project Program Management Unit,	Ministry of Agriculture
P. Emmersyn Harris		Liberian Institute of Certified Public Accountants (LICPA)
Peggy Mayers	Director	Public Procurement and Competition Commission
Peggy Varfley Meres	Executive Director - Public Procurement and Concessions Commission (PPCC)	Public Procurement and Concessions Commission
Peter Ofori-Asumadu	Project Manager urban projects -	Monrovia City Corporation (MCC)
Ramses Kumuyah,	Executive Director LACE	LACE Office
Richard Dorley	Director Central Bank	Bank of Liberia (CBL)
Richard Panton		Liberian Institute of Certified Public Accountants (LICPA)
Roosevelt Jayjay		Ministry of Land Mines and Energy

Salia Hussein	Project Accountant, Project Financial Management Unit,	Ministry of Finance
Sam Gotomo		Ministry of Gender
Sam Hare	Deputy Minister	Ministry of Youth and Sport
Samuel Kofi Woods -	Minister of Public Works	Ministry of Public Works
Samuel Z. Joe	Director, Aid Management Unit,	Ministry of Finance
Sheriff	Director, Fiscal Unit	Ministry of Finance
V. Larry Reeves	Procurement Officer - Ministry of Public Works	Ministry of Public Works
Walter McCarthy	Deputy Minister for Administration (and former Director of Mines)	Ministry of Land Mines and Energy
Willard A. Russel, I	Minister	Ministry of Transport
William Allen	Director	Civil Service Agency
William Hagbah	Director, Resource Management Unit	Ministry of Finance

Development Partners

Atilio Pacifici	Ambassador - Head of Delegation	Delegation of the European Union in Liberia
Christopher Lane	International Monetary Fund (IMF) Resident Representative in Liberia	IMF
Cires Afonso Adolfo		European Commission
Claudia Hermes	Resident Representative in Liberia	German International Cooperation (GIZ)
Dejene Sahle	Senior Technical Expert	Employment Intensive Investment Programme, International Labour Organization
Dominic Sam	Resident Representative, United Nations Development Programme (UNDP)	UNDP
Dr. Mark Marquardt	Chief of Party, Tetra Tech, Agriculture and Rural Development	Liberia Land Commission
Emily Stanger		UN Women
Fazlul Haque	Deputy Representative	United Nations Children's Fund (UNICEF)
Francis Kai Kai,	Chief of Civil Affairs	United Nations Mission in Liberia (UNMIL)
Giorgio Kirchmayr	European Union, Acting Head of Operations	European Union
Giorgio Kirchmayr	European Union	European Union
Giorgio Kirchmayr		European Commission
Guglielma da Passano	Chief Technical Advisor Liberia	UN-HABITAT Liberia Office, Land Commission
Henry Donso	Acting Resident Representative	ILO
Izeduwa Derex-Briggs	UN Gender Theme Group (Chair)	UN Women
Jennifer Ketchum		US Coast Guard
Kenneth Hasson		USAID
Kimberly Rosen	USAID	USAID

Lansana Wonneh		World Food Programme (WFP)
Lara Eldrige		WFP
Marc Vansteenkiste		ILO
Margaret Kilo	Resident Representative	African Development Bank
Moses Wogbeh		Forest Development Authority
Patricia Rader	Resident Representative, United States Agency for International Development (USAID)	USAID
Paula Vasquez	Head of operations, European Union	European Union
Robert Chakanda	Food Security Coordinator	Food and Agriculture Organization (FAO)
Stanley Kamara	National Economist for Liberia	UNDP
Tesfu Taddese	Civil Affairs of Officer	UNMIL,
Tiago de Valladares Pacheco	Emergency Coordinator	Food and Agriculture Organization (FAO)
Tiago de Valladares Pacheco	Emergency Coordinator	Food and Agriculture Organization (FAO)
Tiago Pacheco		Food and Agriculture Organization (FAO)
Winley Nanka	Auditor General	General Auditing Commission (GAC)
Zainab H. Al-Azzawi	Monitoring and Evaluation Specialist	UNICEF

Civil Society Organizations

Alex Hartman	Project Coordinator	Norwegian Refugee Council
Alfred Brownell	Director	Green Advocates,
Amanda Rawls	Carter Center	Carter Center
Art Blundell	Forestry Expert	World Bank
Cerue Garlo		Women Non-governmental Organizations (NGOs) Secretariat
Gregory Kitt	Project Manager	Norwegian Refugee Council
Salifu M.M. Sledge	Country Director	Oxfam
Silas Siakor	Director	Sustainable Development Institute
Thomas Doe Nah	Center for Transparency and Accountability in Liberia (CENTAL), Executive Director	CENTAL

Private Sector

Allesandra Baillie	Head of Corporate Social Responsibility	Buchanan Renewables,
Francis A. Dennis Jr.	Former President and Chief Executive Officer	Liberian Bank for Development and Investment (LBDI)
Franklin B. Cole	Credit Manager	International Bank
Fu Yan Quan	Country Manager, China Chongqing International Construction Corporation (CICO)	CICO

Matteneh-Rose L. Dunbar	Administrator	RANTO, Petroleum Liberia Limited
Maxwell Kemaya	President	Liberia Business Association,
Mr. John A. Kokulo	General Manager	MAKO Business Inc.
T. Nelson Williams	Managing Director	Liberia Petroleum Refinery Corp
Vijay Maira	General Manager	Liberian Agricultural Company

Charles Taylor	Procurement Specialist	Ghana Country Office
Coleen R. Littlejohn	Senior Operations Officer	World Bank
Daniel Kobina	Advisory Services Coordinator for Liberia	International Finance Corporation (IFC)
David deGroot	Consultant	World Bank
Deryck R. Brown	Senior Governance Specialist	World Bank
Diji Chandrasekharan Behr	Natural Resources Economist	World Bank
Fanny Missfeldt-Ringius	Senior Energy Economist	World Bank
Flavio Chaves	Natural Resources Management Specialist	World Bank
Giuseppe Zampaglione	Country Manager	World Bank
Gylfi Palsson	Lead Transport Specialist	World Bank
Inguna Dobraja	Country Manager - World Bank	World Bank
Ishac Diwan	Former Country Director for Liberia	World Bank
Ismail Arslan	Senior Evaluation Officer	World Bank
Jaime Jaramillo-Vallejo	Lead Economist	World Bank
Jenny Hasselsten	Urban development specialist -	World Bank
Jim Smyle	Consultant	World Bank
Joel Hellman	Director	World Bank
Jumoke Jagun-Dokunmu	Country Manager for Liberia	IFC
Kobina E. Daniel	IFC Legal Advisor, Investment Climate Team for Africa	IFC
Kulwinder Singh Rao	Senior Highway Engineer	World Bank
Laura Figazzolo	Consultant	World Bank
Louis Tian-Pierquin	Agriculture and Rural development	World Bank
Luigi Giovine	Lead Operations Officer	World Bank
Mats Karlsson	Director	World Bank
Mattias Lundberg	Senior Economist	World Bank
Michelle Rebosio	Social Development Specialist	World Bank
Natalie Lahire	Senior Education Economist	World Bank
Neeta Hooda	Senior Carbon Finance Specialist	World Bank
Nyaneba Nkrumah	Senior Natural Resources Management Specialist	World Bank

World Bank Group (cont.)		
Ohene Owusu Nyanin	Country Manager	World Bank, Monrovia
Oliver Braedt	Senior Rural Development and Natural Resources Specialist	World Bank
Paola Agostini	Senior Economist	World Bank
Renee M. Desclaux,	Senior Finance Officer (LRTF contact)	World Bank
Rianna L. Mohammed-Robert	Health Specialist	World Bank
Roberto Panzardi,	Senior Public Sector Management Specialist	World Bank
Sergiy Kulyk	Country Program Coordinator	World Bank
Steve Webb	Consultant	World Bank
Tuuka Castren	Senior Forestry Specialist	World Bank
V.S.Krishnakumar	Regional Procurement Manager	World Bank
William Reno	Consultant	World Bank
Winter Chinamale	Procurement Specialist	World Bank
Yi-Kyoung Lee	Health Specialist	World Bank

Bibliography

Civil Service Agency, Republic of Liberia. 2008. "Civil Service Reform Strategy 2008 – 2011. Smaller Government, Better Service." June 2008. Monrovia, Liberia: Civil Service Agency.

De Groot, D., Antti Talvitie, and Utkirdjan Umarov. 2011. "Liberia: World Bank Country Level Engagement on Governance and Anti-Corruption." Working Paper 2011/8. Independent Evaluation Group: Washington, D.C.

Dwan, Renata and L. Bailey. 2005. "Governance and Economic Management Assistance Program." A Joint Review by the Department of Peacekeeping Operations' Peacekeeping Best Practices Section and the World Bank's Fragile States Group." The World Bank Fragile States: The LICUS Initiative and United Nations.

Government of Liberia. Ministry of Planning and Economic Affairs. "External Trade of Liberia." Various issues: 1971–81.

———. 2009. Ministry of Transport and Public Works, Republic of Liberia. "National Transport Policy and Strategy." Monrovia: Ministry of Transport and Public Works. Liberia: Ministry of Transport and Public Works.

International Monetary Fund. 2011. "Liberia-Seventh Review under the Extended Credit Facility Arrangement." IMF Country Report No. 11/345. Washington, DC: International Monetary Fund.

———. 2008. "Liberia Poverty Reduction Strategy Paper." IMF Country Report No. 08/219 . Washington, DC: International Monetary Fund.

———. 2007. "Interim Poverty Reduction Strategy. " February 2007. IMF Country Report No. 07/60. Washington, DC: International Monetary Fund.

National Transitional Government of Liberia. 2004. "Results-focused Transition Framework progress review report". Report No. 30049. September 2004. World Bank: Washington, DC.

Oxford Policy Management. 2009. *Liberia Extractive Industries Transparency Initiative (EITI) Validation.* Liberia: Oxford Policy Management.

World Bank. 2004. "Project Appraisal Document on a Trust Fund for Liberia (RFLIB). Proposed Technical Assistance Component for Infrastructure Rehabilitation in the Amount of US$5 Million to the Republic of Liberia. December 28, 2004." Report No: 31071 –LR. Washington, DC: World Bank.

———. 2005a. "Expanding Opportunities and Building Competencies for Young People: A New Agenda for Secondary Education." Education Policy Paper. Washington, DC: World Bank.

———. 2005b. *Fragile States: Good Practices in Country Assistance Strategies.* Report No 34790. Washington, DC: World Bank.

———. 2007a. "International Development Association Program Document for a Proposed Grant in the Amount of SDR 263.1 Million (US$416.4 Million Equivalent) to the Republic of Liberia for a Reengagement and Reform Support Program." Report No. 40307-LR. November 20, 2007. Washington, DC: World Bank.

———. 2007b. *Liberia: Gender Needs Assessment.* Washington, DC: World Bank.

———. 2007c. *Rapid Social Assessment.* Social Development Notes. Community Driven Development. No. 107. March 2007. Washington, DC: World Bank.

———. 2008. "Doing Business 2009, Comparing Regulations in 178 Economies" Washington, DC: World Bank.

———. 2009a. "Doing Business 2010, Reforming Through Difficult Times." Washington, DC: World Bank.

———. 2009b. "Emergency Project Paper on a Proposed Grant in the Amount of US18.4 Million to the Republic of Liberia for an Emergency Monrovia Urban Sanitation Project." Report No. 47632-LR. October 6, 2009. World Bank: Washington, DC.

———. 2010. "Project paper on a Proposed Additional Grant in the Amount of SDR 13.6 Million (US$20 Million Equivalent) from the Pilot Crisis Response Window Resources (As Part of a Total of US$47 Million Equivalent, Including US$27 From Liberia Reconstruction Trust Fund) to the Republic of Liberia for the Urban and Rural Infrastructure Rehabilitation Project." Report No. 54950-LR. June 14, 2010. Washington, DC: World Bank.

———. 2011a. "Doing Business 2012. Doing Business in a More Transparent World". www.doingbusiness.org. Washington, DC: World Bank.

———. 2011b. "Report on the Observance of Standards and Codes (ROSC). Republic of Liberia." Accounting and Auditing. February 14, 2011. World Bank: Washington, DC.

World Health Organization. 2004. *The World Health Report.* Geneva: World Health Organization.

Attachment: Government Comments

From Meetings Held in Monrovia, June 11–12, 2012

An IEG delegation comprising Messrs. A. Khadr and C. Leechor visited Liberia on June 11-12, 2012 to discuss the draft report: Liberia Country Program Evaluation (CPE) with representatives of the government. Four separate round-table meetings were held to cover the contents of the country program supported by the World Bank Group, including the three pillars (rebuilding core state functions, rehabilitating infrastructure, and facilitating pro-poor growth) and cross-cutting themes (capacity building, gender, and the environment). The following is a summary of the discussions.

The participants by and large agreed with the findings of the report, including the country context, assessments of relevance and efficacy, as well as the ratings. Some participants specifically endorsed the interpretations of Liberia's history in the CPE, including the causes and devastation of the civil war. Some helped clarify particular circumstances under which the engagement of the World Bank Group took place and provided updates on recent developments. Some pointed out that, in some areas such as decentralization, the contribution of the World Bank Group should have been given more attention. No objections were raised concerning the validity of the findings. Most representatives thanked IEG for sharing the draft report, reaching out to individual agencies and giving them an opportunity to voice their concerns.

Among the issues and recommendations discussed at the meetings are:

Capacity development. Many representatives highlighted the formidable challenge of capacity building. While agreeing with IEG that much progress has been made, they cautioned that it is too early to declare victory. Much more work remains to be done and continuing support of the World Bank Group will be needed.

Procurement capacity. Participants from a broad range of agencies agreed with the assessment of the report that greater efforts to build procurement capacity should have been made early on. They highlighted the importance of doing so in the future. Some pointed out, however, that a new procurement training program has now been initiated with the assistance of the World Bank Group as part of the public financial management school at the Ministry of Finance.

Internal coordination. Some participants suggested that in the future the World Bank Group should consider supporting the government in improving "internal coordination of efforts" across ministries, department and agencies. This assistance might be considered an extension of the harmonization and alignment agenda already being pursued by the World Bank Group.

Sustainability. Some participants said that interventions of the World Bank Group would be more helpful if more attention is given to ensuring the sustainability of outcomes. Sustainability should be a core feature in the design of World Bank Group projects, but so far this has not been the case. Some pointed out the example of a breakdown when three-year assistance is given to support five-year programs, as with the training in medical schools. In addition, it was recommended that a clear timeframe be developed so that IDA credits can be expeditiously disbursed to the national system, as has already been done by some of the development partners such as the IMF and U.S. Millennium Challenge Corporation.

Land administration. A representative pointed out that while land records and titling remain a chronic and fundamental issue in Liberia, some progress has nonetheless been made. For example, land dispute resolution centers have been set up in five towns. In addition, the harmonization of land records has been initiated to reconcile the differences that exist between those of the National Archive and the Ministry of Lands, Mines and Energy. It was also noted that shortfalls in the funding for land administration may limit further progress in the future.

Employment and the private sector. Participants welcomed the report's recommendation for more concerted effort to promote job creation, noting that the private sector has a key role to play in this regard. However, an enabling environment for businesses is needed. They pointed out that today the insecurity of land tenure and overlapping claims on land remain a deterrent to private investment. Entrepreneurs among the Liberian Diaspora are reluctant to return to Liberia because of this issue.

Mainstreaming cross-cutting themes. Agencies responsible for capacity building, gender and the environment said that these themes need to be mainstreamed to a greater extent across projects and public sector agencies. So far, these themes have been incorporated in a small number of projects and in a few government agencies (mainly the Ministries of Health and Education).

Implementation support. Improving implementation support, as discussed in chapter 7 of the report, is a topic that generated a large number of comments, including the following:

- Many participants experienced delays in getting technical advice or approval from task team leaders not based in Liberia. They urged the World Bank Group to empower the country office, especially the country manger, and strengthen the field presence of staff to enhance the responsiveness of World Bank Group staff and the implementation of projects.

- In some projects, no provisions have been made to cover the costs of fuel and utilities, making it very difficult for the supervising agencies to carry out their responsibilities.

- Regarding infrastructure, it was noted that the goal posts of a project often shifted when a new task team leader arrived. As a result, it would be a good idea for project management units to develop detailed implementation manuals to ensure continuity in the face of inevitable personnel changes.

- In the case of cross-cutting themes, some participants experienced difficulties in finding a counterpart at the World Bank Office in Liberia. They urged that the World Bank Group increase its visibility in this area to achieve the results envisaged. (This suggestion corresponds to one of the explicit recommendations of the report.)

In addition, some participants requested clarifications on the meanings and implications of IEG ratings. For example, one representative asked if a moderately unsatisfactory rating implied a reduction of the support from the World Bank G in the future. The IEG representatives explained that there were no such implications. In the CPE context, a rating summarizes IEG's assessment of the extent to which relevant objectives of the country program have been achieved. When a rating is below satisfactory, this is often an indication that a new approach is needed.

Representatives of the following ministries, departments and agencies of the government of Liberia participated in the discussion:

- Civil Service Agency;
- Forest Development Authority;
- Governance Commission;
- Land Commission;
- Liberia Agency for Community Empowerment;
- Ministry of Agriculture;
- Ministry of Commerce;
- Ministry of Education;
- Ministry of Finance;
- Ministry of Gender and Development;
- Ministry of Health and Social Welfare; and
- Ministry of Public Works.